T0215508

Data-Driven Alexa Skills

Voice Access to Rich Data Sources for Enterprise Applications

Simon A. Kingaby

Apress®

Data-Driven Alexa Skills: Voice Access to Rich Data Sources for Enterprise Applications

Simon A. Kingaby
La Vergne, TN, USA

ISBN-13 (pbk): 978-1-4842-7448-4   ISBN-13 (electronic): 978-1-4842-7449-1
https://doi.org/10.1007/978-1-4842-7449-1

Managing Director, Apress Media LLC: Welmoed Spahr
Acquisitions Editor: Jonathan Gennick
Development Editor: Laura Berendson
Coordinating Editor: Jill Balzano

Cover image designed by Freepik (www.freepik.com)

Distributed to the book trade worldwide by Springer Science+Business Media LLC, 1 New York Plaza, Suite 4600, New York, NY 10004. Phone 1-800-SPRINGER, fax (201) 348-4505, e-mail orders-ny@springer-sbm.com, or visit www.springeronline.com. Apress Media, LLC is a California LLC and the sole member (owner) is Springer Science + Business Media Finance Inc (SSBM Finance Inc). SSBM Finance Inc is a **Delaware** corporation.

For information on translations, please e-mail booktranslations@springernature.com; for reprint, paperback, or audio rights, please e-mail bookpermissions@springernature.com.

Apress titles may be purchased in bulk for academic, corporate, or promotional use. eBook versions and licenses are also available for most titles. For more information, reference our Print and eBook Bulk Sales web page at http://www.apress.com/bulk-sales.

Any source code or other supplementary material referenced by the author in this book is available to readers on GitHub via the book's product page, located at www.apress.com/9781484274484. For more detailed information, please visit http://www.apress.com/source-code.

Printed on acid-free paper

This book is dedicated to all who have caught or want to catch the vision of ambient computing.

About the Author

Simon A. Kingaby is a software developer, programming professor, and public speaker residing in middle Tennessee. He believes that voice user interfaces will change the world and that tools like Alexa are just the tip of the iceberg. He spends his days moving data for Deloitte Global and teaching DataViz and FinTech at universities around the country. In 2016, he published his first Alexa skill and has been enthralled by voice development ever since. In 2017, his uncle suddenly went blind, and Simon began exploring ways Alexa could be used to help the blind with skills from "What's the time?" and home navigation skills to smart home skills like "Turn on the coffee pot." In 2019, that same uncle committed suicide, and Simon turned his attention to mental health issues and using Alexa to help identify and prevent suicidal behavior. Now he is focused on enabling developers to use their programming abilities to build data-driven Alexa skills that will make a real difference in the world.

About the Technical Reviewer

Jose Rivera has been in the IT industry for over 20 years, ranging from help desk, DBA, programming, and business intelligence and analytics. He mentors junior developers when joining companies and works with leads in making architecture reviews on programming solutions.

Acknowledgments

My thanks to my family, especially my wife, who supported me through this process. Thanks to my friends who read through the chapters and provided edits and recommendations. Special thanks to José and Joan for testing the code. Thanks to the Alexa Evangelists, Jeff Blankenburg and Justin Jeffress, who taught me so much. Thanks to the Alexa Community for their support and encouragement, especially Tradelast, Goldzulu, Oxygenbox, and Xeladotbe (see also `https://apl.ninja`).

Introduction

Welcome to the wonderful world of data-driven Alexa skills. Come along as we take a journey beyond the typical Hello World examples and design and build innovative, custom, data-driven Alexa skills for your home or business that integrate Alexa with online APIs, rich data sources, and powerful applications. If you have basic Python skills, this book will show you how to build data-driven Alexa skills. You will learn to use data to give your Alexa skills dynamic intelligence, in-depth knowledge, and the ability to remember.

Data-driven Alexa Skills takes a step-by-step approach to skill development. You will begin by configuring a skill in the Alexa Skill Builder Console. Then you will develop an advanced custom skill that uses the latest Alexa Skill Development Kit features to integrate with lambda functions, Amazon Web Services (AWS), and Internet data feeds. These skills enable you to link user accounts, query and store data using a NoSQL database, and access stock prices and more via web APIs.

What you learn from this book will help you to integrate Alexa with software-as-a-service and platform-as-a-service applications and environments such as Salesforce, ServiceNow, Microsoft Azure, and AWS.

This book is for the next generation of Alexa skill developers who want to use data to make Alexa smarter, more relevant, and more helpful. To move closer to the goal of ambient computing, Alexa will need to access and combine data from many sources in many ways. If you imagine the day when Alexa can intelligently manage your email, the day when she can reconcile your schedules from Outlook, Google, Apple, and Calendly, the day when you can ask her to tell you your net worth, or the day when you can ask her to log a ticket in ServiceNow, this book is for you.

Part I: Getting Started

In this first part of the book, we will introduce you to voice user interface development. Then we will build a Routine and a couple of Alexa skills from Blueprints. Then we set up some accounts you will need so that you can develop Alexa skills. Now you are ready to create a skill, starting with creating an Alexa Conversations voice user interface, followed by coding and testing the back end in Python and VS Code. In the last chapter of Part I, you will publish your new skill to the Alexa Skills Store!

INTRODUCTION

Chapter 1: Voice User Interfaces

An introduction to the world of voice user interface development. Chapter 1 includes a brief history of voice development leading up to today's voice landscape. It also answers the questions: Why voice? Why Alexa? Why now?

Chapter 2: Routines and Blueprints

The easiest way to create new skills for Alexa is with Routines and Blueprints. This chapter walks you through the process of creating these no-code skills.

Chapter 3: The Developer Accounts

You will need to create and configure a lot of accounts to develop Alexa skills. This chapter guides you through the creation of these accounts.

Chapter 4: Creating the VUI for a Custom Data-Driven Skill

Now that the accounts are set up, we're ready to create the base Alexa skill. For the remainder of Part I, we will create a Body Mass Index skill. In this chapter, we configure the voice user interface, including the conversational dialog, the user utterances, the slot values, and Alexa's responses.

Chapter 5: Writing the Back-End Code

With the VUI created, we're ready to write some code. Of course, you will need to install the tools, including VS Code and Anaconda, among others. Chapter 5 lists the tools you'll need and where to find them on the Internet. Then it walks you through configuring an Anaconda environment for Python development. Next, we create the back-end code for the BMI Alexa skill. We end the chapter by testing our code.

Chapter 6: Publishing an Alexa Skill

After creating the VUI in Chapter 4 and coding the back-end in Chapter 5, you will be ready to publish your new Alexa skill to the Alexa Skills Store. By the end of Chapter 6, you will have done just that!

Part II: Custom Skill Development

After creating your first skill in Part I, we take a deep dive into many of the components of the skill development process. Building a 90-year calendar skill, we will cover the Alexa Interaction Model including Intents, Slots, and Utterances. We will use the Alexa Presentation Language to draw the 90-year calendar on devices with screens. We'll use account linking to allow us to gather the events of your life safely and securely. We'll create a custom lambda function – the brains of our skill. Lastly, we use a DynamoDb persistence layer to store your information so that Alexa remembers you.

Chapter 7: Custom Alexa Skills

Now that you've created an Alexa-hosted skill in Part I, we are ready to create a fully custom skill and see how to use some of the more advanced features of the Amazon Web Services (AWS) cloud as your Alexa skill back end. You'll need some AWS accounts and services to get started.

Chapter 8: Beyond Hello World

With the accounts set up and the basic requirements defined, we're ready to design the voice user interface. Dialog design is notoriously difficult, but there are tools, like Botmock, that make it much easier. In this chapter, we lay out the dialog for the 90-year calendar skill.

Chapter 9: Configuring the VUI

After designing the dialog in Botmock, we are ready to transfer the design into a new Alexa skill.

Chapter 10: Using APL to Present on Screens

With the dialog sorted out, the next step is to create the visualization for Alexa devices with screens. For this, we need to use the Alexa Presentation Language, which is covered in Chapter 10.

Chapter 11: Coding the Lambda Function

Now that the VUI and the APL have been created and written, we can write the back-end code. For this, we will use a fully custom lambda function. We will build out the intent handlers, do the math to draw the calendar, and create the dataset to bind to the APL template.

Chapter 12: Unit Testing an Alexa Skill

With the code written, we should probably do some testing. In Chapter 12, we look at several ways to test the intent handlers and Alexa's responses. These include unit testing the code in the lambda function and in VS Code, as well as testing Alexa's natural language understanding and automated speech recognition.

Chapter 13: Storing the Data

With the skill working as designed, we are ready to take it to the next level by capturing the events of your life. This will be done with account linking to ensure that the data is safely and securely stored in a DynamoDB NoSQL database. The chapter ends with some suggestions for next steps to build out the remainder of the 90-year calendar skill.

Part III: Using APIs in Advanced Skills

Now that you've learned how to create Alexa skills, we will begin working with Application Programming Interfaces (APIs). These are a common way of gathering data over the Internet. We will use two APIs in particular to build a Personal Net Worth skill that will tell you the value of your home and investments. Of course, such a skill will have its hands on some of your personal data, but all that data will be safely ensconced in a secured database and encrypted for your protection. In all cases, you will have the option of using a test account for development purposes, so no REAL data need be involved at all.

Chapter 14: A Personal Net Worth Skill

Imagine Alexa being able to tell you your net worth. By using account linking and DynamoDB, we can safely store your personal data. In this chapter, we flesh out the VUI and work out the back-end lambda function. But once we have the dialog model sorted out, how do we get the value of your assets? The answer is found on the Web using APIs.

Chapter 15: The Real Estate API

Using a website named Rapid API, we find several APIs that can price our homes. Realty Mole stands out with its Sales Price Estimator. In this chapter, we figure out how to get the price of your home using the address we gave to Alexa in Chapter 14.

Chapter 16: The Stock Market API

After selecting one of the hundreds of stock price APIs to choose from, we plug it into our lambda function. This chapter expands on the unit testing done in Chapter 12, as we test several different scenarios to ensure your stock portfolio is properly valued. The chapter ends with some suggestions for improving our skill.

Chapter 17: What's Next?

Within this book, you have worked with various data sources, including databases like DynamoDb, and APIs like the Realty Mole Property API. In addition, you have created and tested lambda functions that are back-end applications in the cloud. These Lambda back-ends can pull data from anywhere and expose it through an Alexa skill interface. What's next? This book is just the beginning of your data-driven Alexa skill journey. I can't wait to hear what you build.

PART I

Getting Started

CHAPTER 1

Voice User Interfaces

Welcome to the incredible world of voice user interfaces (VUIs). You are embarking on a fantastic voyage of discovery. Are you new to VUI? Do you have a little bit of Python under your belt? Do you want to learn how to design and build innovative, custom, data-driven Alexa skills for your home and business? Have you already published your first dice rolling skill? Are you an experienced Alexa skill builder and want to integrate Alexa with online APIs (Application Program Interfaces), rich data sources, and powerful applications? If you answered "Yes," then this book will show you how to analyze, build, test, and deploy data-driven Alexa skills. You will learn how to use the tools, techniques, and code so that you quickly level up, first building a simple calculator skill, on up to the final project, where you will create a FinTech (Financial Technology) skill that uses APIs to tell you your personal net worth.

Why Voice User Interfaces?

A Voice User Interface (VUI) is any system that allows you to interact with a smart device using your voice. Smart devices could include your computer, car, phone, tablet, home, or even your vacuum cleaner. Traditionally, we get out of bed to flip on light switches, go to the kitchen to turn on the coffee pot, and press some buttons to send a text to the children that it's time to get up for school. With VUIs, you can control all these things using your voice by instructing your smart speaker to do them for you.

Alexa is the voice technology built into every Amazon Echo smart speaker and many other devices from Amazon's partners. Smart devices that work with Alexa enable you to use your voice to control a lot more than just your smart speaker. It has taken a long time to get to a point where we have the computing power in a small, relatively inexpensive device, and where we have widespread access to the Internet, to enable smart speaker technology to work effectively. In the next section, we'll take a trip down memory lane to learn about some of the history of VUIs and how we got to where we are today.

© Simon A. Kingaby 2022
S. A. Kingaby, *Data-Driven Alexa Skills*, https://doi.org/10.1007/978-1-4842-7449-1_1

A Brief History of VUIs

For over 200 years, scientists have pursued the dream of fully conversational interactions with smart devices. In 1773, the German scientist Christian Kratzenstein succeeded in producing vowel sounds using resonance tubes connected to organ pipes.[1] Today, we have reached a point where the ubiquity of chatbots and smart devices is making voice interactions commonplace in the daily lives of millions of people worldwide. It has been an exciting journey of discovery to get here.

In the 1930s, Bell Labs researcher Homer Dudley developed the first computerized speech synthesizer.[2] Called VODER (Voice Operating Demonstrator), the operator, Helen Harper, used it to sound out words through a combination of ten keys, a pedal, and a wrist plate. It took Helen about a year to learn how to make VODER speak. In Figure 1-1, Helen is operating VODER at the 1939 World's Fair.

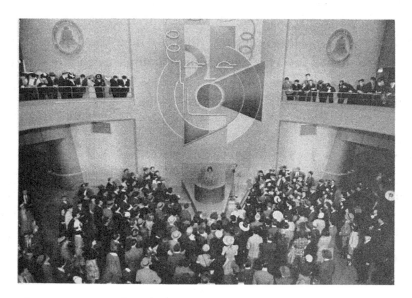

Figure 1-1. *The VODER at the 1939 World's Fair. Public Domain*

---

[1] J. Ohala. "Christian Gottlieb Kratzenstein: Pioneer in Speech Synthesis." August 17–21, 2011. www.academia.edu/24882351/Christian_Gottlieb_Kratzenstein_pioneer_in_speech_synthesis

[2] K. Eschner. "Meet Pedro the "Voder," the First Electronic Machine to Talk." June 5, 2017. www.smithsonianmag.com/smart-news/meet-pedro-voder-first-electronic-machine-talk-180963516/

In 1952, Bell Labs pioneered speech recognition with a system named "Audrey" that could recognize the digits from 0 to 9. IBM followed in the early 1960s, with "Shoebox," a machine that could understand 16 spoken words and performed arithmetic on command.[3] In Figure 1-2, scientist and inventor William C. Dersch demonstrates the Shoebox.

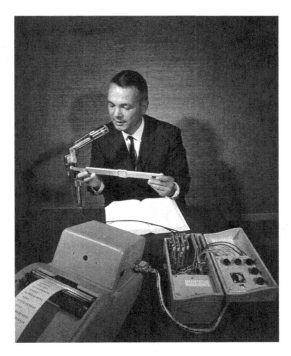

Figure 1-2. *IBM engineer William C. Dersch demonstrates Shoebox in 1961. (Courtesy of International Business Machines Corporation)*

During the Cold War in the 1960s and 1970s, labs all over the world were developing speech recognition technology. For example, from 1972 through 1976, DARPA (Defense Advanced Research Projects Agency) established the Speech Understanding Research (SUR) program to create a computer that could understand continuous speech.[4] Several

---

[3] "IBM Shoebox," in IBM Archives, Exhibits, IBM special products (vol. 1). 1960-1962. www.ibm. com/ibm/history/exhibits/specialprod1/specialprod1_7.html

[4] J. Makhoul, "Speech processing at BBN" in IEEE Annals of the History of Computing, vol. 28, no. 1, pp. 32–45, Jan.–March 2006, doi: 10.1109/MAHC.2006.19

projects under the SUR program were quite promising, though none met the program's performance goal. Computers in the 1970s just weren't powerful enough to handle machine learning and artificial intelligence models needed to do anything more than the most rudimentary speech recognition.

The 1980s were a time of significant change. Not only were PCs becoming ubiquitous and Windows becoming the de facto standard operating system, but speech synthesis and recognition was moving from pattern-based systems to algorithmic and statistical model-based systems. It was during this time that we refined the Hidden Markov Model (HMM). In his 2004 paper on HMMs, Sean Eddy explains, "HMMs are a formal foundation for making probabilistic models of linear sequence 'labeling' problems... HMMs are the Legos of computational sequence analysis."[5]

In 1982, doctors James and Janet Baker launched Dragon Dictate for DOS-based computers. This software was expensive, but it allowed people to dictate, albeit slowly, directly into the tool, instead of typing. In the late 1980s, with the introduction of deep neural networks, we began to have the mechanism, if not the computing power, to take speech recognition to the next level.

Around 1990, DARPA got back in the game, and a variety of speech vocabularies, both simulated and recognized, were developed. In 1997, 15 years after the launch of Dragon Dictate, the Bakers released the much more sophisticated and faster Dragon Naturally Speaking 1.0.[6] Extending beyond dictation, Naturally Speaking also offered voice control of your PC and text-to-speech capabilities so that the computer could read aloud your digital documents.

In 2005, IBM and Honda worked together to put IBM's Embedded ViaVoice software in Honda's Acura (sedan) and Odyssey (minivan) product lines.[7] Automobile manufacturers have been working hard to bring a voice-only experience to drivers.

---

[5] Sean R Eddy. "What is a hidden Markov model?" Nature Biotechnology 22, 1315–1316 (2004). https://doi.org/10.1038/nbt1004-1315

[6] "History of Dragon Naturally Speaking Software." 2012. www.voicerecognition.com.au/blogs/news/a-short-history-of-naturally-speaking-software

[7] "World-Class In-Car Speech Recognition System for Navigation in 2005 Honda Cars." 2004. https://phys.org/news/2004-09-world-class-in-car-speech-recognition-honda.html

In 2008–2010, Google launched voice search for its Web app and mobile devices, enabling users to speak their search criteria. Google's voice-to-text technology converted the spoken word into text and submitted it to their best-in-class search engine. In a paper written at that time, the voice search team at Google said:

> *A goal at Google is to make spoken access ubiquitously available. We would like to let the user choose - they should be able to take it for granted that spoken interaction is always an option. Achieving ubiquity requires two things: availability (i.e., built into every possible interaction where speech input or output can make sense), and performance (i.e., works so well that the modality adds no friction to the interaction).*
>
> *—Schalkwyk et al.*[8]

In the fall of 2011, four years after the first iPhone launched, Apple announced the integration of Siri, the voice-activated personal assistant.[9] Siri allowed users to interact with their iPhone by voice. Making calls, sending a text, setting appointments, getting directions, turning on and off iPhone features, and much more became accessible by merely saying, "Hey Siri," and commanding her to act. Siri came from two decades of research and development by Adam Cheyer, who, with cofounders Dag Kittlaus and Tom Gruber, created a little company and a voice-assistant app that sold through the Apple App Store. After refining the app, growing the company, and much negotiation, the founders sold Siri Inc. to Apple for a reported $200 million.[10]

A few years later, in 2014, Microsoft launched Cortana, their version of a voice assistant, first for the Windows Phone, but eventually for Windows 10 Mobile, Windows 10 PCs, Xbox One, and for both iOS and Android.[11] Cortana is now one of the most widely distributed, though not necessarily widely used, voice user interfaces in the world.

---

[8] Johan Schalkwyk, Doug Beeferman, Françoise Beaufays, Bill Byrne,

Ciprian Chelba, Mike Cohen, Maryam Garret, Brian Strope. "Google Search by Voice: A case study." Google, Inc. 2010.

https://static.googleusercontent.com/media/research.google.com/en//pubs/archive/36340.pdf

[9] Catherine Clifford. "Here's how Siri made it onto your iPhone." 2017. www.cnbc.com/2017/06/29/how-siri-got-on-the-iphone.html

[10] Erick Schonfeld. "Silicon Valley Buzz: Apple Paid More Than $200 Million for Siri To Get Into Mobile Search." 2010. https://techcrunch.com/2010/04/28/apple-siri-200-million/

[11] Jez Corden. "A brief history of Cortana, Microsoft's trusty digital assistant." 2017. www.windowscentral.com/history-cortana-microsofts-digital-assistant

Also, in that same time frame, 2014, Amazon launched Alexa on the Amazon Echo smart speaker,[12] and the race to put smart devices in every home on the planet was on! Echo devices were the first widely distributed smart speaker technology that combined voice activation with simple commands and attractive features. Users could say, "Alexa, what's the time?" Or, "Alexa, shuffle my playlist." And she would respond appropriately. See Figure 1-3 for a sampling of the things you can ask Alexa to do.

Figure 1-3. *Amazon Echo smart speaker with the Alexa voice assistant*

Consumers worldwide are getting into smart technology, and the market has grown by leaps and bounds, as we'll see in the next section.

Today's VUI Landscape

There are currently five major players in the global Smart Speaker market. Combined, they account for 88% of the total unit sales. This market grew by 60.3% from 2018 to 2019, up 47 million units from 78 million to 125 million units.[13] The most prominent players in the smart speaker industry are (see Figure 1-4)

[12] Aaron Pressman. "Alexa Turns 5: What Amazon's Kindergarten-Aged Assistant Can Teach the Rest of Tech." 2019. https://fortune.com/2019/11/06/amazon-alexa-echo-5-anniversary-dave-limp-interview/

[13] "Global smart speaker Q4 2019, full year 2019 and forecasts." Canalys 2020. https://canalys.com/newsroom/-global-smart-speaker-market-Q4-2019-forecasts-2020

1) Amazon. The leader in this space for the last two years, with a 30% market share, Amazon's Alexa smart speakers, screens, and devices are sold all over the world. There are over 100,000 skills available in the Alexa Skills Store, making Alexa the most versatile smart speaker on the market.

2) Google. American search giant Google offers the Nest series of smart speakers and screens and has a 19% market share. Formerly Google Home, these devices use the Google Assistant voice service, with Google Search built right in.

3) Baidu. China's top search engine company, Baidu, acquired Raven in 2017. The Raven H smart speaker was expensive, but in 2018, they unveiled the lower-cost Xiaodu smart speaker to a lot of fanfare and sold 10,000 devices in 90 seconds. Baidu now has a 14% market share. Their smart speakers connect to the open-platform personal assistant service DuerOS. Even though shipping costs and tariffs are still on the rise, there is no denying that these smart speakers are attractively priced, especially at home in China.

4) Alibaba. Chinese online retailer Alibaba introduced the Tmall Genie in 2017. This smart speaker connects to Alibaba's personal assistant service, AliGenie. Alibaba now offers over 10,000 different smart devices in its catalog.

5) Xiaomi. Chinese electronics manufacturer, Xiaomi, offers smartphones and smart speakers under its Mi brand name. The Mi AI Speaker connects to Xiaomi's Xiao AI virtual assistant.

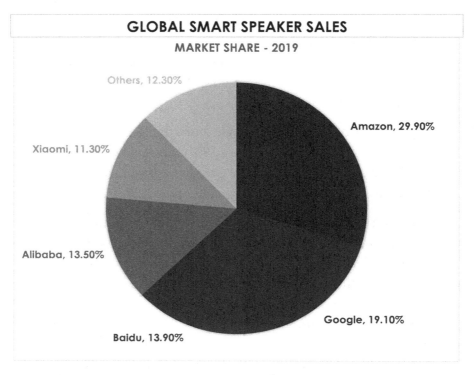

Figure 1-4. *Global market share percentages (Source: Canalys)*

Although not selling as many Apple HomePod smart speakers as the big five players, Apple's Siri VUI is also on every iPhone and iPad in the world, earning it a significant spot in the industry.

Many other firms are investing heavily in voice, such as Microsoft (their voice assistant Cortana is on every Windows PC in the world), Sonos (which uses Google Assistant), Samsung (with their own Bixby personal assistant), and IBM (with its Watson technology). Vendors of sound and entertainment technology, such as Bose (with both Amazon Alexa and Google Assistant built in), Belkin (Google Assistant), and Facebook (Alexa), are launching their own voice-enabled devices or partnering with someone to do so.

In other markets and industries, voice is also becoming more common. For example, the United States Army is developing the Joint Understanding and Dialogue Interface, JUDI, to enable soldiers to interact with smart robots via wireless microphones using informal language (see Figure 1-5). The robots will use their sensor data to help interpret the given commands.

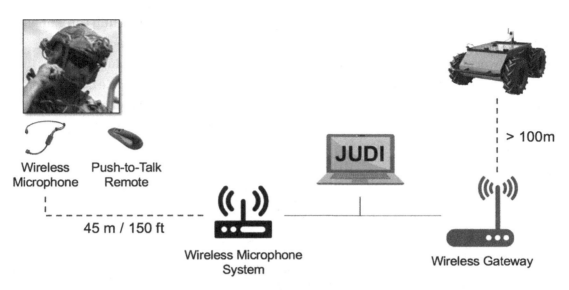

Figure 1-5. *JUDI – A voice interface for soldiers to control robots wirelessly (US Army photo)*

In the automobile industry, VUIs are must-have accessories that consumers expect to see in newer cars. Car manufacturers are offering a wide range of solutions, including embedding Alexa and Google Assistant in the automobile. Meanwhile, the device manufacturers are bringing Alexa to cars with plug-in adapters like the Roav Viva, Garmin Speak, and Amazon Echo Auto.

Not only are industry and government investing in voice, but the American consumer is getting into the game too. Approximately one-third of American homes now have smart technology, including smart speakers, smart TVs, smart lights, and smart plugs. In the next section, we'll identify some of the innovative ways to use smart tech in our homes.

Smart Homes

"Alexa, turn on my home office."

"OK," she responds. As if by magic, the overhead light and ceiling fan come on, the computer boots up, and the printer starts whirring. The oscillating fan comes on; the candle wax warmer glows, sending the strong scent of vanilla into the room; and the desk lamp turns on. Similarly, a simple utterance of "Alexa, shut down the house for the night," and the lights in the fish tank dim, the garage door and front door lock, the thermostat drops the temperature by 2 degrees, and the lights throughout the house are turned off.

Welcome to the smart home. By connecting your smart speaker to a hub (probably your smartphone) and to wireless devices sprinkled throughout your home, you can control power states (on/off), dimmers, volumes, etc. Anything with a plug can be plugged into a smart socket so it can be turned on and off by a simple voice command to your smart speaker; see Figure 1-6. Replace light bulbs and light switches with smart devices that connect wirelessly to your hub, and you can easily control them by a simple command to your smart speaker.

Figure 1-6. *Smart plugs and smart bulbs work with Alexa in the smart home*

Smart devices are great for monitoring things too. Smart smoke and CO_2 detectors, security cameras, motion detectors, and video doorbells are common. Baby monitors, smartwatches, and heart monitors are also available. Integrating with the home's utilities, smart thermostats, water systems, leak detectors, and lighting can save a lot of money on bills. In the home entertainment category, there are smart TVs and smart remotes that make the home theater much more navigable. In the kitchen and laundry room, there are smart stoves and fridges, smart washers and dryers, and smart microwaves and coffee machines. In the few years since the launch of the Amazon Echo, there have been thousands of products built to "work with Alexa." There are some intriguing smart devices among those products. For example, iRobot's Roomba is a voice-controlled robot vacuum cleaner. Whirlpool's selection of Smart Electric

Ranges has voice control and Scan-to-Cook Technology. And, Kohler's Numi 2.0 Intelligent Toilet is Alexa enabled for automatic flushing and hands-free seat closing. Yes, intelligent, talking toilets are here! With such novelties, you might be asking yourself why?

Why Voice? Why Alexa? Why Now?

Why Voice? We have reached a point where voice technology is both ubiquitous and functional. It is growing in reach and ability daily. We are past where it was a novelty. We are heading toward a future where voice is a standard part of the business world. It will not be long before executives expect quick, frequent updates from their smart speaker. Voice is just natural. It's so easy to say, "Alexa, run the numbers for the past hour." Or perhaps, "Alexa, will we make our sales target today?" These are the types of skills we will be building in this book.

Why Alexa? Other than being the industry-leading smart speaker, the main reason to build custom skills for Alexa is that it's relatively easy to do. With knowledge of Python or JavaScript, you will have custom skills up and running in a day or two. Several of the other players seem to have gone out of their way to make it challenging to create custom skills. As you get into the Alexa documentation, you will see that it is quite thorough, as is the documentation for the Amazon Web Services that integrate with Alexa. With an approachable platform, good docs, familiar programming languages, and a compelling market story, Alexa is a strong choice for data-driven skill development.

Why Now? Voice is new enough that there is a lot of discovery, invention, and research happening to move the platform forward. It is also mature enough that we've solved most of the infrastructure and hardware problems. The APIs are well defined. Most of the tooling is in version 2.0 or later. Now is a great time to learn this new technology. The consumer use cases have been well established for a couple of years now. The business use cases have yet to be determined. Now is the best time to join the leading edge and build data-driven Alexa skills.

Summary

In this chapter, we have learned about Voice User Interfaces, their past, and their present. We've discovered Alexa and smart home technology. Lastly, we answered the three why's: Why Voice? Why Alexa? Why Now?

With this foundation, we are ready to start building Alexa skills. In the next chapter, we will configure a Routine and then create a custom skill using a Blueprint.

CHAPTER 2

Routines and Blueprints

Now that we know about VUIs and smart technology, let's dive a little deeper into what Alexa is all about and see how to create Routines and custom skills from Blueprints.

What Is Alexa?

Alexa is Amazon's Voice User Interface for smart speakers, smart screens, and other smart devices. By speaking simple commands to your Alexa-enabled device, you can elicit an intelligent response. You can ask Alexa to

- Tell you the time
- Translate "Hello" into French
- Roll a d6, 2d20, or any number of dice with any number of sides
- Tell you a story
- Shuffle your playlist
- Tell you the weather
- Wake you up in 40 minutes (I like this one)
- Give you a daily news brief
- List your next three to-do items
- Tell you yesterday's market close
- Read your email
- Get a summary of hot-button issues that you need to look at today
- Tell you the projected sales for tomorrow
- And hundreds of other requests

© Simon A. Kingaby 2022
S. A. Kingaby, *Data-Driven Alexa Skills*, https://doi.org/10.1007/978-1-4842-7449-1_2

In the Alexa Skills Store, there are tens of thousands of additional skills you can enable so that Alexa can play games with you, inspire you, help you plan a trip, educate you, control your smart home, and so much more. For example, Alexa's weather feature can tell you the temperature, if it's raining or going to rain. The Big Sky skill adds air quality, humidity, UV Index, wind speed, weather facts, and much more. For premium users, Big Sky also offers custom weather alerts, radar imagery (on smart screens), and the weather at additional addresses.

In addition to the free and premium skills in the Alexa Skills Store, there are several ways to customize Alexa without building skills. In particular, Amazon Routines and Alexa Blueprints are code-free and available to anyone who wants to create a custom Alexa experience.

Alexa Routines

When you find yourself repeatedly asking Alexa to do several things in a row, you should consider creating an Alexa Routine. For example, if, every morning, you turn on the lights, raise the thermostat by 2 degrees, and start the coffee pot, you can create a routine for that.

To create a routine, you will use the Alexa app on your smartphone (see Figure 2-1) and follow these instructions:

1. Select the main menu icon.

2. Select *Routines*.

3. Click the + button to add a routine.

4. Click the + button next to *Enter routine name*, enter a name, and click *Next*. (Note: This is not what you say to trigger the routine. That gets entered later.) The routine name has a limit of 50 characters.

5. Click the + button next to *When this happens*.

6. Click the icon for the trigger action you want, for example, *Voice*. Then enter or select the appropriate action. For Voice, this is the trigger phrase, such as "Fire it up," "Start the Coffee," or even "Pink Flamingo." Then click *next*.

7. Click the + button next to *Add action.*

8. Select the actions you want Alexa to do when the routine runs. For example, choose Smart Home, then All Devices, then TV, then Power On.

9. Add as many actions as you need in the routine.

10. Drag actions up and down using the hamburger icon (the two stacked lines at the right) to rearrange the order they happen in the routine.

11. Click *Save* to finish configuring the routine and create it.

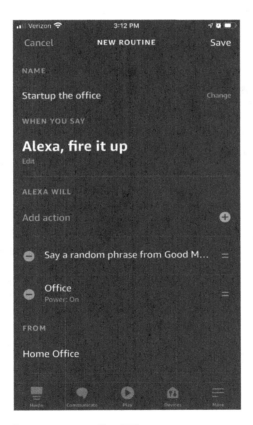

Figure 2-1. *Using the Alexa app on the iPhone to create a routine*

Similarly, a routine could save you time at work. You could create a routine that lists any production failures that happened overnight and still need attention (from the Company Heartbeat Skill), then provides today's revenue projections (from the Sales Forecasting Skill), then lists over budget projects (from the Project Management Skill), and concludes with the top three fires you need to put out (from your Daily Planner Skill).

Creating a routine is a way of queuing several Alexa skills into one trigger. It is not the same as creating a custom skill. So how can we make a custom skill? In the next section, we'll look at using Alexa Blueprints to do just that. No code is needed.

Alexa Blueprints

The easiest way to create custom skills for your Alexa is to start with an Alexa Blueprint. While Routines work with existing skills, Blueprints make personalized skills based on one of the many templates provided. For example, you can create skills for the home from the Chore Chart or Pet Sitter blueprints. Or you can create skills for the office from the Flash Briefing or Onboard Guide blueprints.

To create a skill from a blueprint, open a browser to `https://blueprints.amazon.com/home` (see Figure 2-2).

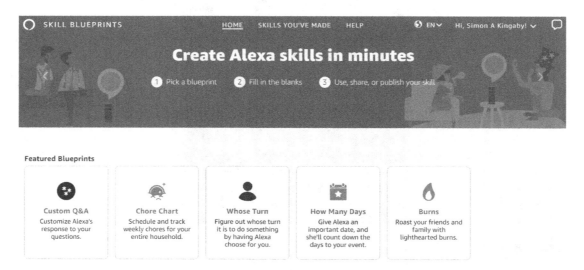

Figure 2-2. *The Alexa Skill Blueprints home screen*

For example, start by selecting the Chore Chart blueprint, which allows you to create a custom chore chart skill using your household members (see Figure 2-3) and your chores (see Figure 2-4). Then click the Make Your Own button.

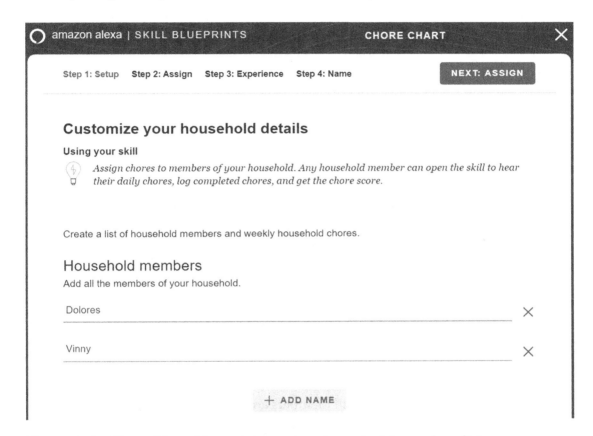

Figure 2-3. *Chore Chart blueprint – custom household members list*

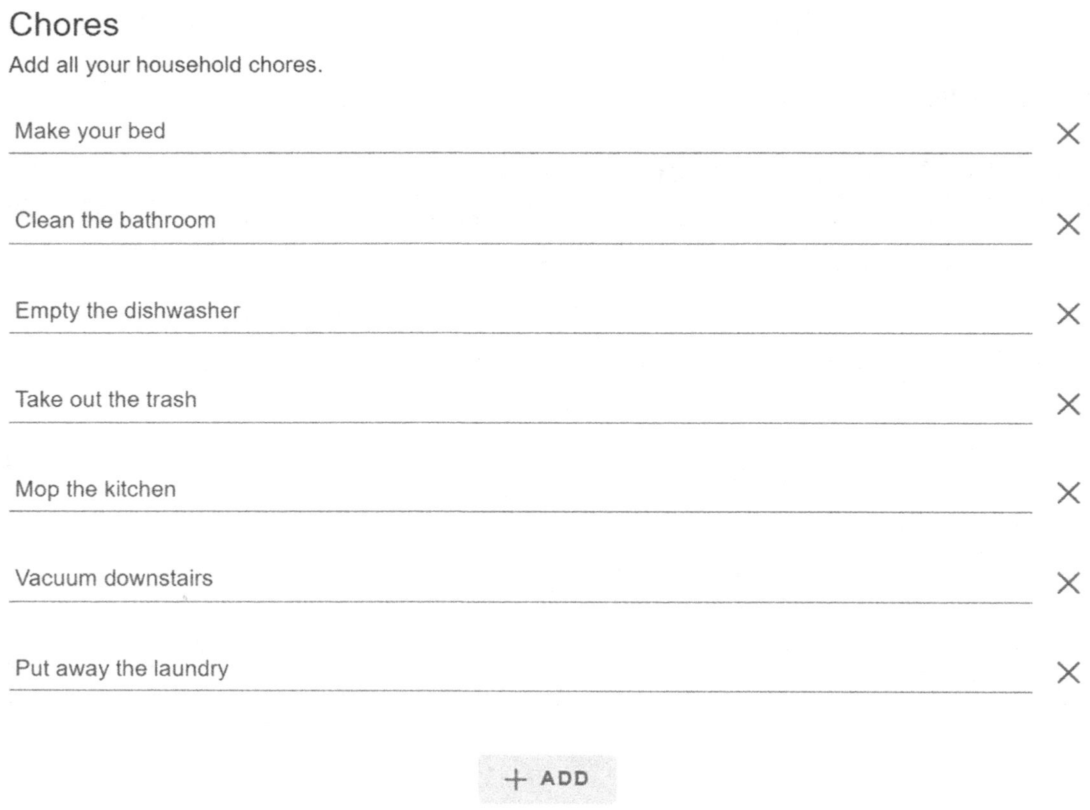

Chores

Add all your household chores.

Make your bed	✕
Clean the bathroom	✕
Empty the dishwasher	✕
Take out the trash	✕
Mop the kitchen	✕
Vacuum downstairs	✕
Put away the laundry	✕

+ ADD

Figure 2-4. *Chore Chart blueprint – custom chores list*

Once you've added your household members and the chores you want doing, click *Next: Assign*. On the next page, *Step 2: Assign*, you can assign and schedule the chores you listed on the first page. In Figure 2-5, I have selected for Vinny to Put away the laundry on Tuesday, Thursday, and Saturday. Vinny will get a reminder on Karen (the Kitchen Echo Dot) at 7:00 p.m.

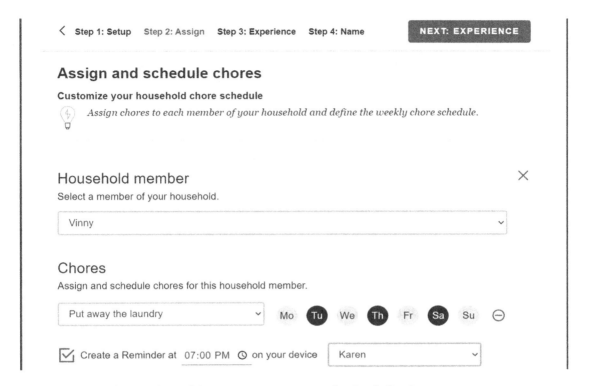

Figure 2-5. *Chore Chart blueprint – assign and schedule chores*

Next, on the *Step 3: Experience* page, you can customize the comments Alexa uses when you open the skill, after you hear your list of chores, and when you finish your tasks. On the *Step 4: Name* page, you can enter a name for your Chore Chart skill, such as Family Chore Chart. Finally, click *Create Skill*. The blueprint will take a couple of minutes to create your new skill. At first, the skill will only be visible to you. Click the *Share With Others* link and then go through the prompts to email the link to the rest of your family.

Another interesting example of the Alexa Blueprint is the Onboard Guide blueprint. To create an Onboard Guide skill, you open a browser to `https://blueprints.amazon.com/home`, scroll to the bottom to the *Business* category, and select *Onboard Guide*, shown in Figure 2-6.

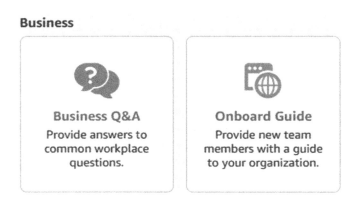

Business

Business Q&A
Provide answers to common workplace questions.

Onboard Guide
Provide new team members with a guide to your organization.

Figure 2-6. *Select the Onboard Guide blueprint*

Click the Make Your Own button; then, in *Step 1: Content*, you'll fill in the Locations of any important resources, Steps for how to do things, and Name and Phone Number of key contacts, as shown in Figure 2-7.

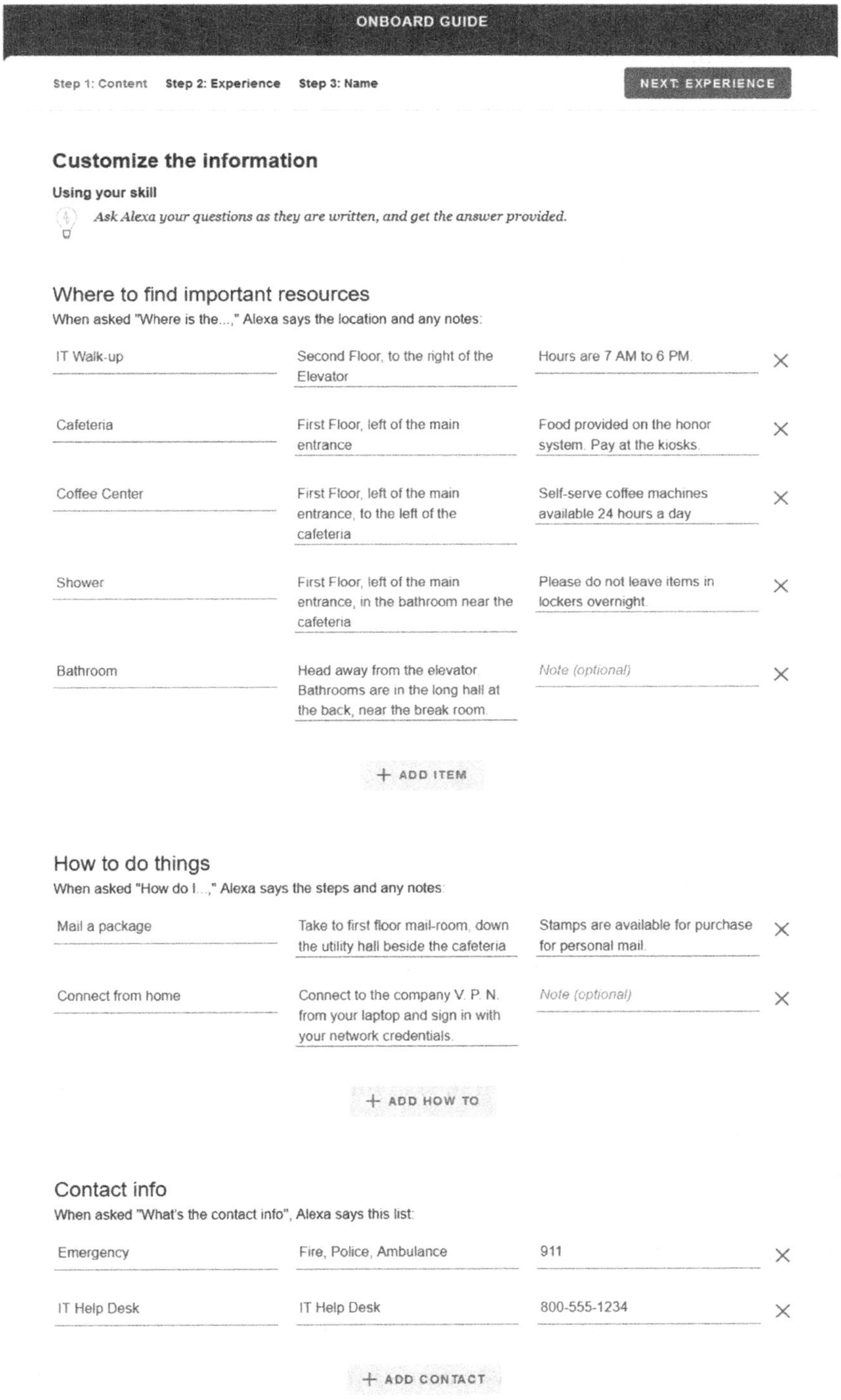

ONBOARD GUIDE

Step 1: Content   **Step 2: Experience**   Step 3: Name   NEXT EXPERIENCE

Customize the information

Using your skill

Ask Alexa your questions as they are written, and get the answer provided.

Where to find important resources

When asked "Where is the....," Alexa says the location and any notes:

IT Walk-up	Second Floor, to the right of the Elevator	Hours are 7 AM to 6 PM.	✕
Cafeteria	First Floor, left of the main entrance	Food provided on the honor system. Pay at the kiosks.	✕
Coffee Center	First Floor, left of the main entrance, to the left of the cafeteria	Self-serve coffee machines available 24 hours a day	✕
Shower	First Floor, left of the main entrance, in the bathroom near the cafeteria	Please do not leave items in lockers overnight.	✕
Bathroom	Head away from the elevator. Bathrooms are in the long hall at the back, near the break room.	*Note (optional)*	✕

+ ADD ITEM

How to do things

When asked "How do I...," Alexa says the steps and any notes:

Mail a package	Take to first floor mail-room, down the utility hall beside the cafeteria	Stamps are available for purchase for personal mail.	✕
Connect from home	Connect to the company V. P. N. from your laptop and sign in with your network credentials.	*Note (optional)*	✕

+ ADD HOW TO

Contact info

When asked "What's the contact info", Alexa says this list:

Emergency	Fire, Police, Ambulance	911	✕
IT Help Desk	IT Help Desk	800-555-1234	✕

+ ADD CONTACT

Figure 2-7. *Step 1 – content for the Onboard Guide*

Next, in *Step 2: Experience*, add some messages to personalize the experience for new employees. For example, see Figure 2-8.

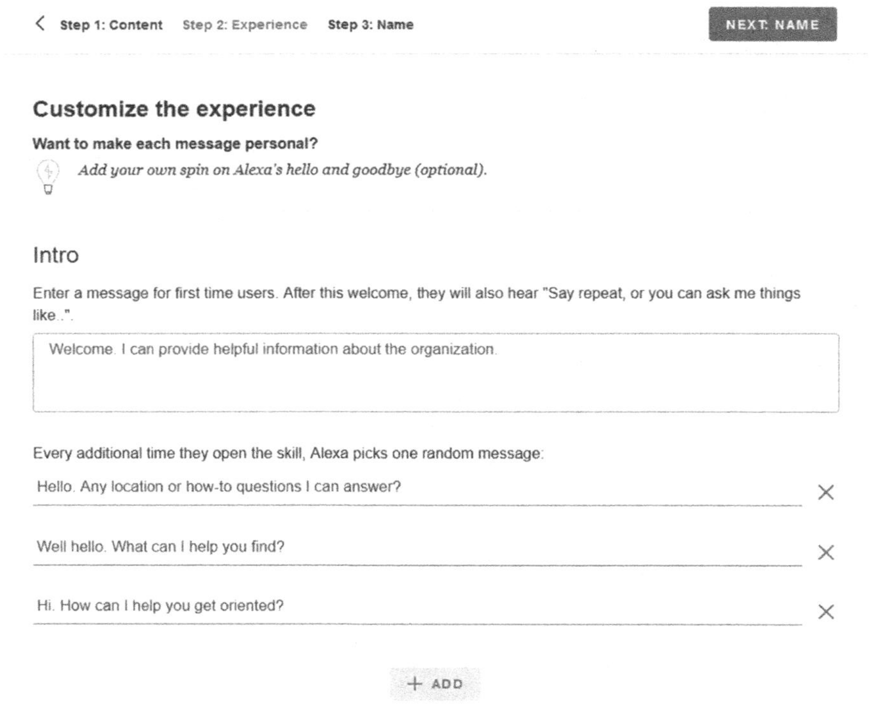

Figure 2-8. *Add some personal touches with Step 2 - customize the experience*

In *Step 3: Name*, give your new skill a name. This is how people will launch your skill, so you might want to call it something easy to remember and easy to say. For example, if you name it "the butler," then to launch the skill, people will say, "Alexa, Open the Butler." Selecting a skill name can be difficult. First, skill names may only contain alphabetic characters, apostrophes, periods, and spaces. So you have to spell out each word and number. So "007" is not a valid choice, but "double oh seven" is. Second, you want your skill name to be unique, easy to say, and easy to remember. This is where it becomes a problem. For example, if you create a skill where the listener can choose from different story endings, you can't call it "choose your own adventure" because that's already a skill name. Worse, any variation on that theme will likely go to the official Choose Your Own Adventure skill instead. It can get tricky to come up with something that is unique, easy to say, and easy to remember.

Finally, click the *Next: Create Skill* button, and the blueprint will take a couple of minutes to create your new skill. Once created, test it thoroughly to make sure it works as expected. At first, the skill will only be visible to you. Click the *Share With Others* link, and then go through the prompts to email the link to the rest of your department or company.

Blueprints are by far the simplest way to create a custom skill for Alexa.

Summary

In this chapter, you learned about Alexa Routines and Blueprints. Routines are a way of combining several Alexa actions into one group with one launch phrase. Blueprints help you implement skills by filling in an existing template – or blueprint – and then sharing the created skill. Both can be useful, but if you want to build custom skills, you will need to work with the Alexa Developer Console and AWS Services. In the next chapter, we set up the accounts you'll need throughout the book so we can build custom skills.

CHAPTER 3

The Developer Accounts

In Chapter 2, you learned how to create Routines and how to configure skills from Blueprints. Now we are going to begin setting up your development environment so that you can start building Alexa skills. First, we will create the accounts you need throughout this book.

Note I highly recommend the use of a password manager, such as Dashlane, 1Password, or LastPass. These will allow you to safely store the passwords you need to access the various accounts you're about to create.

Creating the Developer Accounts

There are four essential accounts you will need when developing data-driven Alexa skills, plus two additional accounts that we'll use throughout this book. Altogether that makes for the following six accounts to create:

1. An Amazon account

2. An Alexa developer account

3. An AWS root user account

4. An IAM developer/administrator account that is NOT the root user

5. A GitHub account

6. A Jira account

In the following sections, you will create each of these accounts and understand why you need them.

© Simon A. Kingaby 2022
S. A. Kingaby, *Data-Driven Alexa Skills*, https://doi.org/10.1007/978-1-4842-7449-1_3

Amazon Account

You will need an Amazon account to access your Alexa device, the Alexa app on your phone, and the Alexa Skills Store. If you do not have an Amazon account, or you wish to create a different one for Alexa development, then you will need a valid email address that you can receive emails at and a smartphone to receive text confirmations. Then, follow these instructions:

1. Go to `https://amazon.com`.

2. If you already have an Amazon account, click on your profile in the top right and select *Switch Account*. Then select *Create Account*.

3. Create an account (Figure 3-1).

Figure 3-1. *Creating a new Amazon account*

Alexa Developer Account

To log in to the Alexa Developer Console, you will need a Developer account. This will be the same Amazon account you just created but configured for Developer access. To do so, follow these steps:

1. Navigate to `https://developer.amazon.com/alexa`.

2. Click *Sign-in* at the top right, and sign in to the Amazon account you created previously.

3. Or select your profile icon at the top right and select Complete Registration.

4. Complete the *Amazon Developer Registration* (Figure 3-2).

Figure 3-2. *Complete the Developer Registration*

5. Complete the profile and answer the survey question about the products that interest you.

6. Then click the *Start exploring the console* option.

You have created an Amazon Developer account, which you can use for a variety of Amazon Developer Services and Technologies (see Figure 3-3).

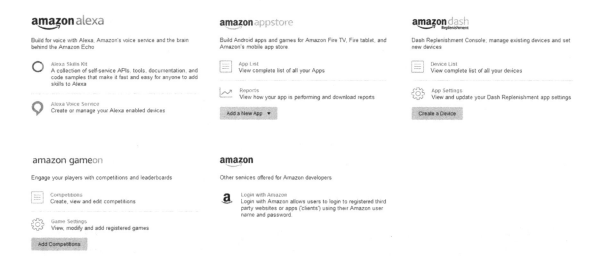

Figure 3-3. *The many services that your Amazon developer account unlocks*

AWS Developer Account

The next account you'll need is an Amazon Web Services (AWS) account. We'll use this account for the back-end services we need to support data-driven Alexa skills. In particular, custom skills use a service called Lambda. Be aware that creating a developer account requires a credit card for payment verification. No charges will be incurred at registration time as you are signing up for a Free Tier account. To get started

1. Navigate to `https://aws.amazon.com/free/` (Figure 3-4).

Figure 3-4. *Signing up for AWS Free Tier*

2. Click *Create a Free Account.*

3. Create an *AWS Account*.

4. Complete the Contact Info and click *Create Account and Continue*.

5. Provide Payment Information and click *Verify and Continue*. You will not incur any charges at this time. AWS will use your payment information to verify your identity and will only charge you for usage in excess of the AWS Free Tier Limits (`https://aws.amazon.com/free/`).

6. Confirm your identity.

7. Select the Basic support – Free plan (Figure 3-5).

Select a support plan

Choose a support plan for your business or personal account. Compare plans and pricing examples ⬀. You can change your plan anytime in the AWS Management Console.

Figure 3-5. *Select the Free support plan*

Welcome to the AWS Management Console (Figure 3-6)!

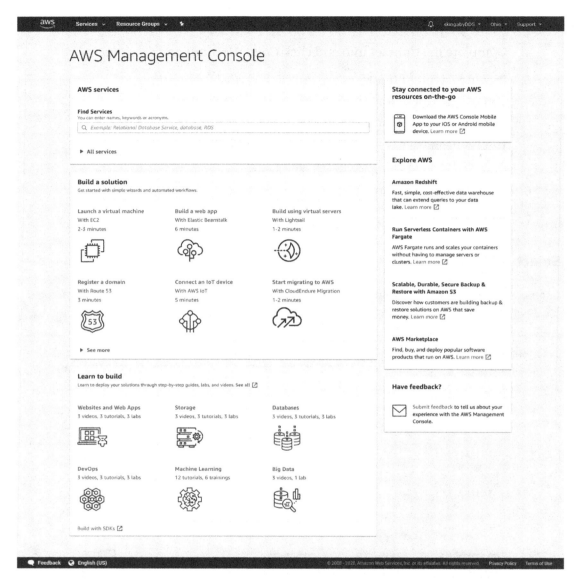

Figure 3-6. *The AWS Management Console*

The AWS account you just created is known as the root user. Think of this as the account with godlike powers to do anything and everything with your AWS services. The first order of business is to create a new user account that is an administrator but is not the root user. The root user will be rarely used and should be safely nestled behind multifactor authentication and a complex password. The next section will create the account you use to log in regularly and create AWS services.

IAM and Account Security

The first Amazon Web Service we'll need to configure is IAM (Identity and Access Management). IAM is where you create users, groups, permissions, etc. Logged in as the root user, we will create an administrator account. You will then log out of the root user account and log in to the administrator account, which you will then use to create, manage, and configure any other AWS services that you need. To make the administrator account, do the following:

1. In the AWS Management Console, search for *IAM*, and select it (Figure 3-7).

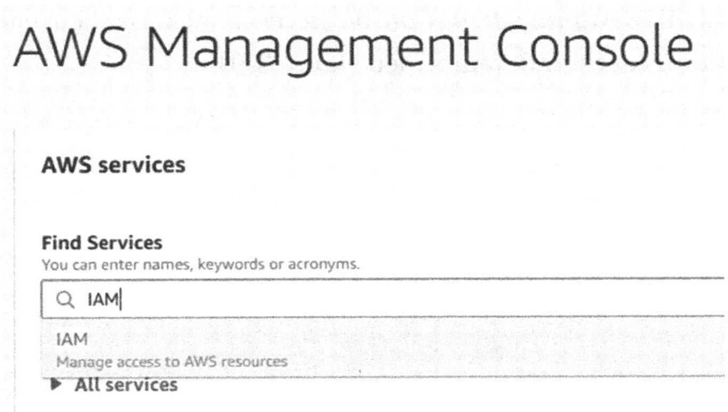

Figure 3-7. *Search for IAM in the AWS Management Console*

2. In the Identity and Access Management (IAM) console, select *Users* in the left menu (Figure 3-8).

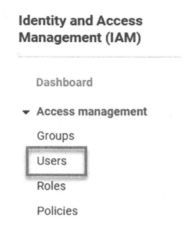

Figure 3-8. *Select Users on the left*

3. Click *Add User* at the top.

4. Enter **administrator** as the user name.

5. Select the *AWS Management Console access* checkbox. Leave the other options at their defaults (see Figure 3-9).

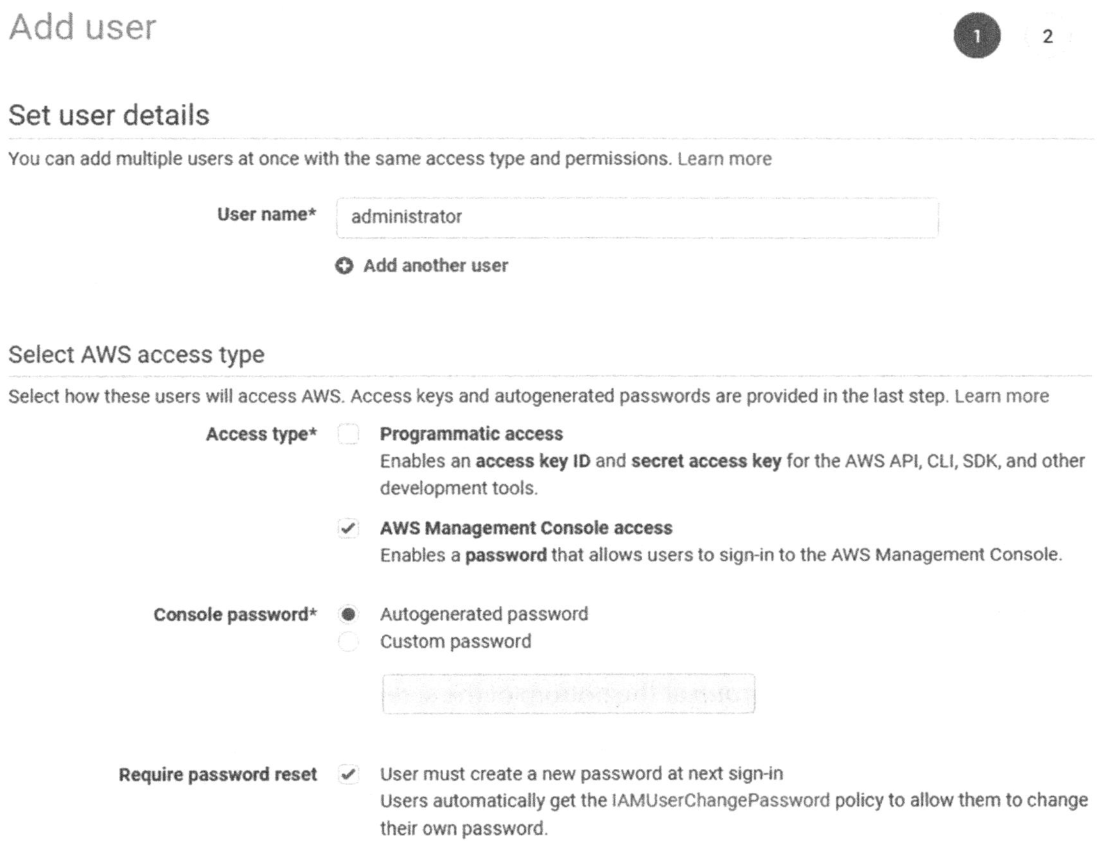

Add user

① ②

Set user details

You can add multiple users at once with the same access type and permissions. Learn more

User name*   administrator

⊕ **Add another user**

Select AWS access type

Select how these users will access AWS. Access keys and autogenerated passwords are provided in the last step. Learn more

Access type*   ☐ **Programmatic access**
Enables an **access key ID** and **secret access key** for the AWS API, CLI, SDK, and other development tools.

☑ **AWS Management Console access**
Enables a **password** that allows users to sign-in to the AWS Management Console.

Console password*   ⦿ Autogenerated password
○ Custom password

Require password reset   ☑ User must create a new password at next sign-in
Users automatically get the IAMUserChangePassword policy to allow them to change their own password.

Figure 3-9. *Adding the administrator user*

6.   Click *Next: Permissions* at the bottom of the screen.

7.   Select *Add User to Group* and click *Create group* (Figure 3-10).

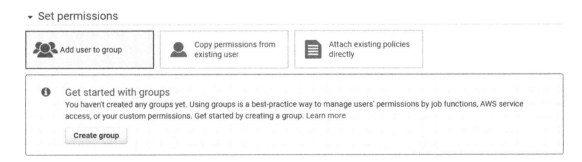

Figure 3-10. *Create a group for the new administrator*

8. Enter **Admins** as the Group Name and select the checkbox next to *AdministratorAccess* in the policy list (Figure 3-11).

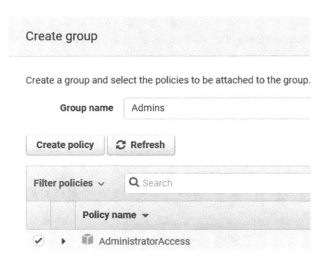

Figure 3-11. *Select the AdministratorAccess policy*

9. Now click *Create group* at the bottom of the screen.

10. Back on the Add user to Group screen, click *Next: Tags* at the bottom of the screen.

11. Then click *Next: Review*.

12. Then click *Create User*.

13.   When the user has been created, download the .csv file. Also, show the generated password and make a note of it for the first sign-in (see Figure 3-12). Optionally, send yourself an email with the login instructions.

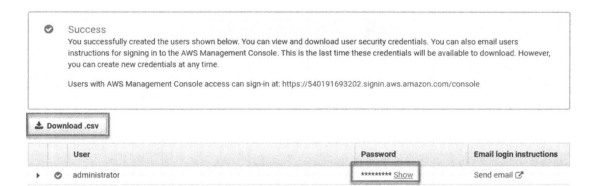

Figure 3-12. *Be sure to download the .csv and note the password*

14.   Open the .csv file you downloaded previously.

15.   Copy the 12-digit number in the URL in the file (Figure 3-13).

```
User name,Password,Access key ID,Secret access key,Console login link
administrator,]Z|vBQwn-sr^,,,https://540191693202.signin.aws.amazon.com/console
```

Figure 3-13. *The downloaded .csv file shows the 12-digit account ID*

16. Next, we'll log out of our root user account and log in as administrator.

17. Select your profile icon in the top right and select *Sign Out* (Figure 3-14).

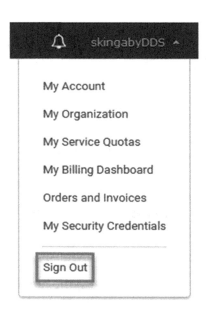

Figure 3-14. *Sign out of the root user account*

18.   Now select the *Sign In to the Console* button in the top right.

19.   From the Sign-in screen (Figure 3-15), select *IAM user*.

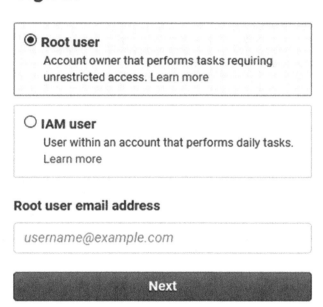

Figure 3-15.   *The AWS sign-in screen*

20. Enter the 12-digit number you copied previously (Figure 3-16). Then click *Next*.

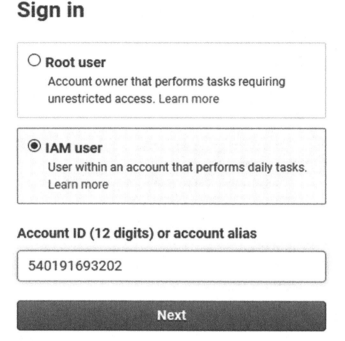

Figure 3-16. *Logging in as IAM user, enter the 12-digit account number*

21. Then enter administrator for the IAM user name and enter the one-time-use password you copied previously (Figure 3-17).

Sign in as IAM user

Account ID (12 digits) or account alias

540191693202

IAM user name

administrator

Password

••••••••••••

Sign in

Figure 3-17. *Sign in as administrator*

22. Then change your password to something suitably complicated for the administrator account for your AWS services.

Welcome back to the AWS Management Console. Whenever you need to administer your AWS services, use this administrator account, not the root user account. Next up, GitHub.

GitHub Access

We will be using GitHub throughout this book as our source code repository. Most of the skills you create will have at least some code that you'll want to store in a safe place. GitHub private repositories are that safe place. As an alternative, you could use Microsoft's Azure DevOps repositories, Amazon's AWS CodeCommit, Atlassian's Bitbucket, or any number of others. We're going to stick with GitHub as it is commonly used throughout business as a standard, and all of the major tools work with it. To start, we need to create a GitHub account:

1. Navigate to `https://github.com`.

2. Click on *Sign up for GitHub*.

3. Enter a username, which is not your email address.

4. Enter your email address.

5. Enter a password.

6. Solve the puzzle.

7. Click *Create account*.

8. Verify your email.

9. Done. You now have a GitHub account.

Jira Account

Atlassian's Jira and Microsoft's Azure DevOps are two of the most popular agile software project management tools. AWS CodeStar and GitHub also have some project management features. Any of these will work for our purposes, so if you have a preference, go for it. However, Jira is commonly used in the open-source community and has less configuration and overhead than Azure DevOps, so throughout this book, we'll be using Jira for requirements and task management. To create a Jira account

1. Navigate to `www.atlassian.com/software/jira`.

2. Click on *Get it free*.

3. Click to select Confluence as a second product (Figure 3-18).

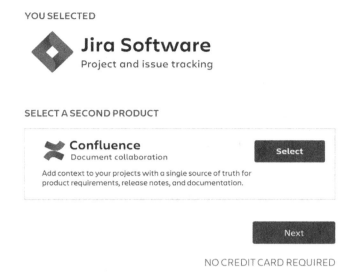

YOU SELECTED

Jira Software
Project and issue tracking

SELECT A SECOND PRODUCT

Confluence
Document collaboration

Add context to your projects with a single source of truth for product requirements, release notes, and documentation.

Select

Next

NO CREDIT CARD REQUIRED

Figure 3-18. *Add Confluence to Jira selection*

4. Click *Next*.

5. Click *Sign up with email*.

6. Enter the required information.

7. Click *Agree*.

8. Verify your email.

9. Give your site a name (Figure 3-19).

Give your site a name

Choose something familiar like your team or company

datadrivenskills-com   .atlassian.net

Figure 3-19. *Create a Jira site name*

10. Answer the survey questions (or click *Skip*).

11. Invite your teammates (or click *Skip*).

12. Select *new to* Jira. Select *new to* agile methodologies. These options will make Jira more user friendly.

13. Select that we spend our time working on *features*.

14. Select we have a *flexible* schedule.

15. Click *Next*.

16. On the next screen, we're going to select *Kanban*. Scrum is a good choice too, but for our purposes, we only need the Kanban template.

17. For your first project name, enter *Data-Driven Skills*, with a key of *DDS*.

18. And that's it. You have a Jira account, site, and project all set up and ready to go.

Summary

In this chapter, we have set up and configured the developer accounts we'll need throughout the book. These accounts capture requirements; manage tasks; store source code; configure the VUI for our custom, data-driven Alexa skills; and build the back-end databases, storage areas, and coding of the logic of the skills. In the next chapter, we will build our first custom skill, a Body Mass Index (BMI) calculator.

CHAPTER 4

Creating the VUI for a Custom Data-Driven Skill

Now that you've configured a routine and created some skills from blueprints and now that you've got the accounts setup, we're ready to build our first custom data-driven Alexa skill. In this chapter, we'll build a Body Mass Index (BMI) calculator. The premise is simple: BMI is a function of height and weight. The math is

$$BMI = \frac{weight\ in\ kilograms}{\left(height\ in\ meters\right)^2}$$

What makes this calculation complicated is that if I ask you your height, you might say: 188 centimeters, 1.88 meters, 6 foot 2 inches, or 74 inches. Similarly, if I ask your weight, you might say 109 kilos, 109 kgs, 240 pounds, or even 17 stone 2 pounds, or just 17 stone.

So let's get to it. First, we're going to create the base skill. Then we'll configure the VUI for that skill in the Alexa Developer Console. In the next chapter, we'll write the back-end code and test our skill to make sure it works as expected. Finally, we'll go through the process of publishing our skill to the Alexa Skills Store.

Step 1: Create the Base Skill

The first step is to create the base skill from a model, method, and template. To start this step, we need to launch the Alexa Developer Console. Navigate to `https://developer.amazon.com/alexa/console/ask`. Welcome to Alexa skill development (see Figure 4-1).

© Simon A. Kingaby 2022
S. A. Kingaby, *Data-Driven Alexa Skills*, https://doi.org/10.1007/978-1-4842-7449-1_4

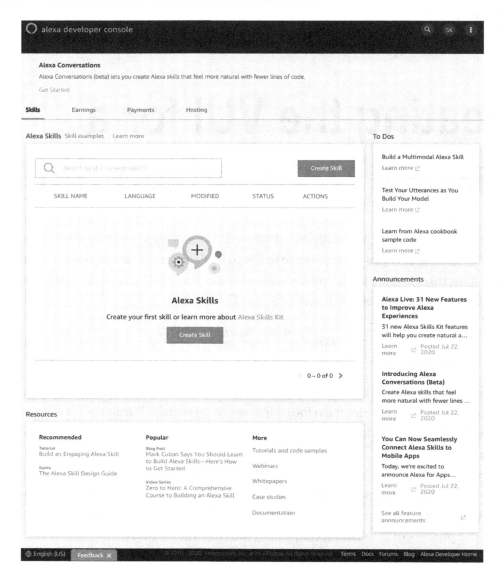

Figure 4-1. *The Alexa Skill Development Console*

Now, click on *Create Skill* and give the skill a name, such as BMI calculator. Then leave the first option at *Custom* because we're building a custom skill, not one of the other types. Then, you can select Alexa-hosted or Provision your own. Alexa-hosted provides the plumbing to the AWS lambda function and several other AWS services. Provision your own does not. We'll have to provision our own for some of the advanced skills in this book, but not yet. Select *Alexa-Hosted (Python)* for the second option, as shown in Figure 4-2.

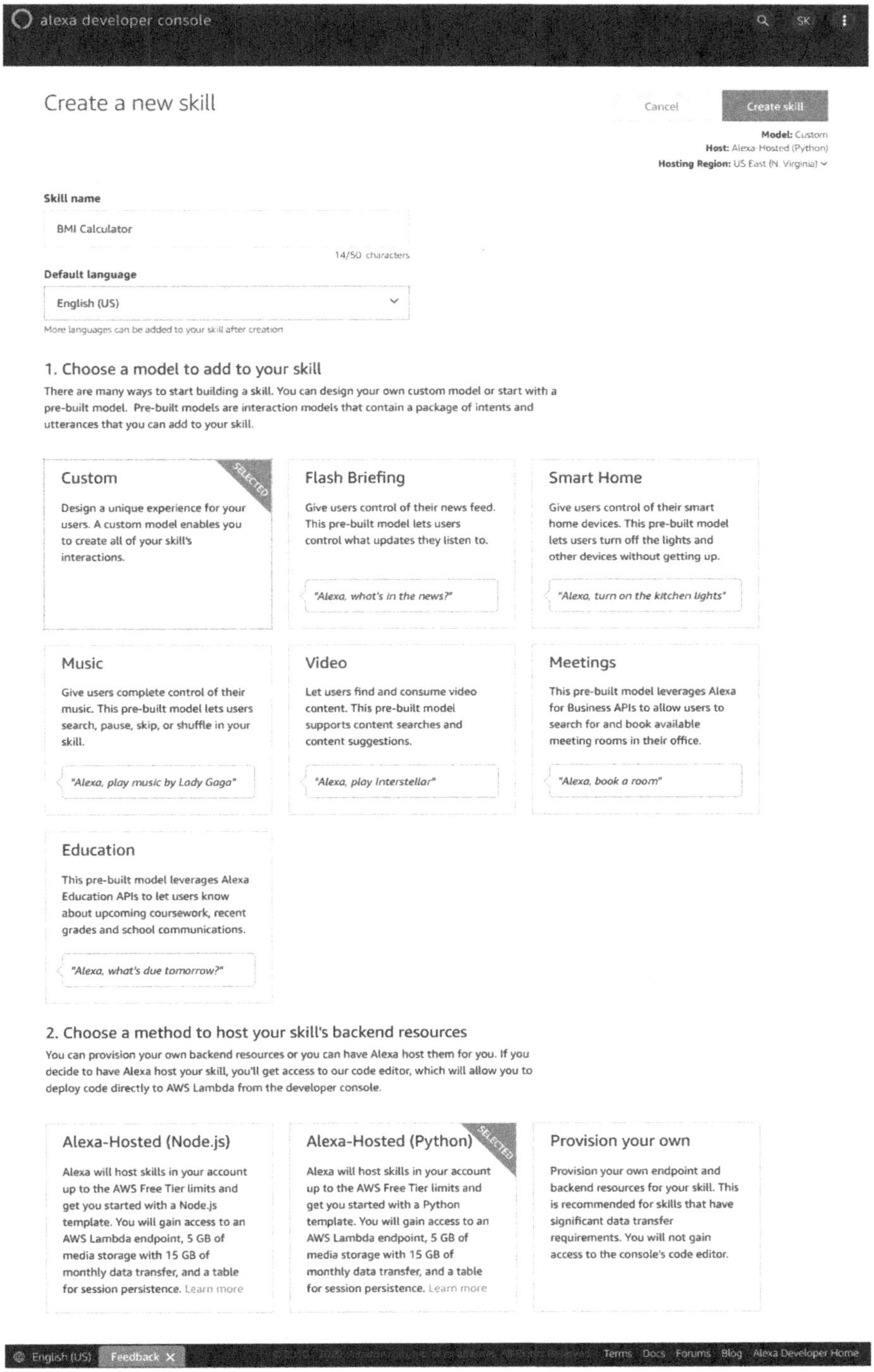

Figure 4-2. *Selecting the model and method for the new skill*

Now click *Create Skill* in the top right. We're going to choose the *Hello World Skill/Start from Scratch* template (I know, I know, but of the options provided, it is the most basic) and click *Continue with template* (Figure 4-3).

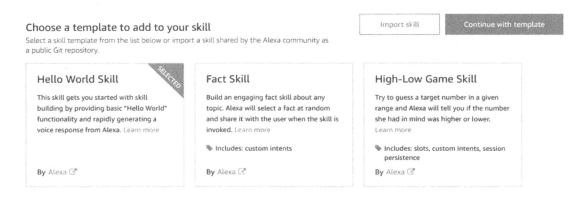

Figure 4-3. *Choosing a template for the new skill*

Woohoo! Your new skill is being created (Figure 4-4).

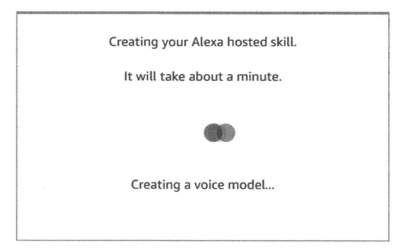

Figure 4-4. *Your skill is being created*

In a minute or two, your new BMI calculator skill will be ready to begin (see Figure 4-5). In the meantime, let's take a tour of the skill interface.

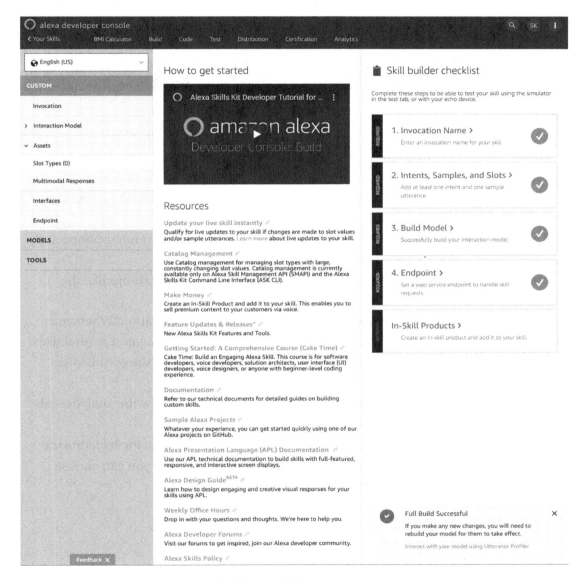

Figure 4-5. *Your new BMI calculator skill*

The Skill Builder Interface

Let's take a look around the Alexa Developer Console. Starting at the top (see Figure 4-6), we have a set of tabs for the main tasks in developing your skill.

Figure 4-6. *The main tasks for developing your skill*

Build: Use this tab to configure the VUI options and create the interaction model for your skill.

Code: Write your back-end code here. For Alexa-hosted skills, this tab is where you write the lambda function. You do not have to go out to AWS for this.

Test: Test your interaction model in this tab. You can turn on your microphone and interact with your skill to make sure it works as expected.

Distribution: Here, you can configure the skill store options and things like the privacy statement.

Certification: This is where you can submit your skill for certification. When you select this tab, your skill will be validated automatically, and it may suggest several fixes. Once you pass the automated validation, you can submit the skill to the certification process.

Analytics: Once your skill is live in the Alexa store, you can review the analytics tab to see how it's doing and to learn how to improve it.

On the left-hand side of the Alexa Developer Console is the menu for selecting the different parts of your interaction model (see Figure 4-7). At the top, you can choose the language of your skill.

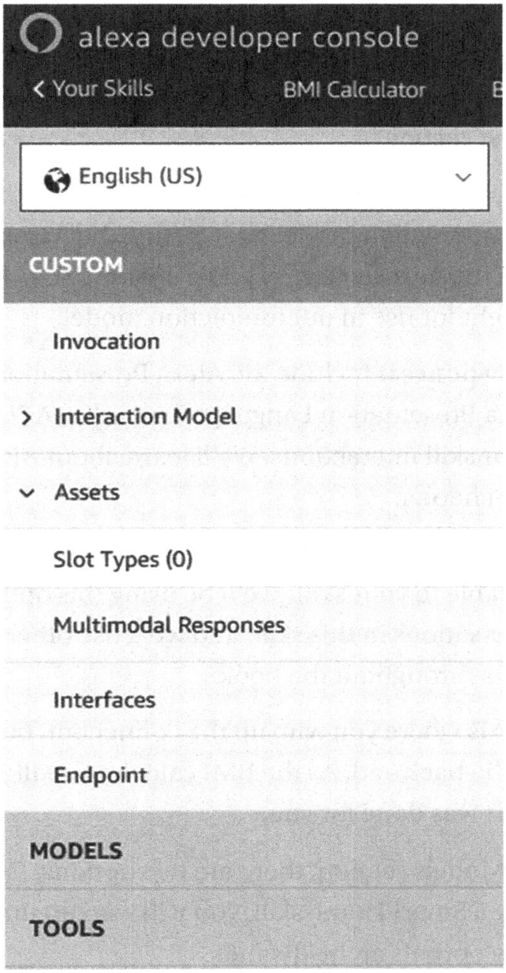

Figure 4-7. *The menu for selecting the components of your interaction model*

Below the language selector, there are three sections: Custom, Models, and Tools. In the Custom section, you will develop your interaction model. The options presented will vary depending on the type of interaction model you choose, but the standard choices are as follows:

> **Invocation:** This is where you assign the invocation name for your skill. If your invocation name is "simon's incredible skill," people will need to say, "Alexa, launch simon's incredible skill," to access your skill.

Interaction Model: Use this option to configure the dialog between your user and Alexa. This option is where you'll spend most of your time writing the intents and utterances for your skill – more on these items in the next section.

Assets: Configure the slot values and other assets you need to complete your interaction model by selecting the Assets menu option. Also, in the next section, we'll be creating slots for the height and weight for use in our interaction model.

Multimodal Responses: Include the Alexa Presentation Language (APL) and Alexa Presentation Language for Audio (APLA) codes returned in your skill interactions. We'll learn about APL and APLA in a later chapter.

Interfaces: Use this option to turn on and off the various interfaces available to your skill. We'll be using this option to turn on Alexa Conversations in this skill, and we'll use other interfaces in other projects throughout the book.

Endpoint: This is where you wire up the connection between the front end and the back end. As the BMI calculator skill is Alexa hosted, this part was done for you.

When you select the Models section, there are two options: Custom and Smart Home. If you are building a Smart Home skill, you will want to turn on that model. We're not, so we can leave these options at the defaults.

In the Tools section, you will find the options for In-Skill Products, Account linking, Permissions, and Languages, all of which we cover in later chapters. We will not need these for the BMI calculator.

In the center panel of the Alexa Developer Console is the *How to get started* video and a list of resources you can use for getting started and learning more.

Finally, on the right-hand side of the console is the Skill builder checklist. This section shows you the status of the various tasks you need to complete to build your skill. With the template we used to create the base skill, most of these are already completed.

With that review of the console, we are ready to get started with configuring the VUI for our BMI calculator skill.

Step 2: Configure the VUI

Let's review the problem statement for the BMI skill found at the beginning of the chapter: Calculate the BMI as a function of height and weight. The math is

$$BMI = \frac{weight\ in\ kilograms}{\left(height\ in\ meters\right)^2}$$

We need a way of asking the user to give us their height and weight so that we can calculate their BMI. Before that, the user needs to launch (or invoke) our skill and ask us to calculate their BMI. We'll take these two steps one at a time.

Invocation Name

The first thing a user has to do is launch your skill. They do this by saying, "Alexa, start/launch/run *<invocation name>*." Create the **Skill Invocation Name** by selecting the Invocation menu item on the left. There are a few rules for the invocation name:

1. Two or more words.

2. It's written in lowercase with spaces between words.

3. Possessive apostrophes are ok, as in "simon's."

4. Abbreviations and acronyms have to be spelled out with periods and spaces between the letters, so "b. m. i." is correct.

5. Numbers have to be spelled out, for example, "one hundred."

6. Invocation names cannot contain any of the Alexa skill launch phrases such as "launch," "ask," "tell," "open," "load," "begin," and "enable." Wake words including "Alexa," "Amazon," "Echo," "Computer," or the word "skill" or "app" are not allowed either.

7. Brand names must be yours to use.

The Skill Invocation Name is how people will launch your skill. As with Routines, the skill name is something you want to be unique, easy to remember, and easy to say. If you look in the Alexa Skills Store (`www.amazon.com/alexa-skills`), you will find a ton of BMI calculators. In order to come up with something unique, I added my first name, so for our BMI calculator, I chose "simon's b. m. i. calculator" as my Skill Invocation Name (Figure 4-8). Notice how the BMI acronym is spelled out. If I just used "simon's bmi calculator," Alexa would be listening for the word, bmi, not the acronym B.M.I.

Skill Invocation Name ⓘ

> simon's b. m. i. calculator

Figure 4-8. *Enter a Skill Invocation Name for your new skill*

Be sure to test your launch phrase several times on an Alexa device. This testing should expose any potential conflicts. For example, a lot of the skills with my name in their launch phrase conflict with the popular game "Simon Says." I have to be careful to come up with unique invocation names.

The next question we need to answer is which interaction model we want to use.

The Interaction Model

There are two options for the **Interaction Model**. First, the default interaction model uses intents to capture what the user intends for the skill to do. An **intent** is a statement that tells or asks Alexa to do something. For example, "What's my BMI?" is an intent. It asks Alexa to begin the process of calculating my BMI. This first intent would be followed by Alexa asking for your height and weight, which you would answer by uttering the ProvideHeightAndWeight intent, where you say the phrase, "I am six foot two and two hundred and forty pounds." This intent would expect you to convey both the height and weight. It would not work for you just to say one or the other. This is where the second interaction model, **Alexa Conversations**, comes in. It is more conversational and allows you to answer the prompt with just your height or your weight. When Alexa notices the missing value, she will then prompt you just for that item.

With the Intent model, the dialog between you and Alexa will go like Figure 4-9.

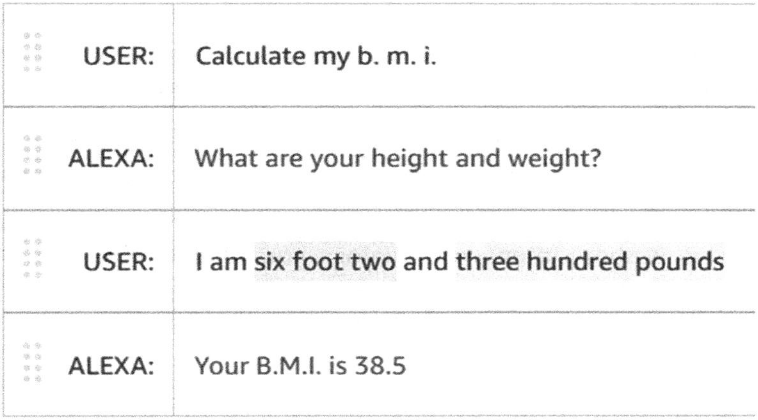

	USER:	Calculate my b. m. i.
	ALEXA:	What are your height and weight?
	USER:	I am six foot two and three hundred pounds
	ALEXA:	Your B.M.I. is 38.5

Figure 4-9. *Intent dialog for the BMI calculator*

Whereas, with the Conversations model, the dialog could go like Figure 4-9, it could also go like Figure 4-10.

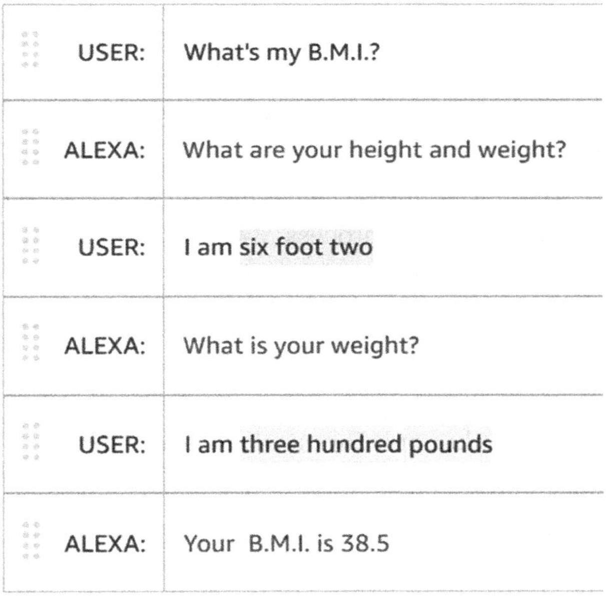

	USER:	What's my B.M.I.?
	ALEXA:	What are your height and weight?
	USER:	I am six foot two
	ALEXA:	What is your weight?
	USER:	I am three hundred pounds
	ALEXA:	Your B.M.I. is 38.5

Figure 4-10. *Conversation dialog for the BMI calculator*

The difference is subtle but significant. For more complex skills, the Conversation Dialog is much more user friendly as it allows the user to answer the prompts in their own way, instead of with the strict interactions required by the Intent model. There's also another advantage: in the Intent model, you, the developer, are responsible for handling all the possible permutations of interaction. In the Conversational model, you show Alexa the basic flow of the conversation, and her A.I. will do the rest. It's also important to note that this is not an all-or-nothing choice; you can have interactions in both models, and, as we shall see, you will need to have at least one intent, even with a Conversation modeled skill.

Now that you know about Intents and Dialogs, you need to understand Slots.

Slots

A Slot is something that the user fills in for Alexa. When you define a slot, you assign it a Slot type. These can be built-in slot types such as AMAZON.City and AMAZON. Artist, more generic slot types such as AMAZON.NUMBER and AMAZON.DATE, or even custom slot types where you provide the slot values as part of the skill configuration process. The cool thing about the built-in slot types is that they handle all the weird and wonderful ways that someone might say, for example, a date. I might say a date as "five ten twenty-twenty," or I might say, "May tenth twenty-twenty," or I might even say, "oh-five ten twenty-twenty." The AMAZON.DATE slot type is designed to handle all these variations and capture for me, the developer, the actual date value 5/10/2020.

In our BMI skill, Height and Weight will be the slots. The user will need to provide those values, much like parameters or variables, and Alexa will then pass on the slot values to the API code to evaluate and process. We have a dilemma, though. How do we represent the numerous possibilities for the Height and Weight slots? At first, we might consider Height and Weight as AMAZON.NUMBERs, in which case, the user could utter

```
I am {Height} centimeters tall and weight {Weight} kilograms.
```

This approach could work, but only for metric measurements. If we allow users to answer in imperial sizes, then we would have to use two slots for the height to allow for feet and inches, that is:

```
I am {Feet} feet and {Inches} inches tall and weigh {Weight} pounds.
```

Or, if the user is a whole number of feet,

```
I am {Feet} feet tall and weigh {Weight} pounds.
```

Then if we allow for weight in stones, we'd need two slots (one required, one optional) for that too, giving us four variations of utterance:

```
I am {Feet} feet and {Inches} inches tall and weigh {Stone} stone and
{Pounds} pounds.
I am {Feet} feet tall and weigh {Stone} stone and {Pounds} pounds.
I am {Feet} feet and {Inches} inches tall and weigh {Stone} stone.
I am {Feet} feet tall and weigh {Stone}.
```

Now we have seven utterances with entirely different slots in them, which means we have to write seven APIs to handle them, which sounds like a lot of work. And no one likes a lot of work if it can be avoided, which, in this case, it can!

Instead of using AMAZON.NUMBER for our slot type, we can instead create Custom Slot Types for Height and Weight that include all the options we want to handle. For example, Table 4-1 shows a sample set of unit combinations.

Table 4-1. *Sample Unit Combinations*

Height	Weight
188 centimeters	45 kilograms
188 c.m.	45 k.g.
1.9 meters	45 kilos
6 foot	180 pounds
6 foot 2	14 stone
6 foot 2 inches	14 stone 3
And so on	And so on

The next problem is Alexa doesn't like you putting numeric values as numbers in custom slots. Instead, we have to spell out the numbers as words. So the example in Table 4-1 should actually be written as shown in Table 4-2.

Table 4-2. *Unit Combinations with Numbers Converted to Words*

Height	Weight
one hundred and eighty eight centimeters	forty five kilograms
one hundred eighty eight c.m.	forty five k.g.
one point nine meters	forty five kilos
six foot	one hundred eighty pounds
six foot two	fourteen stone
six foot two inches	fourteen stone three
And so on	And so on

By creating custom slots with all these different values in them, we allow the user to say whatever quantity and units tickle their fancy, and we can translate them all into usable values for our BMI calculation. But that's a lot of slot values, isn't it? Yes, and that's why this particular skill is actually a data-driven skill!

Creating the Custom Slot Values

To create the lists of slot values, I, for one, have no intention of typing up all the possibilities. Instead, let's look at the Custom Slot's bulk edit feature. This feature allows you to define a list of values in a CSV (comma-separated values) file. I know a tool that creates CSV files quite well: Microsoft Excel (or any spreadsheet, I suppose). I wonder if Excel can convert numbers to words.

Nope. It can't. But wait, a quick Internet search turned up a function that Microsoft support wrote[i] to do precisely that, but for dollars and cents. That is, it can spell out the numbers $1,234.56 as one thousand two hundred thirty-four dollars and fifty-six cents.

---

[i] Microsoft Support Article: Convert numbers into words. https://support.microsoft.com/en-us/office/convert-numbers-into-words-a0d166fb-e1ea-4090-95c8-69442cd55d98

This could work. We could modify the SpellNumbers function not to do dollars and cents, instead just showing the spelled-out numbers. Once changed, we can add that function to Excel as a code module and use it in our slot generation. Like this:

1. Open Excel.

2. Open a Blank Workbook.

3. Press Alt-F11 to open the Visual Basic for Applications window (Figure 4-11).

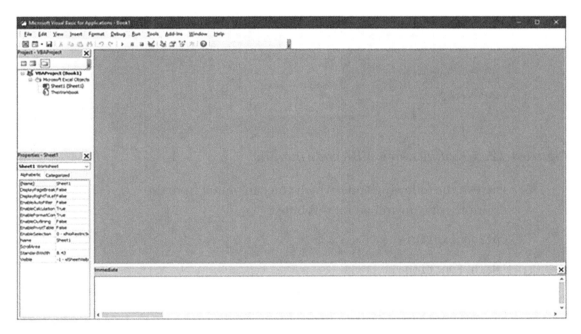

Figure 4-11. *The Visual Basic for Applications window*

4. Right-click on the VBAProject (Book1) and choose Insert | Module (see Figure 4-12).

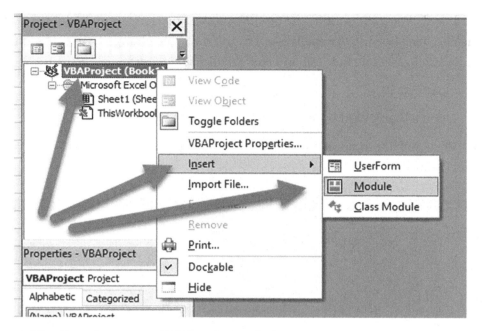

Figure 4-12. *Creating a new VBA code module*

5. Paste in the following code, which you can obtain from the example code download for this book:

```
Option Explicit

'Main Function
Public Function SpellNumber(ByVal MyNumber, Optional AddAnds = False)

    Dim Dollars, Cents, Temp
    Dim DecimalPlace, Count
    ReDim Place(9) As String

    Place(2) = " Thousand "
    Place(3) = " Million "
    Place(4) = " Billion "
    Place(5) = " Trillion "

    ' String representation of amount.
    MyNumber = Trim(Str(MyNumber))

    ' Position of decimal place 0 if none.
    DecimalPlace = InStr(MyNumber, ".")
```

```
' Convert cents and set MyNumber to the dollar amount.
If DecimalPlace > 0 Then
    Cents = GetTens(Left(Mid(MyNumber, DecimalPlace + 1) &
    "00", 2))
    MyNumber = Trim(Left(MyNumber, DecimalPlace - 1))
End If

Count = 1
Do While MyNumber <> ""
    Temp = GetHundreds(Right(MyNumber, 3))
    If Temp <> "" Then
        Dollars = Temp & Place(Count) & Dollars
    End If
    If Len(MyNumber) > 3 Then
        MyNumber = Left(MyNumber, Len(MyNumber) - 3)
    Else
        MyNumber = ""
    End If
    Count = Count + 1
Loop

Select Case Dollars
    Case ""
        Dollars = "Zero"
    Case "One"
        Dollars = "One"
    Case Else
        Dollars = Dollars
End Select

If AddAnds Then
Debug.Print (Right(Trim(Dollars), 7) = "Hundred")

    If Right(Trim(Dollars), 8) <> "Trillion" Then
        Dollars = Replace(Dollars, "Trillion ", "Trillion and ")
    End If
```

```vb
            If Right(Trim(Dollars), 7) <> "Billion" Then
                Dollars = Replace(Dollars, "Billion ", "Billion and ")
            End If
            If Right(Trim(Dollars), 7) <> "Million" Then
                Dollars = Replace(Dollars, "Million ", "Million and ")
            End If
            If Right(Trim(Dollars), 8) <> "Thousand" Then
                Dollars = Replace(Dollars, "Thousand ", "Thousand and ")
            End If
            If Right(Trim(Dollars), 7) <> "Hundred" Then
                Dollars = Replace(Dollars, "Hundred ", "Hundred and ")
            End If
        End If

    SpellNumber = Trim(Dollars)
End Function

' Converts a number from 100-999 into text
Function GetHundreds(ByVal MyNumber)
    Dim Result As String
    If Val(MyNumber) = 0 Then Exit Function

    MyNumber = Right("000" & MyNumber, 3)
    ' Convert the hundreds place.
    If Mid(MyNumber, 1, 1) <> "0" Then
        Result = GetDigit(Mid(MyNumber, 1, 1)) & " Hundred "
    End If
    ' Convert the tens and ones place.
    If Mid(MyNumber, 2, 1) <> "0" Then
        Result = Result & GetTens(Mid(MyNumber, 2))
    Else
        Result = Result & GetDigit(Mid(MyNumber, 3))
    End If
    GetHundreds = Result
End Function
```

```
' Converts a number from 10 to 99 into text.
Function GetTens(TensText)
    Dim Result As String
    Result = "" ' Null out the temporary function value.
    If Val(Left(TensText, 1)) = 1 Then ' If value between 10-19...
        Select Case Val(TensText)
            Case 10: Result = "Ten"
            Case 11: Result = "Eleven"
            Case 12: Result = "Twelve"
            Case 13: Result = "Thirteen"
            Case 14: Result = "Fourteen"
            Case 15: Result = "Fifteen"
            Case 16: Result = "Sixteen"
            Case 17: Result = "Seventeen"
            Case 18: Result = "Eighteen"
            Case 19: Result = "Nineteen"
            Case Else
        End Select
    Else ' If value between 20-99...
        Select Case Val(Left(TensText, 1))
            Case 2: Result = "Twenty "
            Case 3: Result = "Thirty "
            Case 4: Result = "Forty "
            Case 5: Result = "Fifty "
            Case 6: Result = "Sixty "
            Case 7: Result = "Seventy "
            Case 8: Result = "Eighty "
            Case 9: Result = "Ninety "
            Case Else
        End Select
        Result = Result & GetDigit(Right(TensText, 1)) ' Retrieve
        ones place.
    End If
    GetTens = Result
End Function
```

```
' Converts a number from 1 to 9 into text.
Function GetDigit(Digit)
    Select Case Val(Digit)
        Case 1: GetDigit = "One"
        Case 2: GetDigit = "Two"
        Case 3: GetDigit = "Three"
        Case 4: GetDigit = "Four"
        Case 5: GetDigit = "Five"
        Case 6: GetDigit = "Six"
        Case 7: GetDigit = "Seven"
        Case 8: GetDigit = "Eight"
        Case 9: GetDigit = "Nine"
        Case Else: GetDigit = ""
    End Select
End Function
```

6. Select the Debug | Compile VBAProject menu option
    (see Figure 4-13).

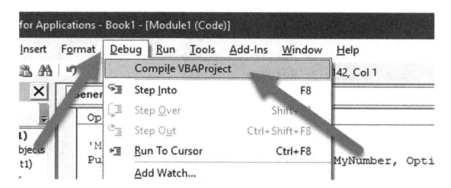

Figure 4-13. *Compiling the VBA module*

7. Select File | Close and return to Microsoft Excel from the menu.

8. Back in the spreadsheet, select File | Save As.

9. Enter a file name, say, SlotValues.

10. Choose a convenient folder.

11. Make sure the file is of type .xlsm (Excel macro-enabled Workbook) (see Figure 4-14). If not, click More options... at the bottom of the dialog and change it in the File Type drop-down.

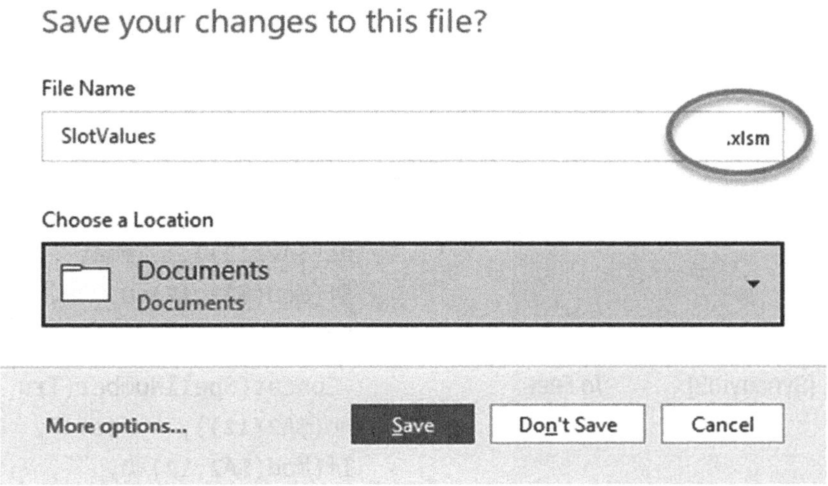

Save your changes to this file?

File Name

SlotValues   .xlsm

Choose a Location

Documents
Documents

More options...   Save   Don't Save   Cancel

Figure 4-14. *Make sure you are saving to a .xlsm file*

12. Click Save.

Now we have a SpellNumber function that we can use to convert numeric values to words. Whew. Take a drink of water. You deserve it.

Next up, let's create the options for the Height tab of our spreadsheet. We're going to need nine column headers, as shown in Table 4-3.

Table 4-3. *Height Columns*

Value	Term	Index	Synonym1 ...	Synonym6
12	Twelve Inches	12	One foot	N/A
30	Thirty centimeters	30cm	Thirty c.m.	N/A

We're going to put the actual number in the Value column. Then we're going to spell out that number in inches or centimeters in the Term column. We're going to index this list by using the inches number as it is and by suffixing "cm" to the metric version. Then we're going to put in the formulae for the synonyms, as shown in Table 4-4.

Table 4-4. *Synonym Formulae for Height*

Units	Col	Conversion	Formula
Imperial	A [Value]	None	Numbers from 12 to 132.
	B [Term]	To Inches	=Concat(SpellNumber($A2), " inches")
	C [Index]	None	=$A2
	D [Synonym1]	To Foot	=Concat(SpellNumber(Trunc($A2/12)), " foot ", If(Mod($A2,12)=0, "", SpellNumber(Mod($A2,12))))
	E [Synonym2]	To Feet	=Concat(SpellNumber(Trunc($A2/12)), " feet ", If(Mod($A2,12)=0, "", SpellNumber(Mod($A2,12))))
	F [Synonym3]	To Foot/Inch	=If(Mod($A2,12)=0, "", Concat(SpellNumber(Trunc($A2/12)), " foot ", If(Mod($A2,12)=0, "", Concat(SpellNumber(Mod($A2,12)), If(Mod($A2,12)=1, " inch", " inches")))))
	G [Synonym4]	To Feet/Inch	=If(Mod($A2,12)=0, "", Concat(SpellNumber(Trunc($A2/12)), " feet ", If(Mod($A2,12)=0, "", Concat(SpellNumber(Mod($A2,12)), If(Mod($A2,12)=1, " inch", " inches")))))
	H [Synonym5]	To Null	=If(Mod($A2,12)=0, "", Concat(SpellNumber(Trunc($A2/12)), " ", SpellNumber(Mod($A2,12))))

(*continued*)

Table 4-4. (*continued*)

Units	Col	Conversion	Formula
	I [Synonym6]	To Inches w/ And in the hundreds	`=If($A2<=100, "", Concat(SpellNumber($A2,True), " inches"))`
Metric	A [Value]	None	Numbers from 30 to 250.
	B [Term]	To Centimeters	`=Concat(SpellNumber($A123), " centimeters")`
	C [Index]	Suffix cm	`=Concat($A123, "cm")`
	D [Synonym1]	To c.m.	`=Concat(SpellNumber($A123), " c.m.")`
	E [Synonym2]	To Centimeters w/ And	`=If($A123<=100, "", Concat(SpellNumber($A123, True), " centimeters"))`
	F [Synonym3]	To c.m. w/ And	`=If($A123<=100, "", Concat(SpellNumber($A123, True), " c.m."))`
	G [Synonym4]	Manual	50cm half a meter 100cm one meter 150cm one and a half meters 200cm two meters 250cm two and a half meters
	H [Synonym5]	Manual	50cm zero point five meters 150cm one point five meters 250cm two point five meters
	I [Synonym6]	Manual	50cm point five meters 100cm a meter 150cm a meter and a half 250cm two meters and a half

Then, copy the formulae down in the appropriate rows. When you're done, the worksheet should look like Figure 4-15.

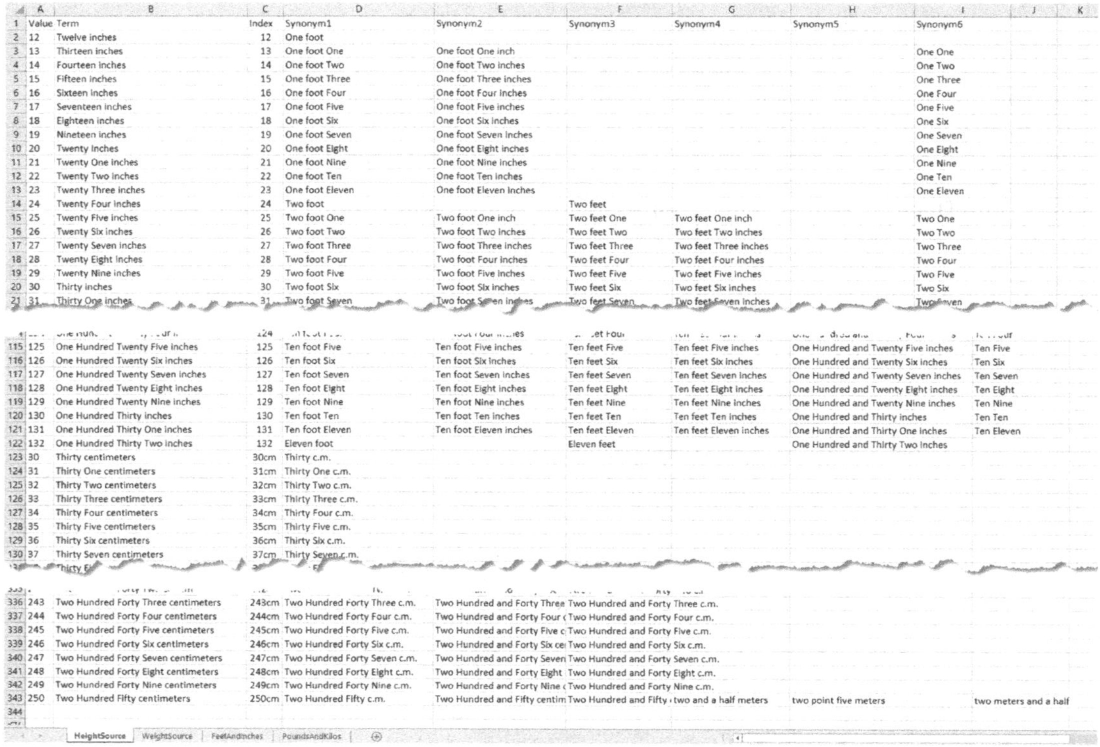

Figure 4-15. *The Height Spreadsheet after completing the formulae*

For weight, we're going to do something similar. We only need three synonyms though, as shown in Table 4-5.

Table 4-5. *Weight Columns*

Value	Term	Index	Synonym1 ...	Synonym3
17	Seventeen Pounds	17lb	One stone three	N/A
20	Twenty kilos	20kg	Twenty kilograms	N/A

Table 4-6 shows the formulae for the synonyms.

Table 4-6. *Synonym Formulae for Weight*

Units	Col	Conversion	Formula
Imperial	A [Value]	None	Numbers from 1 to 600.
	B [Term]	To Pounds	`=Concat(SpellNumber($A2), " pounds")`
	C [Index]	Suffix lb	`=Concat($A2, "lb")`
	D [Synonym1]	To Stone and Pound(s)	`=If($A2<14, "", Concat(SpellNumber(Trunc($A2/14)), " stone", If(Mod($A2,14)=0, "", Concat(" ", Spellnumber(Mod($A2, 14)), " pound", If(Mod($A2,14)=1, "", "s")))))`
	E [Synonym2]	To Stone	`=If($A2<14, "", Concat(SpellNumber(Trunc ($A2/14)), " stone", IF(Mod($A2,14)=0, "", Concat(" ", SpellNumber(Mod($A2, 14))))))`
	F [Synonym3]	To Pounds w/ And	`=If($A2<=100, "", Concat(SpellNumber($A2, True), " pound", If($A2=1,"","s")))`
Metric	A [Value]	None	Numbers from 1 to 275.
	B [Term]	To Kilos	`=Concat(SpellNumber($A602), " kilo", If($A602=1, "", "s"))`
	C [Index]	Suffix kg	`=Concat($A602, "kg")`
	D [Synonym1]	To Kilograms	`=Concat(SpellNumber($A602), " kilogram", If($A602=1, "", "s"))`
	E [Synonym2]	To Kilos w/ And	`=If($A602<=100, "", Concat(SpellNumber($A602,True), " kilo", If($A602=1, "", "s")))`
	F [Synonym3]	To Kilograms w/ And	`=If($A602<=100, "", Concat(SpellNumber($A602,True), " kilogram", If($A602=1, "", "s")))`

The Weight Spreadsheet should look like Figure 4-16 when it's complete.

	Value	Term	ID	Synonym1	Synonym2	Synonym3
2	1	One pound	1lb			
3	2	Two pounds	2lb			
4	3	Three pounds	3lb			
5	4	Four pounds	4lb			
6	5	Five pounds	5lb			
7	6	Six pounds	6lb			
8	7	Seven pounds	7lb			
9	8	Eight pounds	8lb			
10	9	Nine pounds	9lb			
11	10	Ten pounds	10lb			
12	11	Eleven pounds	11lb			
13	12	Twelve pounds	12lb			
14	13	Thirteen pounds	13lb			
15	14	Fourteen pounds	14lb	One stone	One stone	
16	15	Fifteen pounds	15lb	One stone One pound	One stone One	
17	16	Sixteen pounds	16lb	One stone Two pounds	One stone Two	
18	17	Seventeen pounds	17lb	One stone Three pounds	One stone Three	
19	18	Eighteen pounds	18lb	One stone Four pounds	One stone Four	
20	19	Nineteen pounds	19lb	One stone Five pounds	One stone Five	
21	20	Twenty pounds	20lb	One stone Six pounds	One stone Six	

	Value	Term	ID	Synonym1	Synonym2	Synonym3
595	594	Five Hundrea... ty Four pouเ็ds	594lb	Fo... ... Six pou...	Forty Two stone Six	Five Hundred and Ninety Four pounds
596	595	Five Hundred Ninety Five pounds	595lb	Forty Two stone Seven pounds	Forty Two stone Seven	Five Hundred and Ninety Five pounds
597	596	Five Hundred Ninety Six pounds	596lb	Forty Two stone Eight pounds	Forty Two stone Eight	Five Hundred and Ninety Six pounds
598	597	Five Hundred Ninety Seven pounds	597lb	Forty Two stone Nine pounds	Forty Two stone Nine	Five Hundred and Ninety Seven pounds
599	598	Five Hundred Ninety Eight pounds	598lb	Forty Two stone Ten pounds	Forty Two stone Ten	Five Hundred and Ninety Eight pounds
600	599	Five Hundred Ninety Nine pounds	599lb	Forty Two stone Eleven pounds	Forty Two stone Eleven	Five Hundred and Ninety Nine pounds
601	600	Six Hundred pounds	600lb	Forty Two stone Twelve pounds	Forty Two stone Twelve	Six Hundred pounds
602	1	One kilo	1kg	One kilogram		
603	2	Two kilos	2kg	Two kilograms		
604	3	Three kilos	3kg	Three kilograms		
605	4	Four kilos	4kg	Four kilograms		
606	5	Five kilos	5kg	Five kilograms		
607	6	Six kilos	6kg	Six kilograms		
608	7	Seven kilos	7kg	Seven kilograms		
609	8	Eight kilos	8kg	Eight kilograms		
		...ne k...		Nine k...ms		

	Value	Term	ID	Synonym1	Synonym2	Synonym3
870	269	Two Hundred Sixty Nine kilos	269kg	Two Hundred Sixty Nine kilograms	Two Hundred and Sixty Nine kilos	Two Hundred and Sixty Nine kilograms
871	270	Two Hundred Seventy kilos	270kg	Two Hundred Seventy kilograms	Two Hundred and Seventy kilos	Two Hundred and Seventy kilograms
872	271	Two Hundred Seventy One kilos	271kg	Two Hundred Seventy One kilograms	Two Hundred and Seventy One kilos	Two Hundred and Seventy One kilograms
873	272	Two Hundred Seventy Two kilos	272kg	Two Hundred Seventy Two kilograms	Two Hundred and Seventy Two kilos	Two Hundred and Seventy Two kilograms
874	273	Two Hundred Seventy Three kilos	273kg	Two Hundred Seventy Three kilograms	Two Hundred and Seventy Three kilos	Two Hundred and Seventy Three kilograms
875	274	Two Hundred Seventy Four kilos	274kg	Two Hundred Seventy Four kilograms	Two Hundred and Seventy Four kilos	Two Hundred and Seventy Four kilograms
876	275	Two Hundred Seventy Five kilos	275kg	Two Hundred Seventy Five kilograms	Two Hundred and Seventy Five kilos	Two Hundred and Seventy Five kilograms

HeightSource **WeightSource** FeetAndInches PoundsAndKilos ⊕

Figure 4-16. *The Weight Spreadsheet after completing the formulae*

We now have our slot values for the Height and Weight slots.

At this point, be sure to save your work and save a second COPY of your workbook!

To export the slot values to CSV files, we need to copy the lists (not including column A [Value]) to a new sheet (or a new workbook) and paste the formulae as values and then export that sheet as a CSV file. Once for Height and once again for Weight. The export process is as follows:

1. At the bottom of the workbook, click the + to add a worksheet. Name it *HeightData*.

2. In the Height spreadsheet, press *Ctrl-Home*, then *Ctrl-End*, then press *Ctrl-Shift-Home*, then *Shift-Right-Arrow*.

3. Now, with the worksheet highlighted, except Column A, we can press *Ctrl-C* to copy everything.

4. Click over to the HeightData tab.

5. Use the Paste button menu to choose *Paste Values* (see Figure 4-17).

Figure 4-17. *Paste values in Excel*

6. Choose *File | Export* from the menus.

7. Pick *Change File Type.*

8. Pick *CSV (Comma delimited) (*.csv).*

9. Click *Save As.*

10. Enter a file name and click *Ok.*

11. Repeat these steps for the Weight file.

Now we're ready to create our custom slot types in the Alexa Developer Console.

1. Using a text editor, like Notepad++, open the HeightData.csv file you just created. Then copy the contents to the clipboard.

2. In the Alexa Developer Console, click on the *Build* tab at the top.

3. Click on the *Slot Types* menu on the left.

4. Click + *Add Slot Type*.

5. Select *Create a Custom slot type with values*.

6. Enter the name Height. Click *Next*.

7. For the Slot Values, click the little *Bulk Edit* link in the middle.

8. Check *The CSV below contains headers*.

9. Paste your data into the box provided (see Figure 4-18).

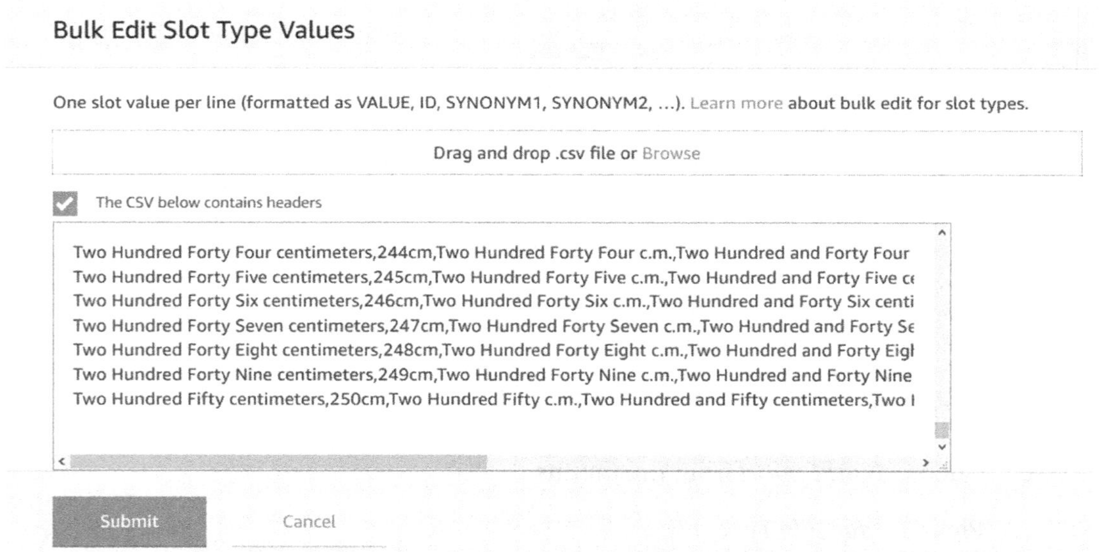

Bulk Edit Slot Type Values

One slot value per line (formatted as VALUE, ID, SYNONYM1, SYNONYM2, …). Learn more about bulk edit for slot types.

Drag and drop .csv file or Browse

☑ The CSV below contains headers

Two Hundred Forty Four centimeters,244cm,Two Hundred Forty Four c.m.,Two Hundred and Forty Four
Two Hundred Forty Five centimeters,245cm,Two Hundred Forty Five c.m.,Two Hundred and Forty Five ce
Two Hundred Forty Six centimeters,246cm,Two Hundred Forty Six c.m.,Two Hundred and Forty Six centi
Two Hundred Forty Seven centimeters,247cm,Two Hundred Forty Seven c.m.,Two Hundred and Forty Se
Two Hundred Forty Eight centimeters,248cm,Two Hundred Forty Eight c.m.,Two Hundred and Forty Eigh
Two Hundred Forty Nine centimeters,249cm,Two Hundred Forty Nine c.m.,Two Hundred and Forty Nine
Two Hundred Fifty centimeters,250cm,Two Hundred Fifty c.m.,Two Hundred and Fifty centimeters,Two I

Submit   Cancel

Figure 4-18. *Bulk editing the height slot values*

10. Click *Submit*.

11. Click *Save* at the top.

Now repeat these steps for the Weight data.

With those slots configured, we are ready to move on to the Dialog configuration.

Configuring the Dialog

When creating an Alexa skill using the Intent model, you would now move on to creating the intents for getting the Height and Weight. However, I'd prefer to let Alexa figure out what the user has or has not told us yet and sort that out by herself, which is where the Conversations model comes in. In this book, we will use both models, but with a preference for the latter. Jumping in the deep end, we're going to start by setting up our dialog as an Alexa Conversation. To do this, we need to (1) turn on the Alexa Conversations tool, (2) build a sample conversation, (3) wire up each step of the sample to the relevant utterances and API calls, (4) create the final intent that will finish the skill, and (5) write the code for the API.

To turn on the Alexa Conversations model

1. Open your skill in the Alexa Developer Console.

2. Select the *Build* tab at the top.

3. Select the *Custom* menu option on the left.

4. Select the *Interfaces* menu under Custom on the left.

5. Scroll down to *Alexa Conversations* and toggle it on.

6. Check the box to *Use Alexa Conversations as the default dialog manager*.

7. Click the *Save Interfaces* button at the top.

Next, we'll identify and define the API that will be used to fulfill our dialog. In other words, what is Alexa going to have to do in the back-end code to fulfill the user's intent. In our case, the API will take two parameters, Height and Weight, and return one value, the BMI. We define this in the Conversation model by doing the following:

1. Select the *API Definitions* option from the menu on the left.

2. Click the *Add API Definition* button at the top.

3. Enter **CalculateBMI** as the *APIName* at the top. (See Figure 4-19.)

API Definitions / CalculateBMI

API Definitions define interfaces with your backend service

Figure 4-19. *Adding the CalculateBMI API definition*

4. Click the *Add Argument* button.
5. Enter **Height** for the *Name*.
6. Select **Height** for the *Slot Type*. (See Figure 4-20.)
7. Click the *Add Argument* button.
8. Enter **Weight** for the *Name*.
9. Select ***Weight*** for the *Slot Type*. (See Figure 4-20.)

Arguments (2)
Arguments are inputs to API Definitions. They are local in scope and connected to dialogs via variables.
Add Argument
NAME
SLOT TYPE
LIST
OPTIONAL
ACTIONS
height
Height
Delete
weight
Weight
Delete

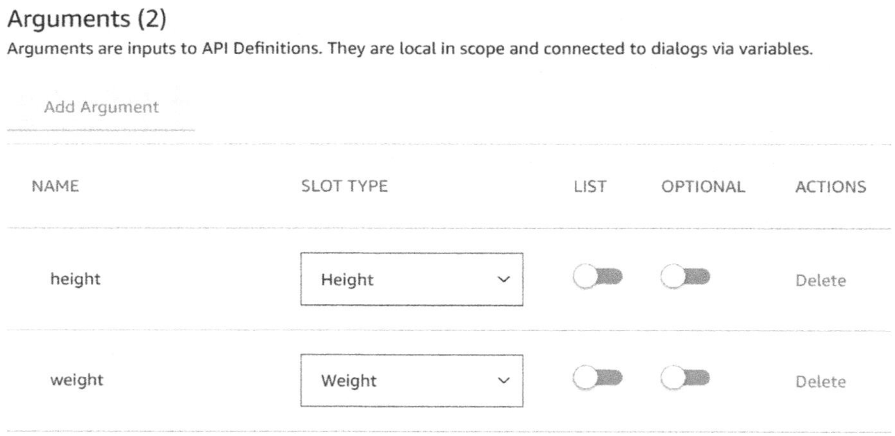

Figure 4-20. *Adding the Height and Weight arguments*

10. We'll come back to the Responses and Return section later.

Next, we're going to type out a sample conversation between the user and Alexa. To do this, follow these steps:

1. Select *Alexa Conversations* on the left menu bar.
2. Select *Dialogs* under that. (See Figure 4-21.)

Alexa Conversations
New
Dialogs (3)

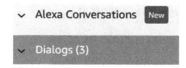

Figure 4-21. *Select the Dialogs tab on the left*

3. Click the *Add Dialog* button at the top.

4. Enter **GetHeightAndWeight** as the *DialogName* at the top.
    (See Figure 4-22.)

Dialogs / GetHeightAndWeight

Figure 4-22. *Enter GetHeightAndWeight as the name of the Dialog*

5. You will now see a table where you can enter the dialog a user
    might have with Alexa to get your skill to work. In our case, this
    will be like Figure 4-23.

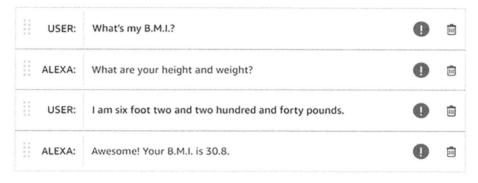

Figure 4-23. *Sample dialog between the User and Alexa*

The next step is to wire up the sample dialog to utterance sets, API
definitions, and responses. An utterance set is what the user might say.
An API definition is how the dialog tells Alexa to figure out the answer.
A response is what Alexa says to the user.

Here is how we will wire up our MainDialog:

6. Select the first line of the dialog (see Figure 4-24).

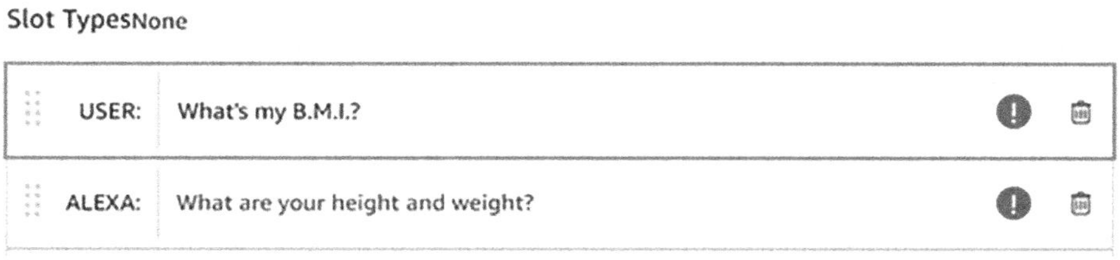

Slot TypesNone

	USER:	What's my B.M.I.?		
	ALEXA:	What are your height and weight?		

Figure 4-24. *Selecting the dialog*

7.   On the right, click the *Dialog Act* drop-down and select *Invoke APIs*. (See Figure 4-25.)

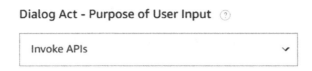

Figure 4-25. *Select Invoke APIs*

8.   This will show the Utterance Set to choose. This is what the user might say to Invoke the API. For example, they might say, "What's my B.M.I.?" as we put in our sample, or they could say, "Calculate my B.M.I." These two options comprise an Utterance Set, and we need to define this set for Alexa Conversations to be able to understand them when a user says them. To do this, we:

a.   Click the *Select an Utterance Set* drop-down and choose *Create New Utterance Set*. (See Figure 4-26.)

Figure 4-26. *Create a new utterance set*

b.   Enter the *Utterance Set Name*: ***InvokeCalculateBMI***. (See Figure 4-27.)

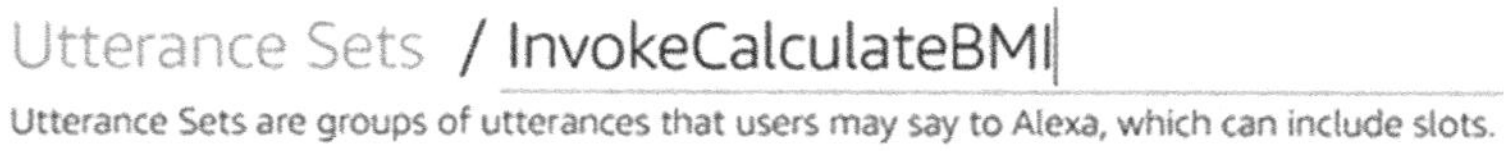

Utterance Sets / InvokeCalculateBMI

Utterance Sets are groups of utterances that users may say to Alexa, which can include slots.

Figure 4-27. *Naming the utterance set*

c.   Skip the *Dialog Act* section and move on to *Sample Utterances*.

d.   Click the *Add Utterance* button.

e.   Enter **Calculate my B.M.I.** in the *What might the user say?* box and then press enter.

f.   Enter another utterance, **What's my B.M.I.** (See Figure 4-28.)

g.   Now click the *Save* button.

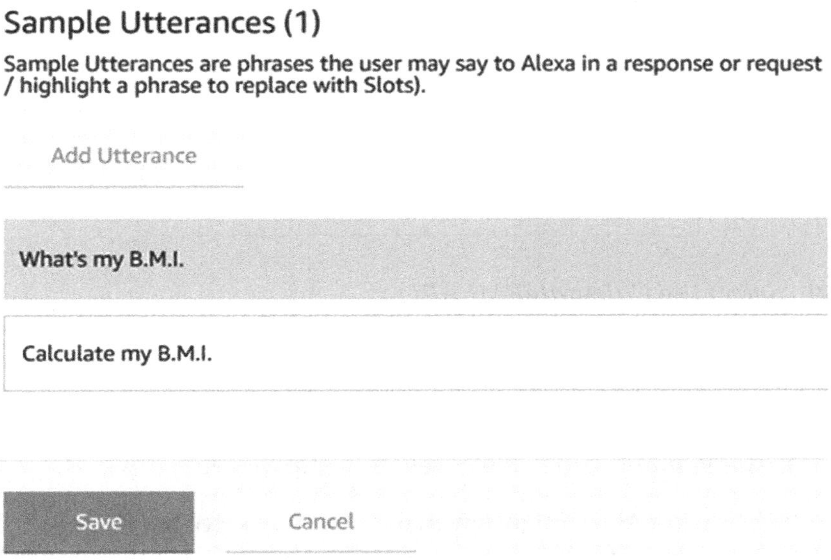

Sample Utterances (1)

Sample Utterances are phrases the user may say to Alexa in a response or request / highlight a phrase to replace with Slots).

Add Utterance

What's my B.M.I.

Calculate my B.M.I.

Save   Cancel

Figure 4-28. *Enter the second utterance and click the Save button*

9.   Back at the Dialog, select the second line of dialog, Alexa's turn.

10. On the right, click the *Dialog Act* drop-down and select *Request Args*. (See Figure 4-29.) This Dialog Act is used when Alexa is requesting arguments (slot values) from the user.

Dialog Act - Purpose of Alexa Response ⓘ

Request Args   ⌄

Figure 4-29. *Select Request Args*

11. Complete the options for the Request Args Dialog Act as follows:

a. First, select the CalculateBMI API that we defined earlier. This API is the API that this conversation will invoke. Select **CalculateBMI** as the *API to Request*. (See Figure 4-30.)

Figure 4-30. *Select the CalculateBMI API*

b. Under *API Arguments to Request*, leave **Height** and **Weight** alone.

c. In the *Response* drop-down, select *Create New Response*.

d. This is what Alexa might say to us to get us to give her our Height and Weight. Under *Response Name*, enter **GetHeightAndWeight**.

e. Scroll down and enter **PromptForHeightAndWeight** as the *Audio Response Name*.

f. The sample dialog we wrote is already entered as the audio prompt, so we can click the *Save* button at the bottom. (See Figure 4-31.)

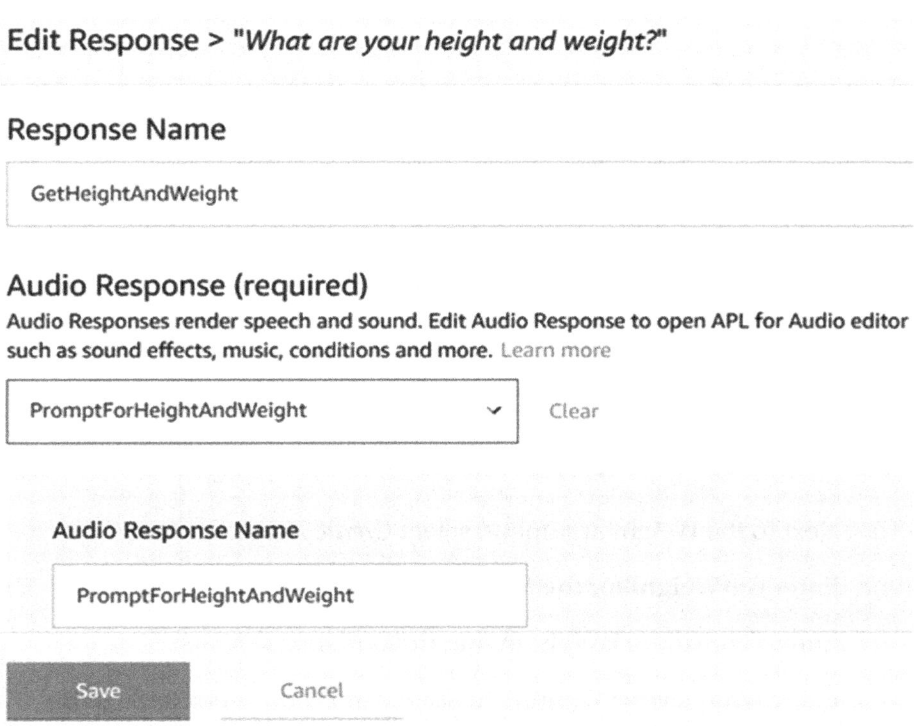

Edit Response > *"What are your height and weight?"*

Response Name

GetHeightAndWeight

Audio Response (required)

Audio Responses render speech and sound. Edit Audio Response to open APL for Audio editor such as sound effects, music, conditions and more. Learn more

PromptForHeightAndWeight   ⌄   Clear

Audio Response Name

PromptForHeightAndWeight

Save   Cancel

Figure 4-31. *Configure the Response*

g. Then we click the *Save* button at the top of the main console.

h. There are two additional responses required. These are for the cases where the user only gives us one of the requested arguments. Alexa needs to prompt for the missing one. Under Additional Responses, there are options for requesting only the Height and only the Weight. We need to repeat previous steps (c) through (g) for each option, as follows:

i. Next to the Height argument, select *Create New Response*.

j. Enter **GetHeight** for the *Response Name*.

k. Enter **PromptForHeight** in the *Audio Response Name*.

l. Under *Alexa Prompts*, click *Add prompt*.

m. Enter **What's your Height?** in the *Alexa Prompts* box.

n. Click *Save*. (See Figure 4-32.)

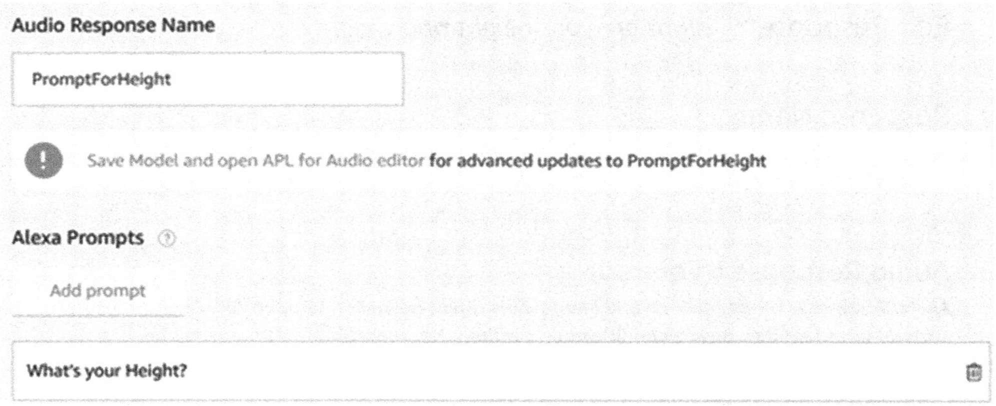

Audio Response Name

> PromptForHeight

(!) Save Model and open APL for Audio editor **for advanced updates to PromptForHeight**

Alexa Prompts ⑦

> Add prompt

What's your Height?   🗑

Figure 4-32. *Entering the Height prompt*

o. Next to the Weight argument, select *Create New Response*.

p. Enter **GetWeight** for the *Response Name*.

q. Enter **PromptForWeight** in the *Audio Response Name*.

r. Enter **What's your Weight?** in the *Alexa Prompts* box and click the + at the end to add it.

s. Click *Create Prompt*.

t. Click *Save*.

u. Your *Additional Responses* should now look like Figure 4-33.

Figure 4-33. *Additional Responses after adding the two responses*

v.   Click the *Save* button at the top of the console to save your progress. (See Figure 4-34.)

Figure 4-34. *Click Save at the top*

12. Next, select the third line of dialog. This is where the user tells us their Height and Weight.

13. First, we'll highlight and identify the slot values the user is giving us:

a.   Select the words *six foot two*. You might have to try a couple of times because the slot prompt is quite eager.

b.   In the Slot Type prompt that pops up, select **Height** as the *Slot Type*.

c.   Click the *Add* button on the right.

d.   Now select the words *two hundred and forty pounds*.

e.   In the Slot Type prompt, select **Weight** as the *Slot Type*.

f.   You should have two highlighted slots, as shown in Figure 4-35.

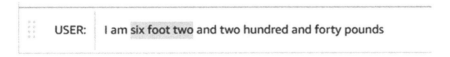

Figure 4-35. *After selecting the slots for the user to fill in*

14. Now that we've identified the slots the user is giving us, we can select the *Inform Args Dialog Act* on the right.

15. In the *Select an Utterance Set* drop-down, select *Create New Utterance Set*.

16. Enter **InformHeightAndWeight** for the *Utterance Set Name*.

17. Under *Sample Utterances*, add **I am {height} and {weight}** and click the Add Utterance button.

18. Add **{height} and {weight}** as another option and click the Add Utterance button.

19. Lastly, enter I am **{height} tall and weight {weight}**.

20. Your sample utterances should look like Figure 4-36.

Figure 4-36. *Sample Utterances for InformHeightAndWeight utterance set*

21. Scroll down to locate the two slots we've added in the utterances, **height** and **weight**. Now select the appropriate *Slot Types*.

22. Click the *Save* button.

23. Now select the Variables from the second line of dialog that will be populated by the user's slot values in the third line of dialog by filling in the Slot ➤ Variable mapping, as shown in Figure 4-37.

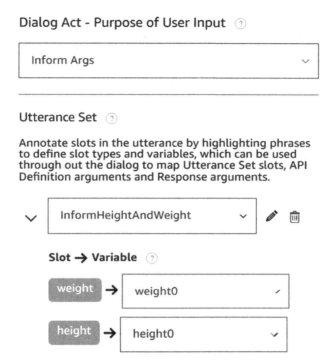

Figure 4-37. *Mapping the Slots to the Variables*

24. Click the *Save* button at the top too.

25. Now we move on to the last line of the dialog; select *Confirm API* as the *Dialog Act*.

26. Select **CalculateBMI** as the *API to Confirm*.

27. Leave the *API Arguments to Confirm* alone. It should say Height and Weight.

28. Confusingly, we're not going to have Alexa respond by saying the BMI at this point; instead, we're just going to select ***bye*** as the *Response*. This will make more sense when we get to the coding section. Alexa Conversations are intended to be an ongoing dialog between Alexa and the user. Each time Alexa speaks, she should prompt or ask the user for something, unless you've come to the end of the Conversation and want to end the session (which we do). In this case, you must Delegate the Dialog to a regular Intent in your skill and not have Alexa prompt for anything else.

The regular Intent handler will set the appropriate flag to end the session. We will do this in the code, and when the API completes, it will Delegate to an Intent, so any response we put in this particular line of the Dialog will be ignored. So we might as well just pick *bye* as the response. (See Figure 4-38.)

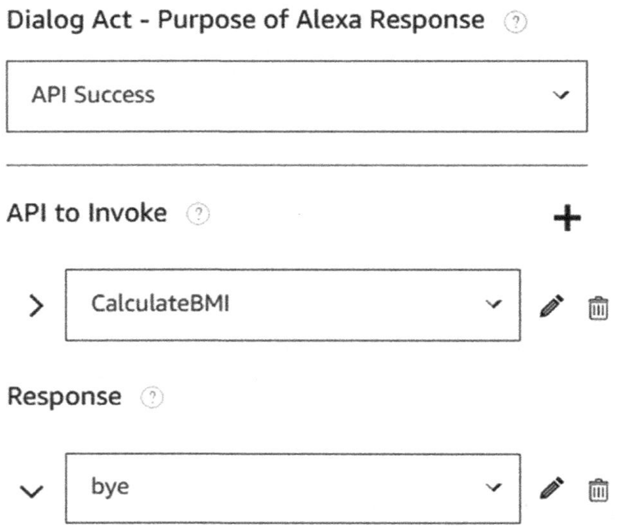

Dialog Act - Purpose of Alexa Response ⑦

    API Success

―――――――――――――――――――――――――――――――――――

API to Invoke ⑦   **+**

    ›   CalculateBMI

Response ⑦

    ⌄   bye

Figure 4-38. *Selecting the 'bye' response*

29. And that's it. We've wired up the dialog.

Next, we need to create the Intent that we'll be delegating to:

1. Select the *Interaction Model* menu option on the left.

2. Select the *Intents* option below that.

3. Click the *Add Intent* button.

4. All we need is an intent to tell the user the BMI and end the session. So let's call it **TellThemTheBMI**.

5. The *Sample Utterance* is going to be simple: **Your B.M.I. is {BMI}**.

6. In the *Intent Slots*, select *AMAZON.NUMBER* for the **BMI** slot type. (See Figure 4-39.)

7. Then click the *Save* button at the top.

Intents / TellThemTheBmi

Sample Utterances (1) ⓘ   🔅 Recommendations 🗐 Bulk Edit ⬆ Export

What might a user say to invoke this intent?	+

Your BMI is {BMI}	🗑

⟨ 1 – 1 of 1 ⟩

Dialog Delegation Strategy ⓘ

Dialog management is not enabled f... ⌄	> Why is this disabled?

Intent Slots (1) ⓘ

ORDER ⓘ	NAME ⓘ	SLOT TYPE ⓘ	MULTI-VALUE ⓘ	ACTIONS
∧ 1 ∨	░ BMI	AMAZON.NUMBER ⌄	◯▮	Edit Dialog | Delete

Figure 4-39. *The TellThemTheBmi intent*

While we're at it, we can delete the Hello World Intent, since we won't need it.

1. Select the *Interaction Model* menu option on the left.

2. Select the *Intents* option below that.

3. To the right of the **HelloWorldIntent**, select the *Delete* option.

4. Click the *Delete Intent* button.

Finally, in the next chapter, you're going to write the back-end code to get this skill to do the math to calculate the BMI.

Summary

In this chapter, we created the base skill for our BMI calculator, set up the data for the slots, defined the dialog, along with the API, utterance sets, and responses. At this point, we've completely built out the VUI for our skill. In the next chapter, we will write and test the back-end code to finish the skill and get it ready for certification.

CHAPTER 5

Writing the Back-End Code

Now that we've created the VUI for our BMI skill, we are ready to write the code in the back end that makes the skill actually do something interesting. In our case, this is calculating the BMI. As we write the code, we'll test our skill to make sure it works as expected. Then, in the next chapter, we'll go through the process of getting our skill certified and published to the Alexa Skills Store.

Before we can write the code, though, we need to install the tools.

Installing the Tools

We're going to need to download and install several tools to work with the back-end code efficiently. These include the following:

- Microsoft Visual Studio Code (User Installer)

  `https://code.visualstudio.com/download`

  After installation, under *Tools and languages*, install support for **JavaScript** and **Python**. See Figure 5-1.

© Simon A. Kingaby 2022
S. A. Kingaby, *Data-Driven Alexa Skills*, https://doi.org/10.1007/978-1-4842-7449-1_5

Figure 5-1. *After installation, click on JavaScript and Python*

- Then, in the extensions marketplace, install the ***Alexa Skills Kit (ASK) Toolkit*** from Amazon Alexa. See Figure 5-2.

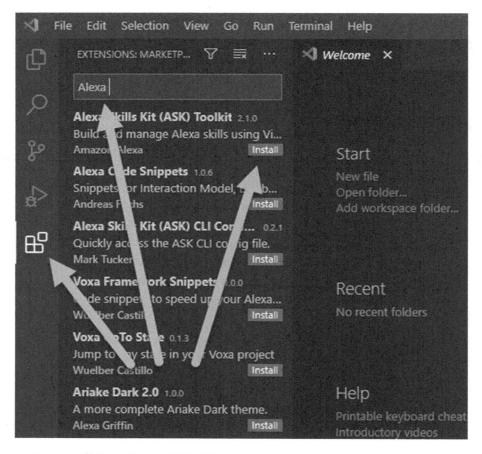

Figure 5-2. *Install the Alexa Skills Kit extension*

- Anaconda

  `www.anaconda.com/products/individual#Downloads`

- Notepad++

  `https://notepad-plus-plus.org/downloads/`

- Firefox Browser

  `www.mozilla.org/en-US/firefox/download/thanks/`

- Git for Windows

  `https://gitforwindows.org`

When Git Setup asks you the following questions, here are the suggested answers:

Choosing the default editor used by Git: Choose Notepad++.

Adjusting your PATH environment: Use Git from Git Bash only.

Otherwise, you can leave the default selections and install Git for Windows.

Once you have all these tools installed, you still need to install the Python modules.

Installing the Python Modules

Throughout this book, we will be adding Python modules to our Anaconda environment. Right now, we need to create that environment and install several modules. To do this, follow these steps:

1. Open an Anaconda Prompt from the Start Menu | Anaconda | Anaconda Prompt option. See Figure 5-3. Note: Do not select the Anaconda PowerShell prompt. You want just the Anaconda Prompt, without the word PowerShell.

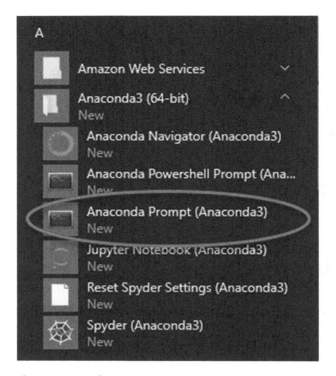

Figure 5-3. *Open the Anaconda Prompt*

2. Once open, you should see the (base) option in front of the
    command prompt, like this:

    (base) C:\Users\UserName>

3. If you don't see the (base) option, try this command: conda
    activate base. If that doesn't work, then you'll need to debug
    your Anaconda install and get it working before you can proceed.

4. Run the following commands, one at a time, at the command
    prompt. Some of these will take a while, so be patient. I will
    be using the name DDS (for Data-Driven Skills) for the virtual
    environment in Anaconda, but any name will do.

    ```
    conda update -n base -c defaults conda
    conda create --name DDS anaconda
    conda activate DDS
    ```

5. After creating and activating the environment, the prompt should look like this:

    ```
    (DDS) C:\Users\UserName>
    ```

6. Next, we need to install Node.js and the Alexa SDK.[1]

    ```
    conda install -c conda-forge nodejs
    pip install ask-sdk
    pip install ask-sdk-local-debug
    ```

7. I have found that the following command is helpful in registering the virtual environment for use in Jupyter Notebooks.

    ```
    python -m ipykernel install --user --name DDS --display-name
    "Data-Driven Skills"
    ```

With these tools installed, we are ready to write and test some code.

Writing the Code

There are two models for the front-end VUI development, and there are two models for the back-end code. When the VUI uses the Intent model, the back end needs to have Request and Intent Handlers. When the VUI uses the Conversation Model, the back end will instead have API Handlers. We'll see all of these in the following sections as we write the code for the BMI calculator skill.

The Code We Have in the Template

Thankfully, the Hello World template that we used to create the BMI calculator comes with quite a bit of boiler-plate code. If we look at the Build tab in the Alexa Developer Console and then select Intents on the left menu, we see a HelloWorldIntent and four Built-in Intents (see Figure 5-4).

---

[1] This installation may require the installation of other components, such as the appropriate Visual C Runtime.

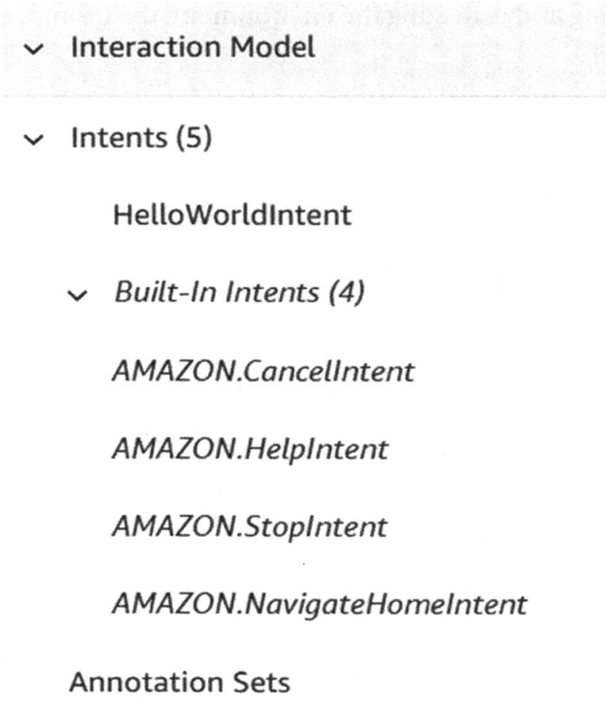

Interaction Model

Intents (5)

HelloWorldIntent

Built-In Intents (4)

AMAZON.CancelIntent

AMAZON.HelpIntent

AMAZON.StopIntent

AMAZON.NavigateHomeIntent

Annotation Sets

Figure 5-4. *The Intents that come with the Hello World Skill template*

Each of these intents, plus the Launch Request that starts the skill, has a Handler in the code that comes with the Hello World Skill template. Now select the Code tab at the top, where we see the lambda function for this skill.

The Lambda Function

In the Code tab, in the Skill Code/lambda folder, is a file called lambda_function.py. (See Figure 5-5.)

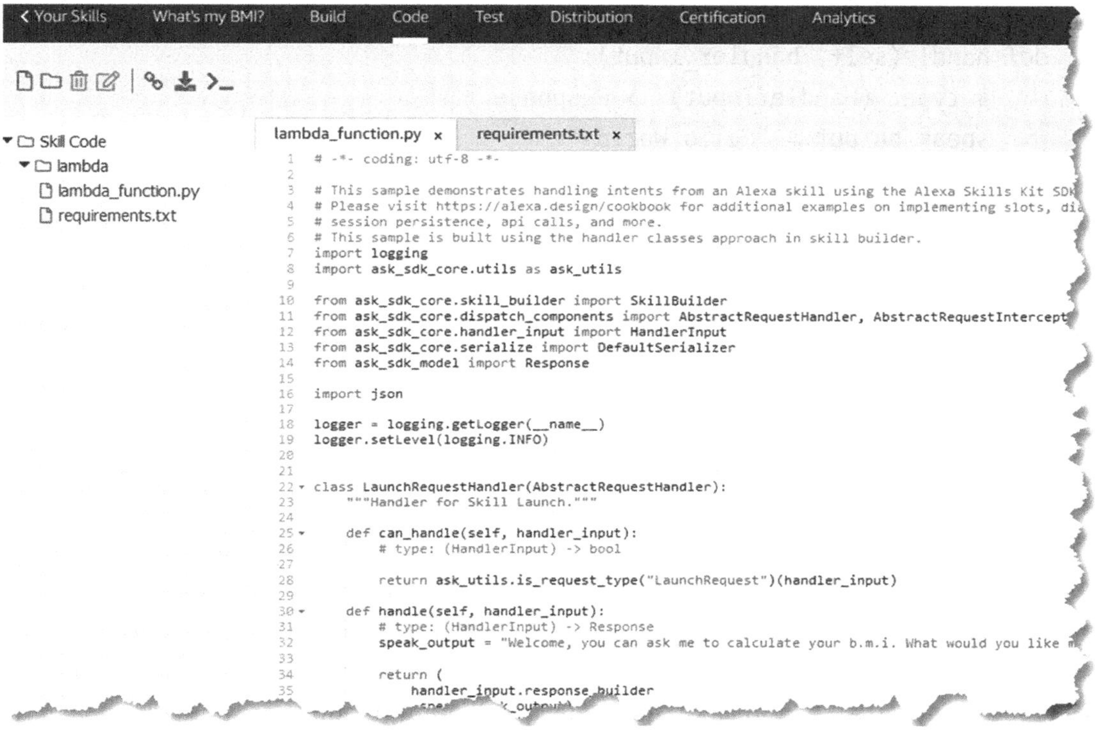

Figure 5-5. *The lambda_function.py file in the Code tab*

This file contains the back end to the skill's VUI, and it is this function where we will find the Request, Intent, and API Handler code. In Amazon Web Services (AWS), **lambda functions** are cloud-based serverless functions. They are scalable and run in the cloud, independent of containers or servers, so they are ideal for building the back end of an Alexa skill.

The **Request and Intent Handlers** are how we create the words that Alexa will speak on her turn in response to the user uttering something that triggers the intent. In Python, each Request, Intent, and API Handler is implemented as a `class` with two methods: `can_handle` and `handle`. The handler classes are called by the VUI through the `SkillBuilder` class and handle, or process, the various requests, intents, and API calls that the VUI makes. For example, the `HelloWorldHandler` looks like this:

```
class HelloWorldIntentHandler(AbstractRequestHandler):
    """Handler for Hello World Intent."""
    def can_handle(self, handler_input):
        # type: (HandlerInput) -> bool
        return ask_utils.is_intent_name("HelloWorldIntent")(handler_input)

    def handle(self, handler_input):
        # type: (HandlerInput) -> Response
        speak_output = "Hello World!"

        return (
            handler_input.response_builder
                .speak(speak_output)
                # .ask("add a reprompt if you want to keep the session open
                for the user to respond")
                .response
        )
```

Notice how in the can_handle function we return True or False based on whether this is the correct handler for the intent called by the VUI. Then, in the handle function, we create the speech that Alexa will say in the line: speak_output = "Hello World!" and return it to the VUI using the response_builder to tell Alexa to .speak(speak_output).

The other main area of interest in the lambda function is at the bottom, where the SkillBuilder is created, and all of the request and intent handlers are added to it, as shown here:

```
sb = SkillBuilder()

sb.add_request_handler(LaunchRequestHandler())
sb.add_request_handler(HelloWorldIntentHandler())
sb.add_request_handler(HelpIntentHandler())
sb.add_request_handler(CancelOrStopIntentHandler())
sb.add_request_handler(SessionEndedRequestHandler())
sb.add_request_handler(IntentReflectorHandler()) # make sure
IntentReflectorHandler is last so it doesn't override your custom intent
handlers

sb.add_exception_handler(CatchAllExceptionHandler())

lambda_handler = sb.lambda_handler()
```

See how the `HelloWorldIntentHandler()` is added as a request handler? This is where we will need to add our request handlers too.

In the next section, we will outline the changes we need to make to the lambda function. If the code seems overwhelming at this point, that's normal. In the rest of this chapter, we'll dig deeper into the lambda function, and you will begin to see how the back end of an Alexa app is formed.

The Changes We Need to Make

There are six things we need to do to modify the template code and make it our own, as shown in Figure 5-6.

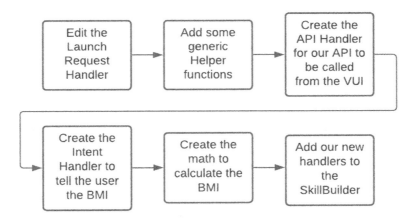

Figure 5-6. *The Code Changes we'll make in this chapter*

The six things we need to change are the following:

1) Modify the Launch Request Handler to make the interaction with Alexa relevant to the BMI calculator.

2) Create some helper functions that we will use in the API Handler.

3) Create the API Handler for the CalculateBMI API we defined in the Alexa Conversations part of the VUI.

4) Create the intent handler for the TellThemTheBMI Intent we defined in the Intents part of the VUI.

5)   Create a function to do the math to calculate the BMI.

6)   Add our new handlers to the SkillBuilder at the bottom of the lambda function.

The next section addresses the first of these changes. Subsequent sections will look at the remaining changes, one by one.

Changing the Launch Request Handler

The first change we need to make to the template code is in the Launch Request Handler (see Figure 5-7).

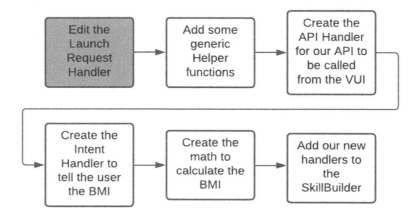

Figure 5-7. *The first change we make is to the Launch Request handler*

In the `class LaunchRequestHandler`, in the `handle` function, it currently shows the speech for Alexa to say as

```
speak_output = "Welcome, you can say Hello or Help. Which would you like
to try?"
```

We need to change that to say instead

```
speak_output = "Welcome, you can ask me to calculate your b.m.i. What would
you like me to do?"
```

The finished class will look like Figure 5-8.

```python
class LaunchRequestHandler(AbstractRequestHandler):
    """Handler for Skill Launch."""

    def can_handle(self, handler_input):
        # type: (HandlerInput) -> bool

        return ask_utils.is_request_type("LaunchRequest")(handler_input)

    def handle(self, handler_input):
        # type: (HandlerInput) -> Response
        speak_output = "Welcome, you can ask me to calculate your b.m.i. What would you like me to do?"

        return (
            handler_input.response_builder
            .speak(speak_output)
            .ask(speak_output)
            .response
        )
```

Figure 5-8. *The finished LaunchRequestHandler class*

The second change is a little more substantial as we add some helper functions that we need for the API Handler.

Creating the Helper Functions

As part of the API Handler, we need to add some helper functions (see Figure 5-9).

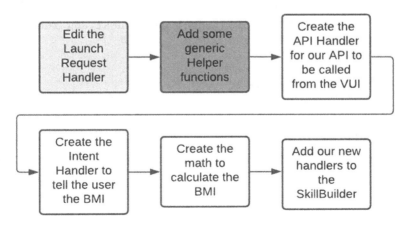

Figure 5-9. *The second change is to add the helper functions*

The helper functions provide support functionality that we will need in our API and intent handlers. Scroll down to the `sb = SkillBuilder()` line in the code.

```
139
140 ▾    def handle(self, handler_input, exception):
141          # type: (HandlerInput, Exception) -> Response
142          logger.error(exception, exc_info=True)
143
144          speak_output = "Sorry, I had trouble doing what you asked. Please try again."
145
146          return (
147              handler_input.response_builder
148                  .speak(speak_output)
149                  .ask(speak_output)
150                  .response
151          )
152
153
154          ⬅━━━━━━━        Helper functions go here.
155
156
157
158    # The SkillBuilder object acts as the entry point for your skill, routing all request and response
159    # payloads to the handlers above. Make sure any new handlers or interceptors you've
160    # defined are included below. The order matters - they're processed top to bottom.
161
162
163    sb = SkillBuilder()
```

Figure 5-10. *Location for the helper functions*

Above the comments there (see Figure 5-10), insert the following code:

```
def isApiRequest(handlerInput, apiName):
    """Helper method to find if a request is for a certain apiName.
    """
    try:
        return ask_utils.is_request_type('Dialog.API.Invoked')(handlerInput) \
            and handlerInput.request_envelope.request.api_request.name ==
            apiName
    except Exception:
        logging.exception("Error")
        return False

def getApiArguments(handlerInput):
    """Helper method to get API request entity from the request envelope.
    """
    try:
        return handlerInput.request_envelope.request.api_request.arguments
    except Exception:
        logging.exception("Error")
        return False
```

```
def getApiSlots(handlerInput):
    """Helper method to get API resolved entity from the request envelope.
    """
    try:
        return handlerInput.request_envelope.request.api_request.slots
    except Exception:
        logging.exception("Error")
        return False
```

These three helper functions wrap the handlerInput parameter in an exception handler in case the requested objects are not present or throw an error. With the helpers in place, scroll back up to right after the HelloWorldIntent, where we will insert the API Handler.

Creating the Calculate BMI API Handler

In this section, we need to create the API Handler for the Alexa Conversations API (see Figure 5-11).

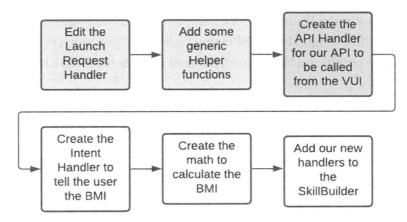

Figure 5-11. *The third change is to add the API Handler*

Recall that we already configured the dialog to call the CalculateBMI API. See Figure 5-12 and Figure 5-13.

API Definitions / CalculateBMI

API Definitions define interfaces with your backend service using arguments as inputs and return as output. Th
turns in a Dialog. Learn More.

Arguments (2)

Arguments are inputs to API Definitions. They are local in scope and connected to dialogs via variables.

Add Argument

NAME	SLOT TYPE
height	Height
weight	Weight

Figure 5-12. *The API definition in the Alexa Conversations model*

In the API definition in Figure 5-12, we named the API: CalculateBMI. It has two arguments: height and weight. In the following dialog configuration (Figure 5-13), Alexa gets the height and weight slot values from the user and passes them to the CalculateBMI arguments.

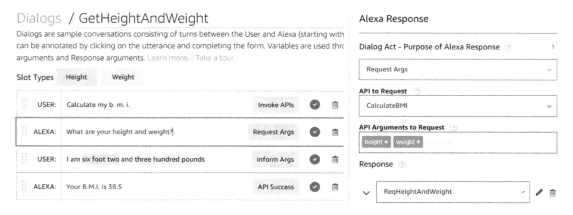

Figure 5-13. *The API request in the Alexa Conversations Dialog*

In the back end, we will need to handle this API call and insert the beginning of the CalculateBMIApiHandler class:

```
class CalculateBMIApiHandler(AbstractRequestHandler):
    """Handler for CalculateBMI API."""

    def can_handle(self, handler_input):
        # type: (HandlerInput) -> bool
        return isApiRequest(handler_input, "CalculateBMI")

    def handle(self, handler_input):
        # type: (HandlerInput) -> Response
        # args = getApiArguments(handler_input)
        # print(args)

        response = ""
        return response
```

Now we need to get the height and weight values out of the handler_input and into variables so we can calculate the BMI. These values are stored in the slots, specifically in the slot ID for the selected Height and Weight. In the preceding class, in the handle function, we need to add the following code, which calls the getApiSlots helper function so that we can get at the slot IDs:

```
slots = getApiSlots(handler_input)
weightId = slots["weight"].resolutions.
    resolutions_per_authority[0].values[0].value.id
heightId = slots["height"].resolutions.
    resolutions_per_authority[0].values[0].value.id
```

We then pass those ID values to the CalculateBMI function that has yet to be defined:

```
BMI = CalculateBMI(heightId, weightId)
```

Remember, at the end of chapter 4, we said that instead of saying the BMI in our API Handler, we would need to delegate that task to an Intent instead. Because our API is a "one shot," which means it only runs through once and then terminates, we need to tell Alexa that we're done. You can't do that in Alexa Conversations. You have to hand off that responsibility (or delegate it) to an intent handler. The intent handler can then end the session.

Here is the code that delegates from Alexa Conversations to the TellThemTheBmi Intent that we created:

```python
responseStr = """
{
    "directives":
    [
        {
            "type": "Dialog.DelegateRequest",
            "target": "skill",
            "period": {
                "until": "EXPLICIT_RETURN"
            },
            "updatedRequest": {
                "type": "IntentRequest",
                "intent": {
                    "name": "TellThemTheBmi",
                    "slots": {
                        "BMI": {
                            "name": "BMI",
                            "value": """ + str(BMI) + """
                        }
                    }
                }
            }
        }
    ]
}
"""

response = json.loads(responseStr)
```

Instead of passing speech text in our response, we're creating a directive of type: Dialog.DelegateRequest. In that directive, we name the TellThemTheBmi Intent as the target Intent Request, passing in the BMI value as a slot to that intent. The directive, as written, is a string; we need to convert it to Json[2] to return it as a response from the handler function. At this point, we have completed the API Handler.

The Complete API Handler

Putting all the pieces together, the CalculateBMI API Handler is defined as follows. This code is available for download from this books's catalog page on Apress.com.

```
class CalculateBMIApiHandler(AbstractRequestHandler):
    """Handler for CalculateBMI API."""

    def can_handle(self, handler_input):
        # type: (HandlerInput) -> bool
        return isApiRequest(handler_input, "CalculateBMI")

    def handle(self, handler_input):
        # type: (HandlerInput) -> Response
        # args = getApiArguments(handler_input)
        # print(args)

        slots = getApiSlots(handler_input)
        weightId = slots["weight"].resolutions.resolutions_per_
        authority[0].values[0].value.id
        heightId = slots["height"].resolutions.resolutions_per_
        authority[0].values[0].value.id

        BMI = CalculateBMI(heightId, weightId)

        responseStr = """
{
    "directives":
    [
        {
            "type": "Dialog.DelegateRequest",
```

---

[2] Json (JavaScript Object Notation) is the standard file protocol for Alexa. All of the messages sent back and forth between your code and Alexa will be in Json format. For an introduction to Json, see www.w3schools.com/js/js_json_intro.asp.

```
            "target": "skill",
            "period": {
                "until": "EXPLICIT_RETURN"
            },
            "updatedRequest": {
                "type": "IntentRequest",
                "intent": {
                    "name": "TellThemTheBmi",
                    "slots": {
                        "BMI": {
                            "name": "BMI",
                            "value": """ + str(BMI) + """
                        }
                    }
                }
            }
        }
    ]
}
        """

        response = json.loads(responseStr)
        return response
```

After completing the API Handler, in the next section, we'll create the handler for the TellThemTheBMI intent – the intent to which the API Handler is delegating.

Creating the Intent Handler

The next change we need to make is to create the intent handler that will tell the user the BMI (see Figure 5-14).

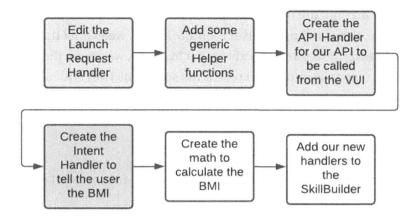

Figure 5-14. *The fourth change is to create the intent handler*

This is the intent that the API delegates to and is named TellThemTheBMI. Recall that we defined it in the VUI like in Figure 5-15.

Figure 5-15. *Definition of the TellThemTheBmi intent*

The TellThemTheBMI intent handler is very similar to the HelloWorld intent handler. The primary purpose of an intent handler is to fashion the speech that Alexa will say in response to the user triggering that intent. In this case, the Conversation API handler is delegating to the intent to trigger it.

In the can_handle function, the intent handler class needs to identify the name of the intent it handles. In our case, this is the name, TellThemTheBMI. The code will look like this:

```
def can_handle(self, handler_input):
    # type: (HandlerInput) -> bool
    return ask_utils.is_intent_name("TellThemTheBmi")(handler_input)
```

In the handle function, the intent handler class needs to create the speech that Alexa will say. In our case, this is telling the user their BMI. First, we extract the BMI value from the slot that the `Dialog.Delegate` directive put it in. Then, we create the speech output. Finally, we use the response_builder to return the speech as Json and to set a flag to end the session so that Alexa knows that our skill has completed. That code will look like this:

```python
def handle(self, handler_input):
    # type: (HandlerInput) -> Response

    BMI = handler_input.request_envelope.request.intent.slots["BMI"].value

    speak_output = f"Awesome! Your b.m.i. is {BMI}"

    return (
        handler_input.response_builder
        .speak(speak_output)
        .set_should_end_session(True)
        .response
    )
```

Now we have the complete intent handler.

The Complete Intent Handler

Putting the pieces together, we have the complete TellThemTheBMI intent handler:

```python
class TellThemTheBmiIntentHandler(AbstractRequestHandler):
    """Handler for Tell Them The BMI Intent."""

    def can_handle(self, handler_input):
        # type: (HandlerInput) -> bool
        return ask_utils.is_intent_name("TellThemTheBmi")(handler_input)

    def handle(self, handler_input):
        # type: (HandlerInput) -> Response

        BMI = handler_input.request_envelope.request.intent.slots["BMI"].value

        speak_output = f"Awesome! Your b.m.i. is {BMI}"
```

```
return (
    handler_input.response_builder
    .speak(speak_output)
    .set_should_end_session(True)
    .response
)
```

Now that we've got the intent and API Handlers written, we can focus on the math.

The Calculate BMI Method

Next, we need to calculate the BMI (see Figure 5-16).

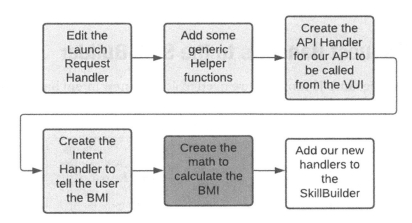

Figure 5-16. *Creating the Calculate BMI method*

We have the slot IDs from the user. These ids are designed to give us the numbers we need. For weight, the id is either *nnn*kg or *nnn*lb. By dropping the last two characters, we get the weight. Similarly, for height, the id is either a whole number of inches or *nnn*cm. The function to handle these four scenarios can be placed after the helper methods we added earlier and will look like this:

```
def CalculateBMI(heightId, weightId):
    # print(heightId, weightId)
    if 'cm' in heightId:
        # centimeters
        meters = float(heightId[0:-2]) / 100.0
```

```
else:
    # inches
    meters = float(heightId) * 0.0254
if 'kg' in weightId:
    # kilograms
    kilos = float(weightId[0:-2]) * 1.0
else:
    # pounds
    kilos = float(weightId[0:-2]) / 2.20462
bmi = round(kilos / meters ** 2, 1)
return bmi
```

And that, lords and ladies, is the end of that. Almost. One final step.

Add the Request Handlers to the Skill Builder

At the bottom of the lambda function, we need to add the new intent handler and the new API Handler to the SkillBuilder (see Figure 5-17).

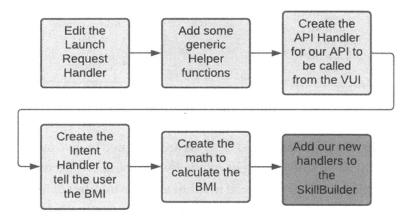

Figure 5-17. *The last step, adding the handlers to the SkillBuilder*

Scroll down to the end of the *lambda_function.py* file and insert the *add_request_handler()* line for each of our new handlers. These should be placed near the top of the list, but after the *LaunchRequestHandler()*, like so:

```
sb = SkillBuilder()

sb.add_request_handler(LaunchRequestHandler())
sb.add_request_handler(TellThemTheBmiIntentHandler())
sb.add_request_handler(CalculateBMIApiHandler())
sb.add_request_handler(HelpIntentHandler())
sb.add_request_handler(CancelOrStopIntentHandler())
sb.add_request_handler(SessionEndedRequestHandler())
```

While we're here, you need to delete the line that adds the request handler for the HelloWorldIntentHandler(). Since we already deleted the Hello World Intent, we won't be needing its handler.

Now, we're finished!

In the top right corner, click Save (this isn't the first time you've done that, right?) and then click Deploy. With the VUI defined and the code deployed, we are ready to start testing!

Testing the Completed Skill

To test your skill, you want to be able to debug the lambda function. There is no way to do this in the Alexa Developer Console. Instead, we need to drop out to an offline tool, such as Visual Studio Code (VS Code). To do this, we're going to connect VS Code to our skill.

Setting Up the Debug Environment

We need to connect Visual Studio Code (VS Code) to our skill VUI for testing. To do this, we will clone the code module from the developer console to your local machine, configure VS Code to be the debugging environment for the skill, and run the lambda function locally in VS Code.

Note   Be sure to enable the Git extension in VS Code before continuing.

Follow these steps to clone your skill into VS Code:

1. Navigate to the Code tab in the Alexa Developer Console.

2. Locate the Skill toolbar (see Figure 5-18), and click the last button (the *Code with offline tools* button).

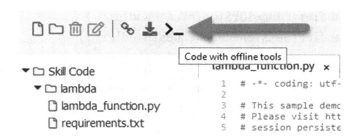

Figure 5-18. *The Lambda Toolbar*

3. Select the Export to VS Code button in the dialog that appears. See Figure 5-19.

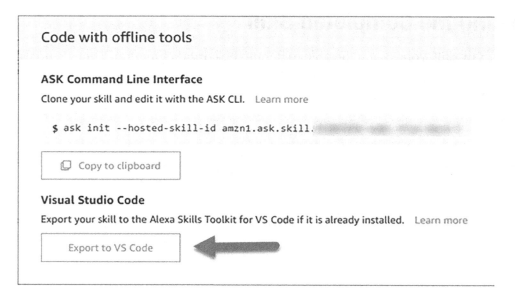

Figure 5-19. *Select the Export to VS Code button*

4. Now allow your browser to open the vscode link in VS Code.

5. Then allow VS Code to open the link too.

6. Create and select a Project Folder on your local machine (this should not be inside another GitHub folder).

7. Wait a minute while the project loads.

8. In VS Code, on the left, in the Explorer tab, you will see your skill. See Figure 5-20.

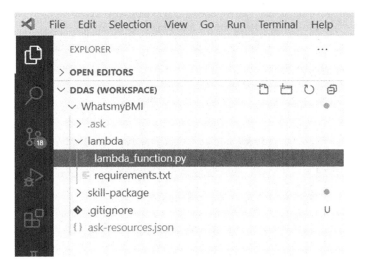

Figure 5-20. *The skill project, loaded in VS Code*

9. Expand the **lambda** folder and select the **lambda_function.py** file. This will open the same code we were working on in the Code tab of the developer console.

Now that you have the skill loaded in VS Code, you can start debugging and testing the lambda code. Scroll down and confirm that you see the `TellThemTheBmiIntentHandler` and the `CalculateBMIApiHandler`.

Before running the code, we need to create a Run Configuration that tells VS Code how to run our function as an Alexa back end. This is done by the following:

10. With the **lambda_function.py** file open, select the *Run* menu in VS Code.

11. Select *Add Configuration...* from the Run menu.

12. Two options say *ASK: Alexa Skills Debugger...* Pick the second one. It is the Python option. This will open a **launch.json** file and add a *Debug Alexa Skill (Python)* configuration. See Figure 5-21.

```
{} launch.json ●

WhatsmyBMI > .vscode > {} launch.json > JSON Language Features > [ ] configurations
  1  {
  2        // Use IntelliSense to learn about possible attributes.
  3        // Hover to view descriptions of existing attributes.
  4        // For more information, visit: https://go.microsoft.com/fwlink/?linkid=830387
  5        "version": "0.2.0",
  6        "configurations": [
  7            {
  8                "name": "Debug Alexa Skill (Python)",
  9                "type": "python",
 10                "request": "launch",
 11                "program": "${command:ask.debugAdapterPath}",
 12                "pythonPath": "${command:python.interpreterPath}",
 13                "args": [
 14                    "--accessToken",
 15                    "${command:ask.accessToken}",
 16                    "--skillId",
 17                    "${command:ask.skillIdFromWorkspace}",
 18                    "--skillHandler",
 19                    "lambda_handler",
 20                    "--skillFilePath",
 21                    "${workspaceFolder}/lambda/lambda_function.py"
 22                ],
 23                "console": "internalConsole"
 24            }
 25        ]
 26  }
```

Figure 5-21. *The launch.json file after adding the ASK (Python) configuration*

13. Save the file to its default location (hidden in the **.vscode** folder).

At this point, you can run the lambda function in VS Code:

14. Select Run | Start Debugging from the menus or press F5 on the keyboard.

If the code doesn't run, you will need to fix any compile errors. These are usually due to typos when entering the code, so carefully double-check the code you've added. When the code builds and runs in debug mode, the status bar at the bottom of VS Code will turn orange, and the debugging toolbar will appear, as shown in Figure 5-22.

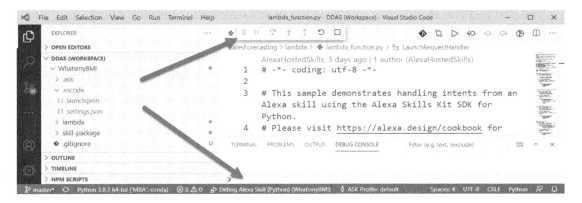

Figure 5-22. *The lambda function running in debug mode*

Now, switch back to the browser, select the Test tab in the developer console, and turn on Skill testing for Development by selecting Development from the drop-down shown in Figure 5-23.

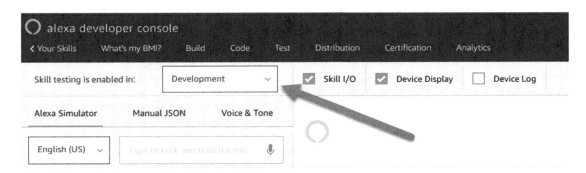

Figure 5-23. *Turn on Skill Testing in Development mode*

You are now ready to test your skill.

Testing the Skill

To test a skill, you will enter or say what you expect the user to say, and Alexa will respond as you've programmed her to do. In this case, we will have a short dialog where she gets your height and weight and tells you your BMI.

The first test you should run is to type the user's statements into the Alexa Simulator tab on the left, as follows.

In the simulator, type "launch *<insert your launch phrase here>*." Note: Your launch phrase is probably not your skill's name. It is the invocation name you entered on the Build tab. Mine was "simon's b.m.i. calculator," so I would enter "`launch simon's b.m.i. calculator`" in the simulator, as shown in Figure 5-24.

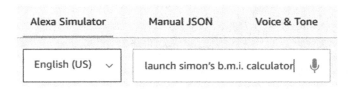

Figure 5-24. *Launching your skill*

Alexa should respond with "Welcome. You can ask me to calculate your b.m.i." as shown in Figure 5-25.

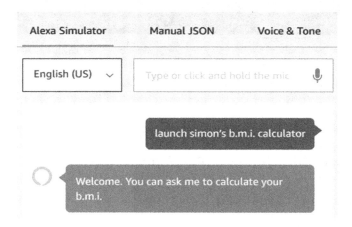

Figure 5-25. *Alexa's response to your launch phrase*

Next, ask Alexa, "what's my b.m.i.?"

She should respond with a prompt for your height, weight, or both, as shown in Figure 5-26.

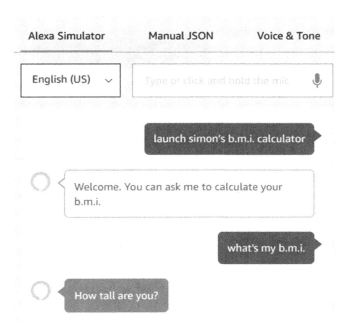

Figure 5-26. *Alexa responds to your inquiry by asking for your height*

Answer her. Enter your height. Don't forget to spell out the numbers as words. For example, six foot two.

After you have told her your height and weight, she will tell you your BMI and end the conversation, like so (Figure 5-27).

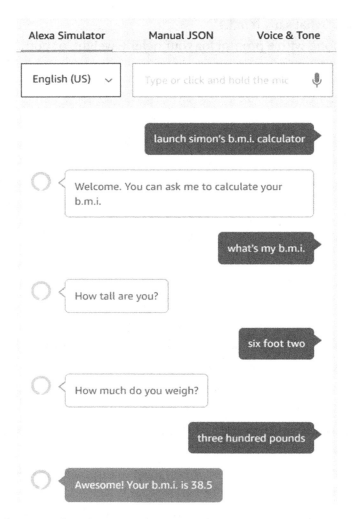

Figure 5-27. *The completed BMI conversation*

At this point, you have an initial test completed, and the skill is working. Give yourself a self-high-five.

If it isn't working, go back and double-check the code in the two functions we wrote and the `SkillBuilder()` code at the bottom of the **lambda_function.py** file. Then retest your skill.

You may find it helpful to add a breakpoint in VS Code by clicking in the margin toward the left of the code window, as shown in Figure 5-28.

```
28  ∨      def handle(self, handler_input):
29             # type: (HandlerInput) -> Resp
30             speak_output = "Welcome, you c
```

Figure 5-28. *Adding a breakpoint to the code*

Once this initial test passes, you should try a few different heights and weights, using various measurement types, debugging as you go.

When you have finished testing the BMI skill, you are ready to publish it to the Alexa Skills Store.

Summary

In this chapter, we wrote and tested the back-end code for the BMI calculator skill. We learned about lambda functions and request, intent, and API Handlers. We set up and used the debug environment on your local machine. All of these concepts will be repeated throughout the book as we get into more complex skills. In the next chapter, we will publish our BMI calculator skill to the Alexa Skills Store.

## CHAPTER 6

Publishing an Alexa Skill

Now that we have a working skill, we are ready to submit it for approval and publishing to the Alexa Skills Store. There are several steps to certification. This chapter will explore these steps and learn how to navigate the process to get our skill certified and published as quickly and efficiently as possible. First, we'll look at the certification process. Then we'll complete the distribution form and validation test. Then we'll talk about some of the rules and requirements for publication. Then we'll examine some of the issues that you may run into and how to remedy them.

The Process

The certification process is relatively straightforward. You complete the distribution details and then submit your skill to an automated validation test, fixing any errors or warnings that appear until the validation passes. Then you submit your skill to the certification team. They will review and test your skill to make sure it meets the certification criteria and will let you know if it doesn't and why it doesn't. After you address their concerns, the skill will be certified and published to the Alexa Skills Store. In the next section, we'll complete the Distribution form and get our skill to pass the validation process.

Distribution and Validation

In Chapters 4 and 5, we created a BMI calculator skill that we would now like to publish. There are a few I's to dot and T's to cross first, though. Select the Distribution tab in the Alexa Developer Console. Then complete the information requested as shown in Figure 6-1.

© Simon A. Kingaby 2022
S. A. Kingaby, *Data-Driven Alexa Skills*, https://doi.org/10.1007/978-1-4842-7449-1_6

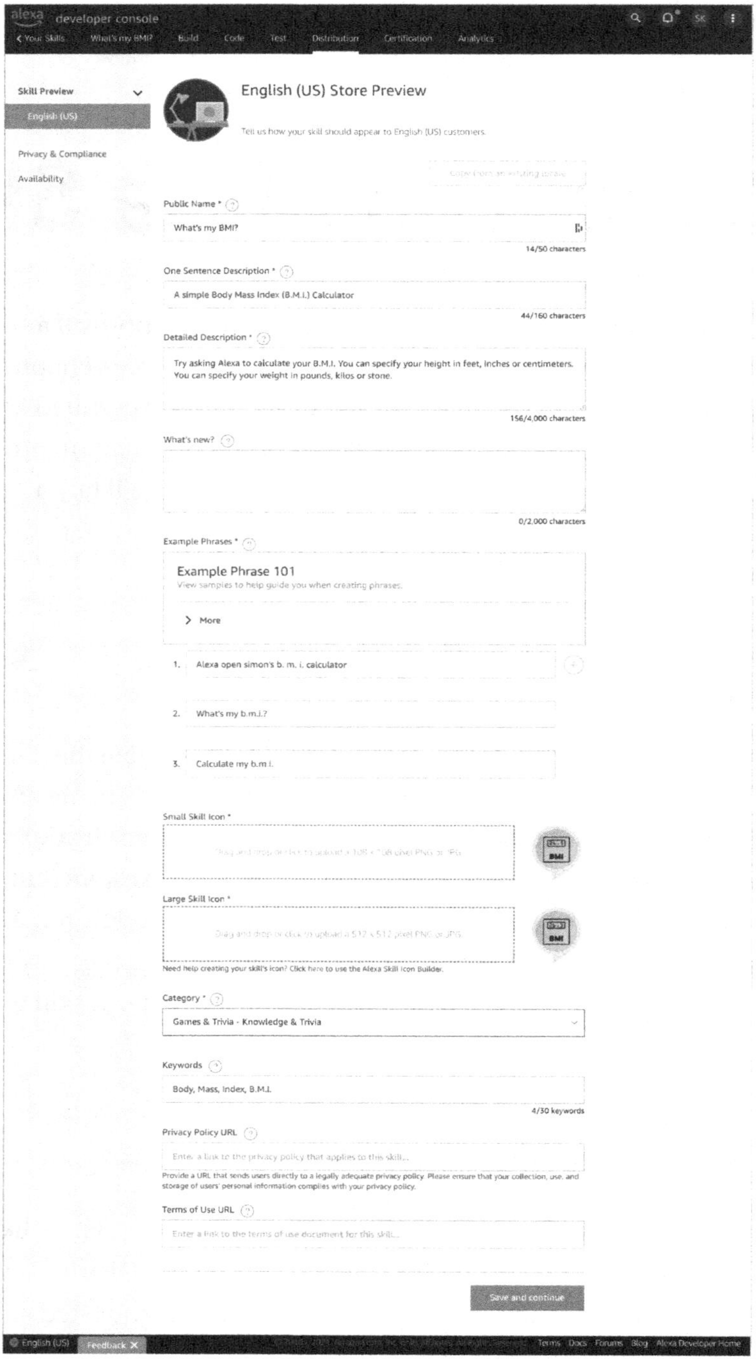

Figure 6-1. *The Distribution tab of the Developer Console*

Skill Preview

In the Skill Preview section are the fields you need to create an entry in the skills store. Things like the name of your skill, a description, and an icon. We'll go through each of these options as follows.

Public Name Enter the name of the skill as you want it to be known to the world. This is probably not your invocation name. Must be less than 50 characters. For the BMI calculator, the public name could be "What's my BMI?"

One Sentence Description A short sentence that describes the skill. Alexa might say this as part of telling someone about your skill. For the BMI calculator, the one sentence description could be "A simple Body Mass Index (B.M.I.) Calculator."

Detailed Description The full description of your skill, including instructions for use and anything you think someone will need to know about your skill if they look it up in the Skill Store. Any hardware requirements, such as a screen, or Echo Buttons, Echo Auto, or Smart Home Devices, should be included here. Note: The Detailed Description appears on the card for your skill in the Alexa app, so consider that as well. For example, see the product card in Figure 6-2.

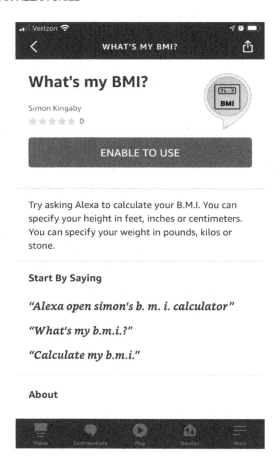

Figure 6-2. *The Product Card in the Alexa app*

For the BMI calculator, the detailed description could be "Try asking Alexa to calculate your B.M.I. You can specify your height in feet, inches, or centimeters. You can specify your weight in pounds, kilos, or stone."

What's New? As this is the first version of our skill, we can leave this blank. As you revise your skill and add features, you would document the changes and fixes in the What's New box.

Example Phrases The example phrases are one of the nit-picky parts of the certification process. You have to ensure that each of your example phrases exactly matches an utterance in the intents or dialog. The first example has to include the wake word, Alexa, and the invocation name. As ours is a conversational skill, the second and third examples do not have to contain those things but instead should show the user how to initiate the dialog with Alexa. For the BMI calculator, the example phrases could be

1. Alexa open simon's b. m. i. calculator

2. What's my b.m.i.?

3. Calculate my b.m.i.

Remember, they have to match the utterances, so the spelling and punctuation should be the same as those used in the Build tab of the Alexa Developer Console.

Small Skill Icon This needs to be a 108 × 108 pixel PNG or JPG, but since it has to fit in a circle, it needs to be a circular icon 108 pixels in diameter. There's a link to the Alexa Skill Icon Builder that will allow you to create your own icon (see Figure 6-3).

Figure 6-3. *The Alexa Skill Icon Builder*

Below the icon editor are hundreds of graphics to choose from to put in your logo (see Figure 6-4), or you could download the icon as a template and edit it in the graphic editor of your choice.

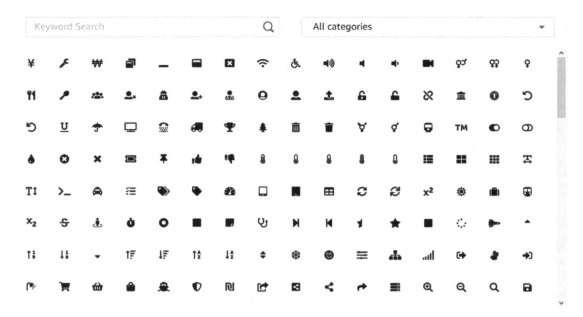

Figure 6-4. *Graphics you can add to your icon*

Large Skill Icon You'll want two sizes of the icon you create: 108 ×108 pixels and 512 × 512 pixels. One for the small skill icon and one for the large.

Category Select the most appropriate category for your skill. This will be the category for your skill in the Alexa Skills Store. For the BMI calculator, the category could be *Games & Trivia – Knowledge & Trivia*.

Keywords Enter a comma-separated list of keywords that will help people find your skill. For the BMI calculator, the keywords could be "Body, Mass, Index, B.M.I."

Privacy Policy URL In the United States, the Federal Trade Commission recommends that any website that shares or collects (stores) consumer data should have a privacy policy. Many states have more stringent requirements. Canada has regulations about privacy online. Then there's the GDPR (the European Union's General Data Protection Regulation), which applies to anyone processing consumer data in the EU or offering services to individuals in the EU.

According to the Better Business Bureau article *BBB Tip: Writing an Effective Privacy Policy for Your Business' Website* (`www.bbb.org/article/news-releases/21390-bbb-tip-writing-an-effective-privacy-policy-for-your-small-business-website`), "Whether or not it's legally required for your business, it's a good idea to develop and maintain a privacy policy... Be sure to do the following:

- Keep it visible.

- Keep it simple.

- Keep it real.

- Keep it current."

There are a variety of privacy policy generators on the Web. For under $100, these will allow you to identify

- What information you collect through your skill

- Why you collect it

- How you collect and store it

- How you protect it

- How they can control or manage their data

- How you will tell users of your skill when the policy gets updated

- Perhaps most importantly, who has access to your information

Having an acceptable privacy policy will help you earn and maintain the trust of your skill's users. Make sure to update your privacy policy when you release a new version of your skill.

Despite all that, since we aren't storing any user-identifiable data, we can leave the privacy policy URL blank for the BMI calculator.

Terms of Use URL Another integral part of the skill is the terms of use, and, like the privacy policy, this helps to build trust. Terms of use are legal agreements between you as a skill developer and a person who wants to use your skill. The person implicitly agrees to abide by the terms of use in order to use your skill. Like the privacy policy, there are a variety of terms of use generators on the Web. The terms of use usually cover

- The users' rights and responsibilities.

- Proper or expected use of your skill. What is the user responsible for doing in their online actions?

- What is misuse or improper conduct? What are the consequences?

- Any payment details, what is paid for, how, subscription fees, etc.

- How the user can opt out and terminate their account.

- Dispute resolution and jurisdiction.

- Limit of liability explaining what you are and are not liable for and how damages will be assessed.

- How a user will know when the terms change.

Make sure to be clear in the terms of use about any personally identifiable information, how it will be handled, and how it can be removed. This is especially relevant if you use account linking in your skill to get access to the users' Amazon accounts. For the BMI calculator, we can leave the terms of use URL blank.

Once you have completed the Skill Preview section, click Save and continue to advance to the Privacy and Compliance section of the Distribution questionnaire.

Privacy and Compliance

The Privacy & Compliance section, shown in Figure 6-5, is a set of questions that broadly identify the functionality of your skill with relation to Privacy and Compliance.

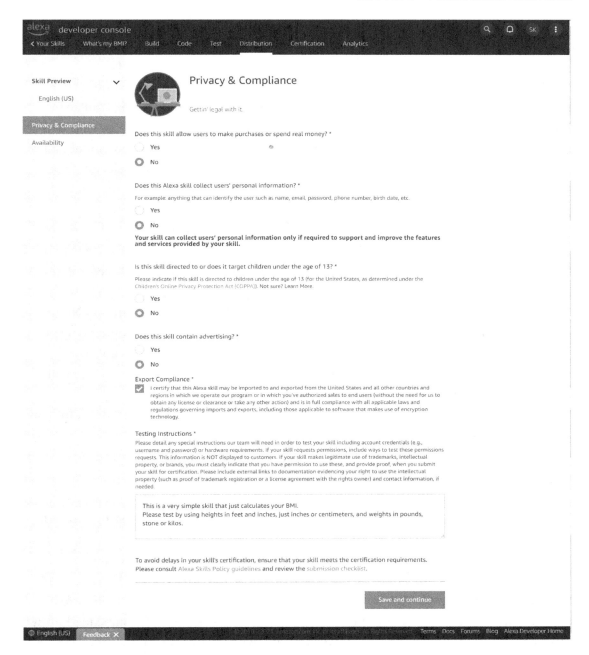

Figure 6-5. *Privacy & Compliance section*

The first few questions are pretty straightforward and are detailed in the following. The Testing Instructions are explained in the next section.

Does this skill allow users to make purchases or spend real money? This includes encouraging people to spend money, for example, encouraging people to go to a website to make a donation or a purchase. For the BMI calculator, we can answer No.

Does this Alexa skill collect users' personal information? This question is tricky, as it covers personal information collected via your skill or account linking. You also need to consider if the personal information is linked to an individual. In our case with the BMI calculator, the data we get (height and weight) is not tied to an individual and is simply for the BMI calculation. We don't store the result either, which is relevant when you consider the term "collect" in the question. Also, you can only collect user data that your skill needs in order to function. For the BMI calculator, we can answer No.

Is this skill directed to or does it target children under the age of 13? There are many rules and laws protecting children, so this question implies that you are aware of those rules and regulations and that your skill adheres to them. For the BMI calculator, we can answer No.

Does this skill contain advertising? For the BMI calculator, we can answer No.

Export Compliance This box is required, so I'm not sure what you would do if your skill weren't "...in full compliance with all applicable laws and regulations governing imports and exports..." I suppose then you wouldn't be able to publish your skill at all. For the BMI calculator, we can check this box.

The next section covers the Testing Instructions box, which is very important for your skill to get past the certification process.

Testing Instructions

As it says in the Testing Instructions prompt, "Please detail any special instructions our team will need in order to test your skill. Include any account or hardware requirements. If your skill requests permissions, include ways to test these permissions requests."

The testing instructions don't need to be exhaustive and fully comprehensive of all possible ways to test your skill, but they should be thorough and precise. Make sure to include steps to test your skill's happy path and any variations thereof. Your skill's happy path is the route through your skill that a user will take if they answer every question correctly and make every choice optimally. Nonhappy paths deviate from the happy path in known ways. In our BMI calculator, we only have one happy path (Alexa asks for height and weight and gets the height and weight) and no nonhappy paths. We also don't handle any error paths. For example, what if Alexa asks for your height, and you say "fish." Include any instructions you can think of to test nonhappy path scenarios that your skill handles. In our case, the testing instructions are relatively straightforward. Some skills may have specific hardware requirements, such as "this skill works best on devices with a screen." Some skills need account linking and other permissions, which need to be listed and tested here. This is also where you put your justification for requiring account linking and additional permissions – the more information you can provide to the skill's certification team, the better.

For the BMI calculator, the testing instructions might be something like this: "This is a very simple skill that just calculates your BMI. Please test by using heights in feet and inches, just inches, or centimeters, and weights in pounds, stone, or kilos." If the BMI calculator skill were any more complicated than it is, these instructions would be insufficient, and we likely wouldn't pass certification with such brevity.

There is a small reminder at the bottom of the screen that you ensure your skill meets all the Alexa policies and certification requirements. It is essential to consider these throughout the skill development process. For the BMI calculator, it meets these requirements, but for some of the skills we will create, these requirements will not be trivial. In the next section, we'll work through the certification checklist.

The Certification Checklist

In the Alexa developer documentation, there is a certification submission checklist (`https://developer.amazon.com/en-US/docs/alexa/custom-skills/certification-requirements-for-custom-skills.html`). You should consider these requirements for every skill you write. They are the following:

1. Ensure your skill meets the Alexa policy guidelines.

2. Ensure your skill meets the security requirements for your method of hosting the service for your skill.

3. Perform all required functional tests.

4. Perform all required voice interface and user experience tests.

5. If your skill includes screen-based interaction, test your skill's screen-based interactions.

6. If your skill includes reminders, ensure that you use the test instructions to describe how you have implemented reminders functionality in the skill.

7. If your skill is eligible for the Works With Alexa Program or the Certified for Humans Program, ensure that your device and skill comply with the Works With Alexa Program Guidelines and the Certified for Humans Program Guidelines.

8. If your skill allows users to make a purchase or spend money on or through Alexa, or any website your skill refers to, ensure you follow the Requirements for Skills that Allow Purchases.

For the full and current requirements, you should review the Amazon Alexa Skills Kit documentation. In the next few sections, we'll elaborate on each of the checklist items.

Alexa Policies

Your skill must adhere to Amazon's Alexa Policies (`https://developer.amazon.com/en-US/docs/alexa/custom-skills/policy-testing-for-an-alexa-skill.html`). Your skill will be rejected if it doesn't. Some of these policies are the following:

1. Trademarks, intellectual property, and brands. You must have the right to use any of these that you use in your skill, and you must document proof of this in your Testing Instructions. For example, if we called our skill the Nike BMI Calculator, we would have to provide evidence of our right to use Nike's name. Without sufficient proof, our skill would fail certification.

2. Child-directed Alexa skills (`https://developer.amazon.com/en-US/alexa/alexa-skills-kit/get-deeper/custom-skills/kid-skills`). You must be an Amazon-approved developer to make skills for children under the age of 13 (or 16 outside the United States and India). There are several legal and policy considerations specific to kids skills, such as the Children's Online Privacy Protection Act ("COPPA") and Amazon's parental consent requirement.

3. Health. There are two kinds of health skills: ones that are HIPAA eligible and ones that aren't. To be eligible to handle Protected Health Information (PHI), your skill must comply with the US Health Insurance Portability and Accountability Act of 1996 (HIPAA). You must also be an Amazon-approved developer for Health skills (`https://developer.amazon.com/en-US/alexa/ alexa-skills-kit/get-deeper/custom-skills/healthcare- skills`). All other health-related skills must include a written disclaimer in the skill description that the skill is not a substitute for professional medical advice. In some cases, the Alexa team will require your skill to provide a verbal disclaimer in the skill as well.

4. Skill recommendations, compensation, and purchasing. If your skill sells anything (digital or physical) (`https://developer. amazon.com/en-US/docs/alexa/custom-skills/requirements- for-skills-that-allow-purchases.html`) or recommends that the user spend money in any way (purchase, donation, etc.), you have to use the Alexa-approved channels to do so. For example, digital goods and services must go through the Alexa In-Skill Purchasing feature (`https://developer.amazon.com/en-US/ docs/alexa/custom-skills/requirements-for-skills-that- allow-purchases.html#digital`). Physical products or services (`https://developer.amazon.com/en-US/docs/alexa/custom- skills/requirements-for-skills-that-allow-purchases. html#non-digital`), or charitable donations (`https://pay. amazon.com/secure-checkout/non-profits`), must use Amazon Pay and account linking correctly.

5. Advertising. Most advertising and promotional messaging in skill responses is prohibited (`https://developer.amazon.com/en-US/ docs/alexa/custom-skills/policy-testing-for-an-alexa- skill.html#5-advertising`). Exceptions include streaming skills that provide audio adverts, in-skill purchasing promotions, and responding to customers' specific requests.

6. Pornography and sex. Sexually explicit material or images are forbidden (`https://developer.amazon.com/en-US/docs/alexa/custom-skills/policy-testing-for-an-alexa-skill.html#cert-pornography-and-sex`).

7. Violence. Extreme violence, organized crime, terrorism, and other illegal activities are forbidden (`https://developer.amazon.com/en-US/docs/alexa/custom-skills/policy-testing-for-an-alexa-skill.html#cert-violence`).

8. Religion, ethnicity, and culture. This policy is mostly about preventing hate crimes (`https://developer.amazon.com/en-US/docs/alexa/custom-skills/policy-testing-for-an-alexa-skill.html#cert-religion`).

9. Emergency services (telecommunications). Your skill can't call 911 or any other emergency responder (`https://developer.amazon.com/en-US/docs/alexa/custom-skills/policy-testing-for-an-alexa-skill.html#9-emergency-services-telecommunications`).

10. Content. This policy is the bucket that prohibits bad behavior (`https://developer.amazon.com/en-US/docs/alexa/custom-skills/policy-testing-for-an-alexa-skill.html#cert-content`). If your skill doesn't promote bad behavior, you will be fine. If it does, then it may get rejected under the content policy.

11. General. This policy (`https://developer.amazon.com/en-US/docs/alexa/custom-skills/policy-testing-for-an-alexa-skill.html#11-general`) is the bucket that asks you to complete the steps outlined in the rest of this chapter and promotes niceness, politeness, and good stewardship of the Alexa brand.

12. Web search skills. If your skill is a search skill, it must search a specific online resource, attribute that source, and comply with all other policies (`https://developer.amazon.com/en-US/docs/alexa/custom-skills/policy-testing-for-an-alexa-skill.html#12-web-search-skills`).

13. Financial skills. Provide a disclaimer about the timeliness of stock quotes, if you provide them. If you access personal financial information, you must meet all the financial skill guidelines. Only US financial skills are allowed. To create a financial or banking skill in the United States, you must contact Amazon to get their approval (`https://developer.amazon.com/en-US/docs/alexa/custom-skills/policy-testing-for-an-alexa-skill.html#13-financial-skills`).

14. Invocation name requirements. There are some very specific requirements for your skill's invocation name (`https://developer.amazon.com/en-US/docs/alexa/custom-skills/choose-the-invocation-name-for-a-custom-skill.html#cert-invocation-name-req`). Note: this is not the skill's name, but rather, this is what the user says to invoke your skill. Mostly, the requirements are that your Skill Invocation Name is clear, precise, and easily repeated by customers. It should also be sensible, practical, and relevant to your skill. It can't include brand/intellectual property terms that you don't own.

15. Security policy – web services. You must use an Amazon-approved certificate authority and present a valid, trusted certificate when establishing the connection.

16. Security policy – account linking. There are many policies specific to account linking. If your skill needs to connect to another system, that's account linking. Linked accounts must be secured and monitored. You must provide a Privacy Policy and Terms of Use URL in the Skill Preview section. Don't forget to include a set of dummy credentials in the testing instructions so that the certification team can test your skill. If your skill is a Smart Home skill, there are additional security requirements, especially if your skill allows unlocking or disarming a device.

17. Security policy – PII handling. Personally Identifiable Information (PII) must only be collected if your skill needs it and, when required, must be handled correctly (`https://developer.amazon.com/en-US/docs/alexa/custom-skills/security-testing-for-an-alexa-skill.html#25-privacy-requirements`).

18. Security policy – voice codes. Certain types of skills, including financial skills and skills that allow purchases over $100, must give the customer an opportunity to set up a voice code (`https://developer.amazon.com/en-US/docs/alexa/custom-skills/security-testing-for-an-alexa-skill.html#voice-code-requirements`).

If your skill meets all these policy requirements, the certification team might reject it anyway. When that happens, they will tell you why. Make the necessary corrections and resubmit or appeal their decision and ask them to reconsider. Most skills will get rejected at least once before the submission is successful, but it is usually not for policy violations. More commonly, it is because of a failure in testing.

Testing Your Custom Skill for Certification

Your skill will go through several rounds of testing before it gets approved by the certification team. Most tests will be focused on the data you enter in the test instructions. You can help make sure your skill passes these tests by doing the following:

1) Review and test your three example phrases. In the Skill Preview page, you must provide three example phrases, as discussed earlier in this chapter. Make sure these work.

2) Make sure your skill description and detail page are accurate. The testers use these items as guidance and verify all the functionality implied in the skill's description and detail pages.

3) Ensure any visual responses (cards, streamed, or Alexa Presentation Language (APL) output) are working as expected.

4) Don't have broken links in your skill. Make sure any external links are working.

5) Provide test credentials linked to your developer account for any skills that use account linking.

6) Make sure your account-linked skill can be enabled, linked, unlinked, and disabled properly.

7) Ensure the audio responses (streamed or Alexa Presentation Language for Audio (APLA) output) are working as expected.

8) If your skill provides a visual interface, make sure it displays appropriately on all the relevant devices and that screen navigation options work as expected.

9) Make sure any API's you incorporate in your skill work as expected.

10) Don't state that your skill is a Test or Trial skill in your skill description. It won't pass. Only production skills will pass certification.

11) Review your intents, utterances, and slots to make sure they are correct, complete, and adhere to voice design best practices.

12) You must test your skill using verbal interactions, not just by typing into the simulator.

13) Test your VUI for smooth flow and good session management. Ensure the intents and slots work together correctly, sound good, and adhere to the Alexa Design Guide recommendations (`https://developer.amazon.com/en-US/docs/alexa/alexa-design/get-started.html`). Ensure that your skill provides supportive prompts when the user doesn't fill all the slots.

14) If you provide a one-shot experience, make sure it works appropriately and ends the session as expected.

15) Ensure that a variety of utterances will engage your skill correctly.

16) Make sure you handle errors gracefully.

17) Your skill must provide a help intent.

18) Your skill must stop, cancel, and end when asked to by the customer.

Whew. That's a lot of policies and tests. Don't worry, though. If your skill is reasonable, polite, nice, and good, it will probably pass the policy requirements, and if it works, it should pass the testing requirements. Later in this book, we will discuss VUI design in depth. We will also learn several different functional testing techniques so that we can ensure the skill works as expected.

For now, we are ready to advance to the next page of the Skill Preview page, Availability.

Availability

Your skill will be available to the public once it is in the skill store. If you have created an Alexa for Business skill, you will have the option to select a particular business organization to publish your skill to.

If you want to Beta Test your skill, which means publishing it to the skill store but with access limited to specific users identified by their email address, you can enter their email addresses. (See Figure 6-6.) The advantage of Beta Test mode is that you can continue to develop your skill, even though it is in the skill store. You can add up to 500 beta testers.

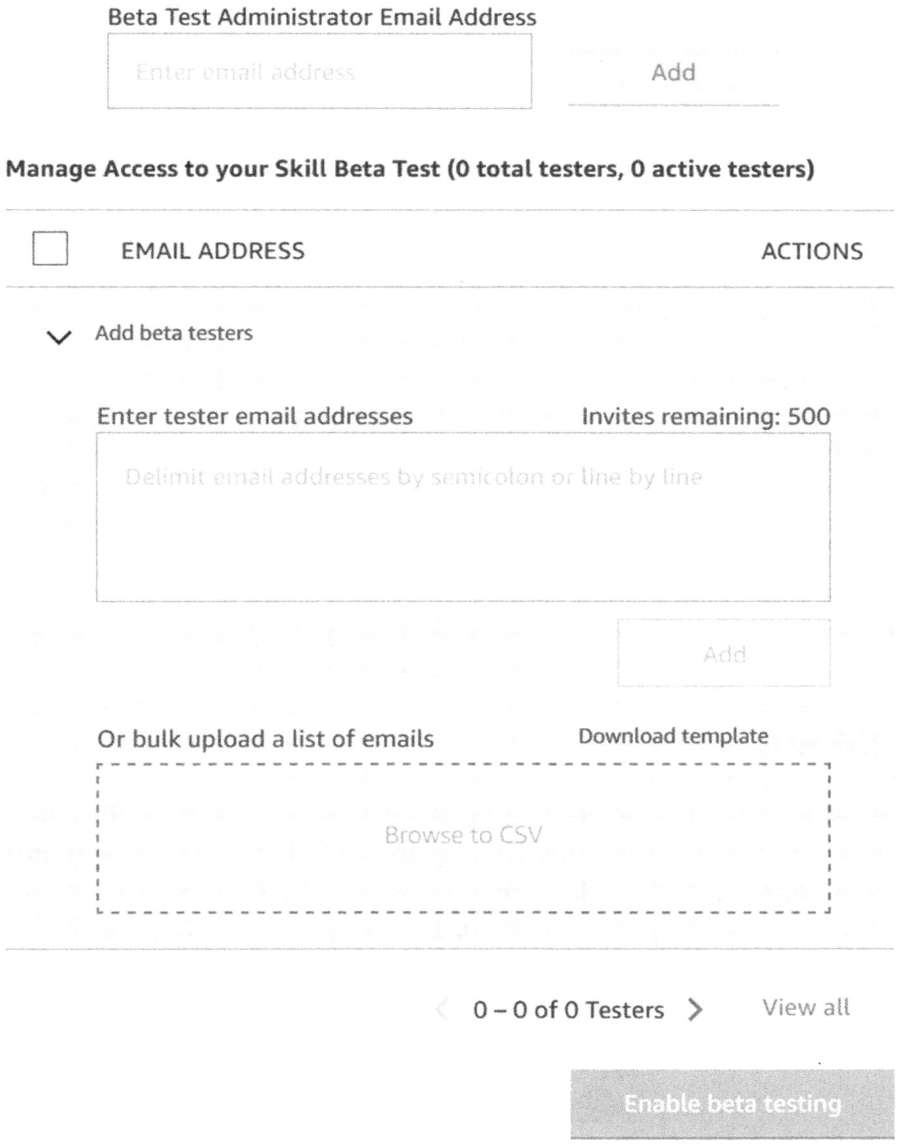

Beta Test Administrator Email Address

| Enter email address | Add |

Manage Access to your Skill Beta Test (0 total testers, 0 active testers)

☐   EMAIL ADDRESS   ACTIONS

∨   Add beta testers

Enter tester email addresses   Invites remaining: 500

Delimit email addresses by semicolon or line by line

Add

Or bulk upload a list of emails   Download template

Browse to CSV

‹   0 – 0 of 0 Testers   ›   View all

Enable beta testing

Figure 6-6. *Adding beta testers to your skill*

If you want your English US skill to be available in other English-speaking countries, you can opt into automated locale distribution. This works for other languages too.

Finally, you need to select which countries your skill is available in – all of them or just specific ones.

At this point, you have completed the presubmission process. Now you are ready to move on to Validation and Submission.

Validation

On the Validation screen, click the Run button to run a series of automated tests that validate your skill. Depending on your skill's complexity, this can take a while. If all is well, you will see a green checkmark appear; see Figure 6-7.

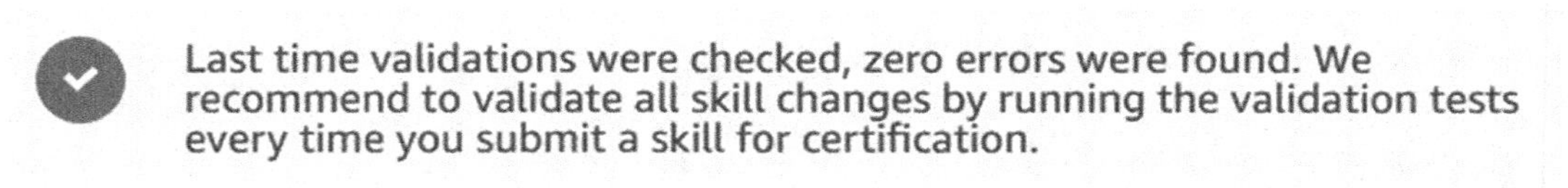

 Last time validations were checked, zero errors were found. We recommend to validate all skill changes by running the validation tests every time you submit a skill for certification.

Figure 6-7. *Your skill has passed Validation*

Quick, before anything changes, click the Submission tab on the left.

Submission

The final decision of the submission process lies before you. Will you certify and publish your skill to the Alexa Skills Store, or did you go through all that effort just to certify your skill so you can publish at a later date? You may want to coordinate the publication with a marketing campaign, in which case, you do just want to certify your skill. So think hard. Make a choice. And click that big blue Submit for review button (Figure 6-8)!

Submit for review

Figure 6-8. *Go ahead, click it. You know you wanna* ☺

Now that you've submitted your skill for review, you can sit back and relax for a few days while the certification team does their job. Then, if your skill is certified, you've got a marketing campaign to write. Otherwise, you will get an email explaining why your skill didn't pass.

Rejection? Now What?

If your skill does not get certified the first time, which is common, the first thing you should do is read the email explaining why it didn't pass. This may seem obvious, but you'd be surprised how many developers just start rewriting their skills. Most rejections are for violating a policy and not for a coding error.

In most cases, if you cannot understand the violation, you can open a ticket by going to the Contact Us page (`https://developer.amazon.com/support/contact-us`). Once you have the ticket number in your email, you can refer to the ticket and your questions therein in the Testing Instructions box on the Distribution tab's Skill Preview page.

The Alexa team has put together a web page detailing the most common reasons for certification failures (`https://developer.amazon.com/en-US/docs/alexa/custom-skills/troubleshooting-common-certification-failures.html`). You can go through this list to get more details and examples of the common failures. Some of these are given here.

The following are some of the common reasons why certifications fail. The reasons are grouped into clusters representing common problem areas.

Problems with the Skill Description

- The skill's detailed description should include all the information required to use the skill.

- The functionality described in the skill description should exist in the skill and work as described.

- Any sample utterances in the description should work in the skill precisely as written.

Problems with Sample Utterances

- Make sure that the three sample utterances in your skill preview work as expected. They should not throw an error. They should provide relevant and correct responses.

- Don't use special characters, numbers, or dates in your sample utterances. Spell things out. For example, if your sample utterance uses a date, type it out: January first, nineteen-eighty.

- The sample utterances must exist as utterances in the skill definition.

- One-shot utterances that are implied by the sample utterances should work too. For example, the sample utterance says, "Six foot two and three hundred pounds." This implies that the user could say, "Alexa, launch my b.m.i. calculator and tell it I am six foot two and three hundred pounds." Alexa should respond to that one-shot utterance with "Your b.m.i. is 38.5."

- Sample utterances should also work if the words are varied a little. For example, the sample "Six foot two and three hundred pounds" should work as shown. But so should "*I am* six foot two and *weigh* three hundred pounds." So should "*I am* six foot two *inches tall*, and *I weigh* three hundred pounds."

- Utterances should be unique across your skill to prevent two intents from conflicting.

- Utterances are in the correct language. For example, if your skill works in English US and Spanish US, make certain the English utterances are in the English locale and the Spanish utterances are in the Spanish locale.

Problems with Skill Session State

- Make sure you test your skill on a device that visually shows you the state of the microphone (such as your smartphone, an Amazon Echo, or an Echo Show). If the blue light is on, Alexa is listening. If Alexa is listening, she should have just asked a question or given a prompt that the customer is expected to respond to.

- If your skill is a one-shot skill, make sure you end the session when Alexa responds. For example:

The customer says, "Alexa, what's my b.m.i.?"

> Alexa says, "What's your height and weight?" – Blue light is on, Alexa is listening.
> The customer says, "Six foot two and three hundred pounds."
> Alexa says, "Your b.m.i. is 38.5." – The blue light should then go off as the session ends. If it stays on, Alexa is listening for a user response, and your skill will fail certification. Make sure you end the session correctly.

Once you have worked through the issues that caused your skill to fail certification, make sure to update your documentation in the Distribution tab's Skill Preview, paying particular attention to the Testing Skills box. Don't hesitate to add commentary explaining your skill's behavior to the testers. You can also send them a message through the Contact Us page to further explain your skill. When you are ready, resubmit your skill for certification. Repeat this process until your skill passes. Sometimes, it can get frustrating as the errors or rejections might seem obtuse. Once I saw a game skill that sold spaceships to its players repeatedly getting rejected, it didn't implement In-Skill Purchasing to pay for the spaceships. Sometimes, you've just got to explain yourself repeatedly until you get through the process. Soon enough, you'll get through the process, and your skill will go live on the Alexa Skills Store.

Summary

In this chapter, you published your skill!

Woohoo, you! Self-high-fives all around.

We filled in the Distribution forms with the required information to pass certification. We went through the certification checklist. We even reviewed the Alexa Policies and some Testing recommendations for certification. We covered what to expect in the submission process and how to handle rejection.

This ends Part I of the book. We have created an Alexa skill from scratch and have gone through the entire data-driven skill-building process from VUI development to publication. In Part II, we will walk through each of these steps in more depth.

PART II

Custom Skill Development

CHAPTER 7

Custom Alexa Skills

Now that you've published your first Alexa skill, let's go back through the steps and look at each of them a little more in depth. In Part I, you created an Alexa skill from VUI development to back-end code to publishing in the Alexa Skills Store. In Part II, we'll develop another skill, and we'll see how to use some of the more advanced features of the Alexa platform.

Alexa Hosted vs. Fully Custom

In Part I, the BMI calculator was an Alexa-hosted skill. This meant the front end, back end, and everything in between were hosted inside the Alexa platform. In particular, the back-end code was hosted in Alexa, so we had to go to the Code tab in the Alexa interface to enter the code for our skill. (See Figure 7-1.)

© Simon A. Kingaby 2022
S. A. Kingaby, *Data-Driven Alexa Skills*, https://doi.org/10.1007/978-1-4842-7449-1_7

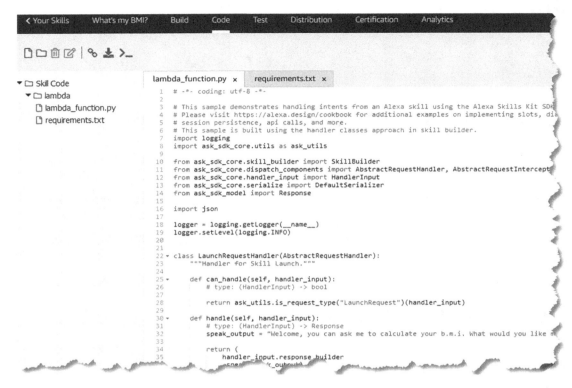

Figure 7-1. *Editing the code for an Alexa-hosted skill*

In this section, we will create a fully custom skill where the code and all the resources we use are hosted as Amazon Web Services (AWS) instead of in the Alexa platform. Alexa-hosted skills are easier to build, but there are some constraints enforced by the Alexa platform. You may need to move to AWS to accomplish what you need for your skill. This is especially true for Media and Data storage. We'll be using both of these in our new skill, so it makes sense to move to AWS in this case. But what is our new skill?

Our New Skill

Several months ago, I was listening to TED Radio Hour on National Public Radio in the car. I don't remember who was on, but it was one of the recap shows where they talk about highlights from the series, including the talks that meant a lot to the commentators. One of them mentioned that they were struck by an idea from one TED speaker – I suppose I should call him a TED talker – slipped in at the end of his talk. After some googling, I found the speaker was Tim Urban and the talk was about procrastination.[1] The idea he presented was a 90-year calendar, something Tim called the Life Calendar, which shows a small box for each week in a 90-year lifespan. At first, you might think that's a lot of boxes. But if you're already 21 years old, you've already crossed off 1,092 of those little boxes. There were only 4,680 boxes to start with. At age 21, you're already 23% done!

Tim Urban's Life Calendar was a life changer for me.

The 90-Year Calendar

As soon as I got home, I fired up Excel and built my own 90-year calendar. After crossing off over half the boxes, I was appalled at how few were left, and I wondered what I had to show for the boxes I had crossed out. Here's what I was looking at (see Figure 7-2).

---

[1] Tim Urban, TED2016, Inside the mind of a master procrastinator. Time: 13:00
www.ted.com/talks/tim_urban_inside_the_mind_of_a_master_procrastinator?language=en.
The Life Calendar comes from Tim's Wait But Why blog, from a 2014 article:
https://waitbutwhy.com/2014/05/life-weeks.html

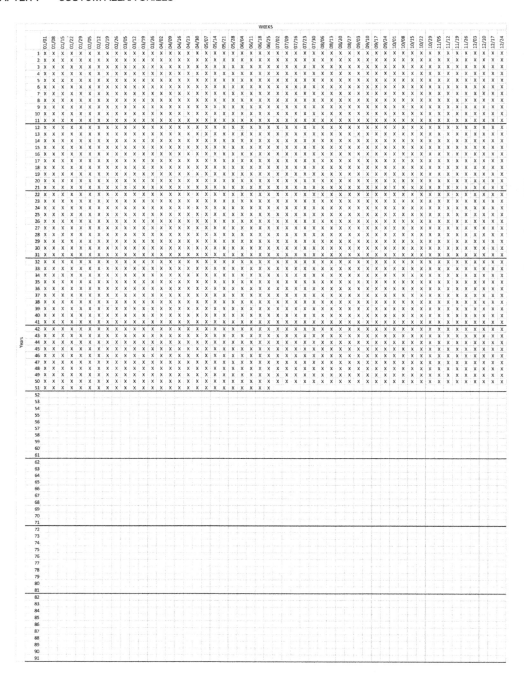

Figure 7-2. *A 90-year life calendar*

But that wasn't all. I made 90-year life calendars for everyone in my household. And then I "enhanced" mine with some of the significant events of my life. It ended up looking something like Figure 7-3.

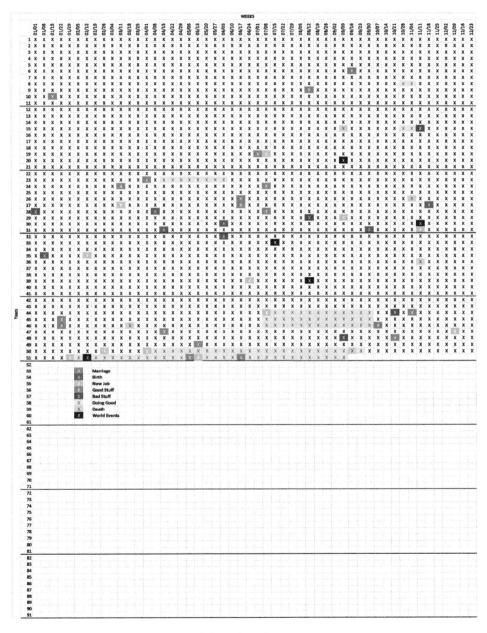

Figure 7-3. *An enhanced 90-year life calendar*

In the next few chapters, we're going to build that enhanced 90-year life calendar as an Alexa skill. Throughout this exercise, we'll learn more about the Alexa development process, and we will use many advanced features, including

- Voice User Interface Design

- Alexa Interaction Model – Intents, Slots, Utterances

- Alexa Conversations and Delegation

- Alexa Presentation Language to draw the 90-year calendar on devices with screens

- Alexa Presentation Language for Audio to enhance our skill with sound effects

- DynamoDb persistence to securely store the events of your life

- S3 Storage to securely link pictures of the events of your life

- Account linking to allow us to gather the events of your life securely

- A lambda function – the brains of our skill

In this chapter, we will create the accounts and AWS services that comprise a fully custom skill. In the following chapters, we will use these AWS services to enable the features of our skill.

VUI Design

The first thing we'll be using is Botmock, a VUI design tool. When designing a conversational interface, it is tempting to pull up Word, Excel, and PowerPoint as these are the tools we are most familiar with. However, each of these has a really hard time representing a VUI. Even advanced tools like Visio and Lucidchart don't lend themselves to mapping the voice experience, which is where tools like Botmock and Voiceflow come in. We'll be using Botmock for this exercise, so you'll need to sign up for their free account.

1. First, go to `www.botmock.com`.

2. Then click to *Try it for Free*.

3. Enter the required information and click *Register*.

Once you've logged in, you'll be in the Free tier, which allows you to create up to two projects. In the next chapter, we'll create a project for the 90-year calendar and learn how to use Botmock to design our voice experience. Next, we'll log in to the Alexa Console and create a skill.

Creating the Alexa Skill

We need to create a custom Alexa skill and turn on several features. So that's what we'll do next. Open the Alexa Developer Console (`https://developer.amazon.com/alexa/console/ask`). Then follow along:

1. Click *Create Skill*.

2. Enter the Skill Name: **90-Year Calendar**.

3. In Choose a model, it's a Custom Skill.

4. In Choose a method, to host your skill's back-end resources, choose Provision your own.

5. Then click *Create Skill* in the top right.

6. In Choose a template: pick **Start from Scratch**.

7. Then click *Choose* in the top right.

The console will create a simple skill with a Hello World intent. Next, we will make some configuration changes, and then we'll come back to the Interaction Model in Chapter 9.

8. Click on *Invocation* in the left navigation bar.

9. Change the *Skill Invocation Name* to something easy to type and to say. During debugging, you will say and type this a lot. Near the end of the creation process, you can make it more appropriate, like Ninety-Year Calendar. For now, stick with a name like **ninety kilo** – two words, easy to type (the keys 90 kilo are all clustered together), easy to say, and easy to remember. (See Figure 7-4.)

Skill Invocation Name ⑦

ninety kilo|

Figure 7-4. *Pick a simple, easy invocation name*

10. Click *Save Model* at the top.

11. In the left nav bar, select *Interfaces*.

12. Scroll down to Alexa Presentation Language and flip it to the **On** setting.

13. Make sure all the hubs and the TV are selected.

14. Scroll down to Alexa Conversations and select it.

15. Do not use Alexa Conversations as the default dialog manager.

16. Scroll back to the top and click *Save Interfaces*.

Now we've created the skeleton for our skill.

We need to navigate back to the Skills List (`https://developer.amazon.com/alexa/ console/ask`). In the Skills List, select *Copy the Skill Id* (see Figure 7-5) and paste it into Notepad++. We'll need it later for the security profile.

Figure 7-5. *Copy the Skill ID for later*

Next, we will need a database to store the life events that Alexa will collect

DynamoDb

When Alexa gathers information, it is transferred as Json documents. We need a place to store these documents. The most likely choice is a NoSQL database, which in the Amazon AWS stack is named DynamoDb. NoSQL has several advantages over a traditional relational database in this case. One, we are going to have one key record with many details associated with it. Two, the data we have will all be in Json format. And three, a NoSQL database will very quickly read and write those Json documents. Therefore, we need to create a DynamoDb table.

1. First, log in to the AWS Developer Console as your admin user, not as the root user. The AWS console is here: `https://console.aws.amazon.com`.

2. Once logged in, search for **DynamoDb** in the Find Services box.

3. After selecting DynamoDb, you are taken to the DynamoDb Console.

4. In the left navigation bar, select *Tables*.

5. To the right, click the *Create Table* button.

NoSQL tables are not like SQL (relational) tables, though they use some of the same nomenclature. Each NoSQL table must have a Partition Key and an optional Sort Key. The Primary Key is comprised of these two attributes and needs to be unique for each item. DynamoDb hashes the Partition Key to determine in which partition of the database to store the item. There may only be one partition in a small database, but there can be many as the database grows. For more information on choosing a Partition Key, check out this document: `https://aws.amazon.com/blogs/database/choosing-the-right-dynamodb-partition-key/`. For our use case, a 90-year calendar for an individual, it seems to make sense to use a Person Id that is unique for each individual as the Partition Key, and we do not have a Sort Key. When completing the table form, enter the following (see Figure 7-6):

6. For Table name, enter **CalendarItem**.

7. For Partition key, enter **PersonId**.

8. Scroll down to the bottom and click *Create*.

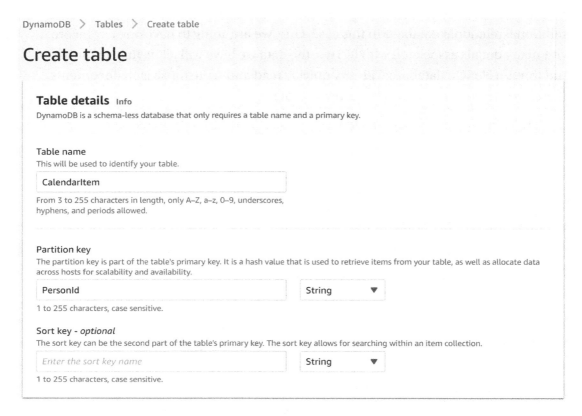

Figure 7-6. Creating the DynamoDb table for calendar items

DynamoDb will take a minute or so to provision the table. When it's finished, copy the ARN for the DynamoDB table to Notepad++ (see Figure 7-7). We'll need it when creating the security Role.

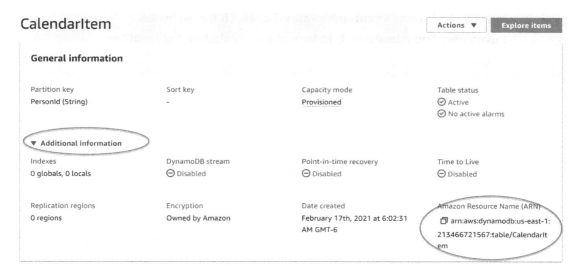

Figure 7-7. Copy the ARN for the DynamoDB table

Next, we will create our S3 storage account.

S3 Storage

While DynamoDb is a great place to store the data about the events of your life, it's not the right place to store the pictures related to those events. Images are a type of binary large object, or Blob data. Blob data is best kept in a file system, where it is easily and cheaply stored. This latter is the main advantage of S3 buckets. Short for Simple Storage Service, S3 is Amazon's cloud solution for file storage. On your local machine, you have disk drives; in S3, you have buckets. Locally, you have folders to contain your files; in S3, you also have folders to organize your objects. To create an S3 bucket for the images we will store for the skill, navigate to the Services menu in the top left corner of any AWS console, and follow these steps:

1. First, log in to the AWS Developer Console as your admin user, not as the root user. The AWS console is here: `https://console.aws.amazon.com`.

2. From the S3 Console, click the orange *Create bucket* button in the top right.

3. For the *Bucket name*: **calendar-pics-12345**. (It has to be all lowercase. The name needs to be unique, so change the numbers as necessary.)

4. Select the correct *Region*.

5. Be sure to leave the *Block all public access* box checked.

6. We do not need *Bucket versioning* (nor the cost associated with it).

7. Since we're storing private pictures, we want *Server-side encryption*, and we can let Amazon manage the key – *Amazon S3 key (SSE-S3)*.

8. Now scroll down and click the orange *Create bucket* button.

   After creating the bucket, we need to edit one of the settings.

9. Select the bucket name link in the list of buckets.

10. Click on the *Permissions* tab.

11. Scroll to the bottom.

12. Next to *Cross-origin resource sharing (CORS)*, click *Edit*.

13. Enter the following JSON:

```
[
    {
        "AllowedHeaders": [
            "*"
        ],
        "AllowedMethods": [
            "PUT",
            "GET",
            "POST",
            "DELETE",
            "HEAD"
        ],
        "AllowedOrigins": [
            "https://www.example.com"
        ],
```

```
        "ExposeHeaders": [
            "ETag"
        ]
    }
]
```

14. Click *Save changes.*

That's all we need to do to the S3 bucket for now. Copy the ARN for the S3 bucket to Notepad++. (See Figure 7-8.) We'll need it when creating the security Role.

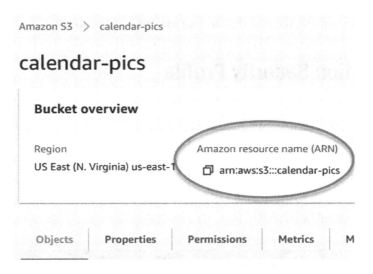

Figure 7-8. *Copy the ARN for the S3 bucket*

We also need to be able to identify the user and give them secure access to their data. This requires account linking, which we'll configure next.

Account Linking

We're going to have two versions of our skill behavior depending on whether the user has linked their Amazon account or not. If it is not linked, the user can create a calendar from their birthday and not store any events. With a linked account, we can securely store events for them so that we can color code the calendar and give them access to their photos.

Account linking[2] is the feature that enables you to link an Alexa skill to a user's Amazon, Microsoft, Google, or other account. Typically, you'll want to link to a user's Amazon account and then use that authentication to access the data in your system.

When the user enables your skill, Alexa creates a User ID for them. If you want to persist session information, the User ID could be an appropriate way to identify the user and store their session info if the data does not need to be secured. On the other hand, to save personal information, linking the account provides a secure authentication layer. When you link the account, Alexa generates a secure Access Token that you can use to identify the user's personal data. This provides a greater degree of security for your skill and allows you to connect safely to external services. To get started, we'll create an application security profile for our skill to use for linking accounts.

The Application Security Profile

The application security profile identifies our Alexa skill as an application and gives us the credentials we need to link our Alexa skill to a user's Amazon account. To create the profile

1. From the Alexa Developer Console (log in using your Amazon account), select your initials from the top-right menu and pick *Settings* (see Figure 7-9).

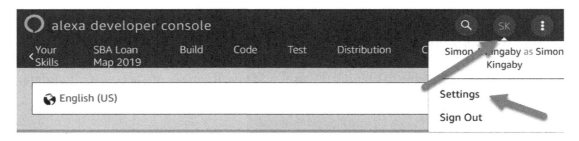

Figure 7-9. *Select the Settings menu option*

2. Select *Security Profiles* from the menu bar.

---

[2] For more information on account linking and how it works, look here: `https://developer.amazon.com/en-US/docs/alexa/account-linking/account-linking-concepts.html`. For some tips specific to account linking for custom skills, look here: `https://developer.amazon.com/en-US/docs/alexa/account-linking/account-linking-for-custom-skills.html`.

3. Click the *Create a New Security Profile* button.

4. Enter a *Name* and *Description* for your Security Profile. For example, "**90-Year Calendar Security Profile**."

5. Click Save.

6. On the Security Profile screen, copy the Security Profile ID to Notepad++. (See Figure 7-10.)

Figure 7-10. *Copy the Security Profile ID*

7. Select the Web Settings tab.

8. Copy the *Client ID* to Notepad++.

9. Click the *Show Secret* button.

10. Copy the *Client Secret* to Notepad++. (See Figure 7-11.)

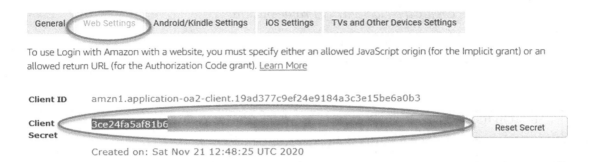

Figure 7-11. *Copy the Client Secret*

Now we have a security profile, and we can set up account linking.

Configure Account Linking

Still in the Alexa Developer Console, switch back to the Skill's Build tab, where we'll plug in the profile credentials as follows:

1. Click on the *Build* tab.

2. Click on *Tools* on the left nav bar.

3. Click on *Account Linking* in the left nav bar.

4. Turn on the option for "Do you allow users to create an account or link to an existing account with you."

5. Turn on the option for "Allow users to enable skill without account linking."

6. Under Security Provider Information, select the option for *Auth Code Grant*.

7. For the *Web Authorization URI*, enter **https://www.amazon.com/ap/oa**.

8. For the *Access Token URI*, enter **https://api.amazon.com/auth/o2/token**.

9. For *Your Client ID*, paste in the previous *Client ID* that you saved to Notepad++.

10. For *Your Secret*, paste in the previous *Client Secret*.

11. For *Your Authentication Scheme,* select **HTTP Basic**.

12. For *Scope,* enter **profile:user_id**.

13. Scroll to the top of the page and click *Save*.

14. The completed form should look like Figure 7-12.

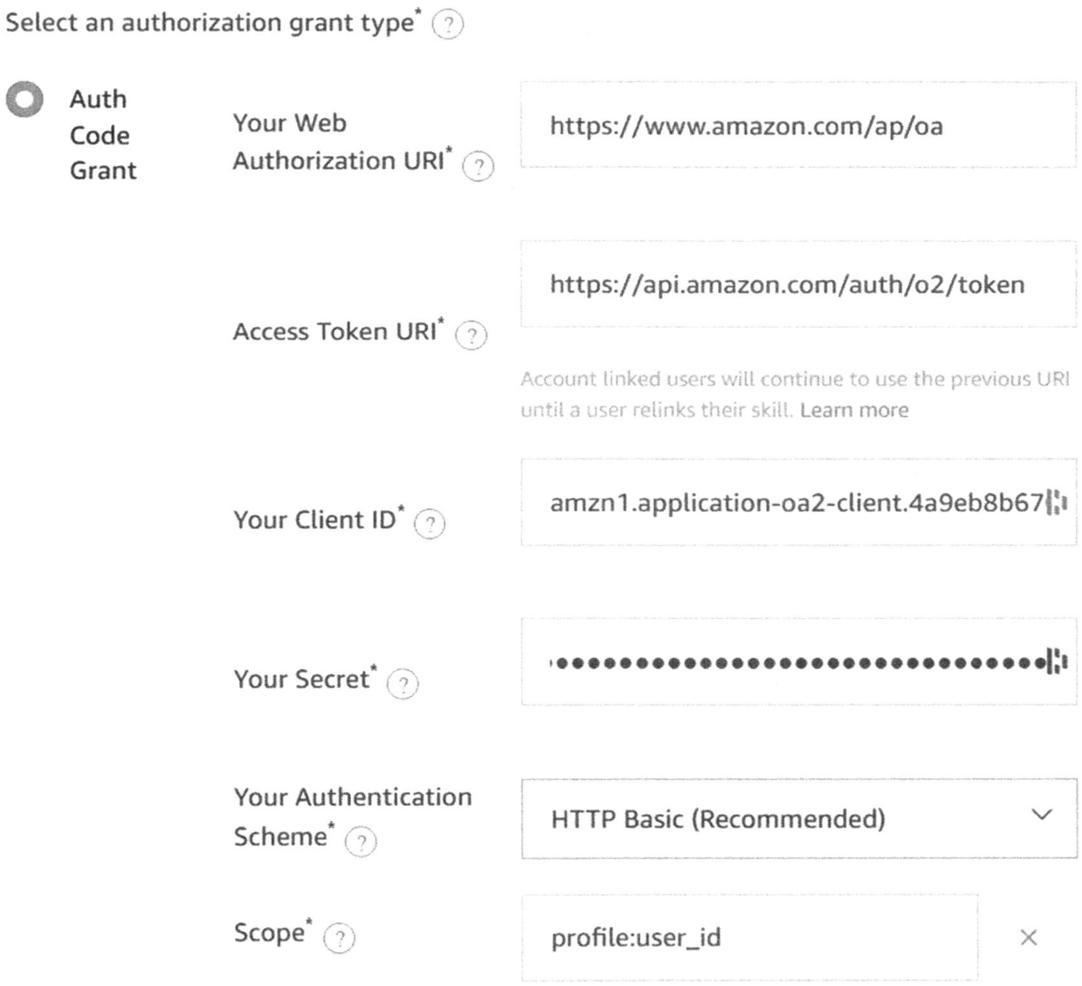

Select an authorization grant type[*] (?)

○ Auth
  Code
  Grant

Your Web
Authorization URI[*] (?)

https://www.amazon.com/ap/oa

Access Token URI[*] (?)

https://api.amazon.com/auth/o2/token

Account linked users will continue to use the previous URI
until a user relinks their skill. Learn more

Your Client ID[*] (?)

amzn1.application-oa2-client.4a9eb8b67

Your Secret[*] (?)

●●●●●●●●●●●●●●●●●●●●●●●●●●●●●●●●●

Your Authentication
Scheme[*] (?)

HTTP Basic (Recommended)   ⌄

Scope[*] (?)

profile:user_id   ✕

Figure 7-12. *The completed account linking form*

Now, we need to copy the Alexa Redirect URLs to the Security Profile
we just created.

15.   At the bottom of the Linked Account screen are three URLs in the
      Alexa Redirect URLs section; see Figure 7-13.

Figure 7-13. *The Alexa Redirect URLs*

16.   Copy these three URLs to the *Allowed Return URLs* section of the
      Security Profile Web Settings tab; see Figure 7-14.

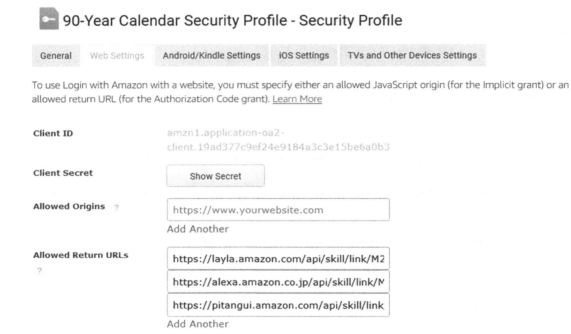

Figure 7-14. *Adding the Allowed Return URLs to the Security Profile*

17.   At the top of the screen, click the *Save* button again.

There's one more step. We need to register our security profile with the
Login with Amazon feature.

18. In your browser, navigate to `https://developer.amazon.com/loginwithamazon/console/site/lwa/overview.html`.

19. In the drop-down, select the **90-Year Calendar Security Profile**.

20. Click *Confirm*.

21. Provide a URL to your Privacy Policy. (If you don't have one, you can see a sample at `https://datadrivenskills.com/privacy-policy`.)

22. Provide an Icon graphic. (Any graphic should do.)

23. Click the *Save* button.

That's it. Account linking is setup. The next step is to create the lambda function for the back end.

The Lambda Function

In Amazon Web Services (AWS), a lambda function is a serverless compute service or cloud function. It does not require us to provision a virtual machine or a container that we would have to manage. The AWS service completely manages the infrastructure resources. This makes lambda functions the go-to solution for Alexa skill back ends. Even in an Alexa-hosted skill, the Code tab contains a lambda function.

There are two steps to creating the AWS lambda function. First, we need to provision a security role that our skill will use to access the lambda function, and then we need to create the lambda function itself.

Creating the Security Role

Before creating the lambda function, we need to create a security role in the IAM (Identity and Access Management) dashboard.

To create the security role, we will need to log in to our AWS account and go to the IAM service:

1. Log in to AWS (`https://aws.amazon.com`). Enter the account number, administrator username, and password. Do not use the root user option.

2. Search for and select the *IAM* service.

3. On the left side, select *Roles* and click *Create role*.

4. Select *AWS Service* at the top and select *Lambda* as the use case in the center. (See Figure 7-15.)

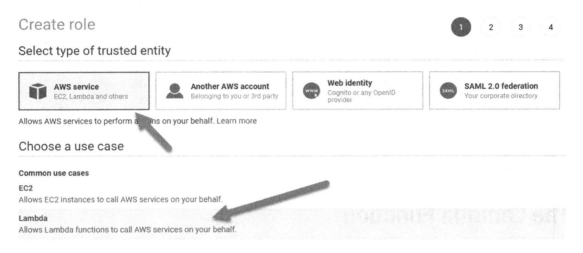

Figure 7-15. *Selecting the lambda service use case*

5. Click Next: Permissions at the bottom right.

6. In the Filter policies box, search for **basic**.

7. Select the checkmark next to the *AWSLambdaBasicExecutionRole*. (See Figure 7-16.)

Figure 7-16. *Selecting the AWSLambdaBasicExecutionRole*

8.   Now click the *Create policy* button at the top.

9.   For *Choose a service*, pick **DynamoDB**.

10.   Under Access level, expand the boxes for Read.

11.   Select GetItem and Query.

12.   Expand the box for Write and select DeleteItem, PutItem, and UpdateItem.

13.   Now select the orange text next to *Resources*.

14.   Next to table, click the *Add ARN* link.

15.   Paste in the *ARN* for the table, or add the *Region*, *Account*, and *Table name* that you saved to Notepad++. (See Figure 7-17.)

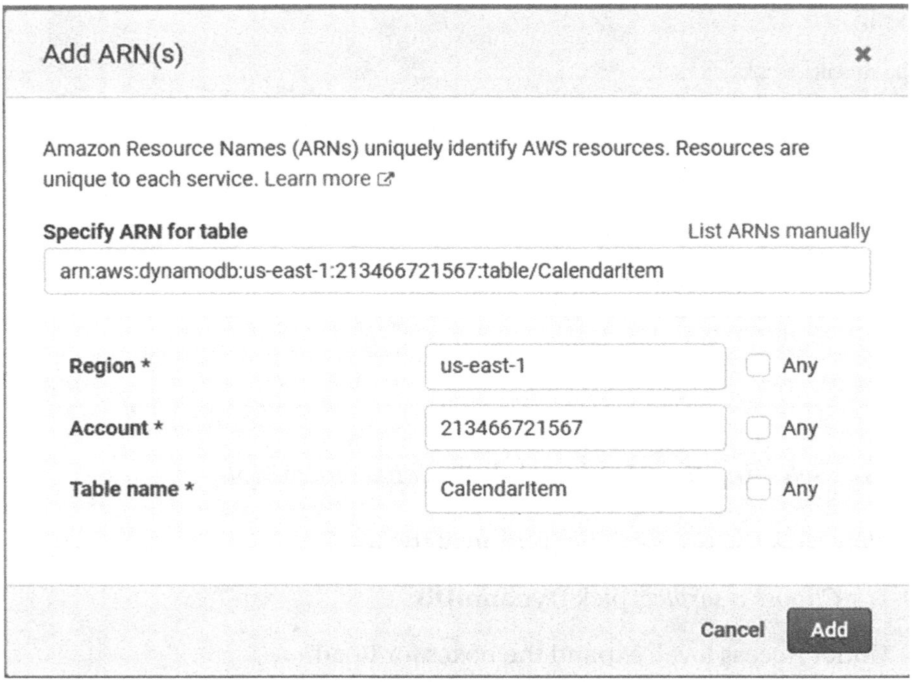

Figure 7-17. *Paste in the ARN for the table*

16.   Click the *Add* button

17.   Click the *Next: Tags* button.

18.   Now click the *Next: Review* button.

19.   Give the policy a name, such as
      CalendarDynamoDBReadAccess.

20.   Click the *Create policy* button.

21.   Flip back to the Create role tab.

22.   Click the *Create policy* button at the top again.

23.   For *Choose a service*, pick S3.

24.   Expand the boxes for Access level List and choose ListBucket.

25.   Expand the boxes for Access level Read and select GetObject.

26.   Now select the orange text next to *Resources*.

27. Next to *bucket*, click the *Add ARN* link.

28. Paste in the ARN for the S3 bucket.

29. Click the *Add* button.

30. Next to *object*, click the *Add ARN* link.

31. Enter the name of the bucket in the *Bucket name* box (**calendar-pics**).

32. Check the *Any* box next to *Object name*.

33. Click the *Add* button.

34. Click the *Next: Tags* button.

35. Click the *Next: Review* button.

36. Give the policy a name, such as **CalendarS3ReadAccess**.

37. Click the *Create policy* button.

38. Flip back to the Create role tab.

39. Refresh the Policy list.

40. Filter the policies by the word **calendar**.

41. Select the two policies we just created. (See Figure 7-18.)

Figure 7-18. *Select both calendar policies*

42. Click *Next: Tags*.

43.   Click *Next: Review.*

44.   Give the *Role a Name,* say, **CalendarLambdaExecutionRole**.

45.   Click *Create role.* (See Figure 7-19.)

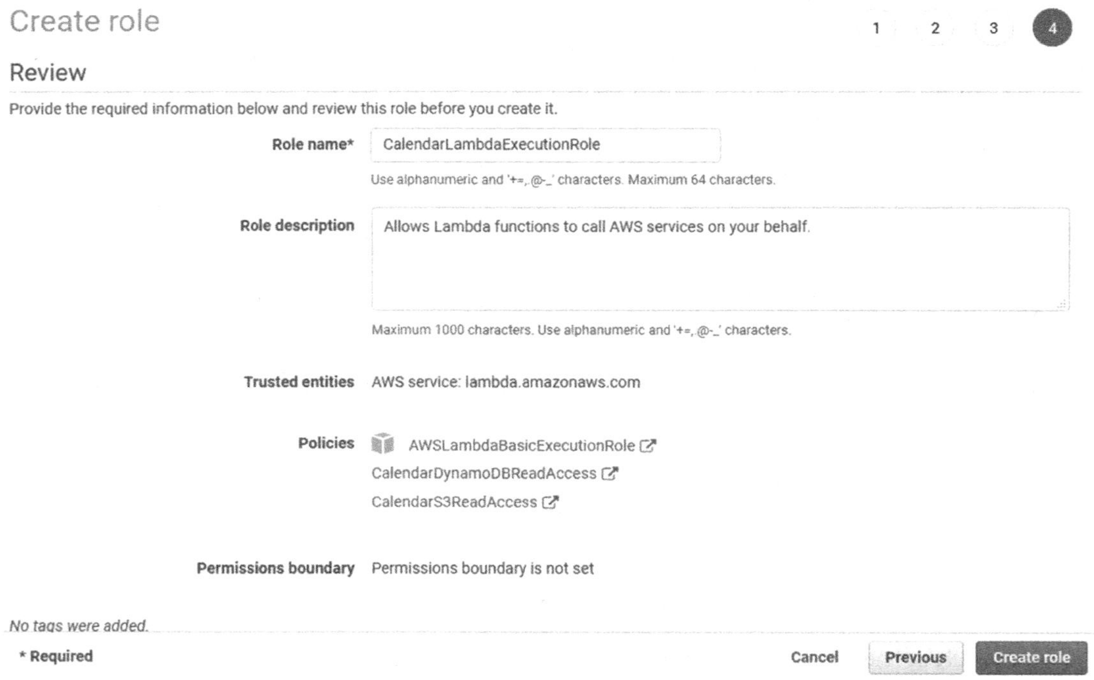

Create role   1   2   3   4

Review

Provide the required information below and review this role before you create it.

Role name*   CalendarLambdaExecutionRole

Use alphanumeric and '+=,.@-_' characters. Maximum 64 characters.

Role description   Allows Lambda functions to call AWS services on your behalf.

Maximum 1000 characters. Use alphanumeric and '+=,.@-_' characters.

Trusted entities   AWS service: lambda.amazonaws.com

Policies   AWSLambdaBasicExecutionRole
                    CalendarDynamoDBReadAccess
                    CalendarS3ReadAccess

Permissions boundary   Permissions boundary is not set

No tags were added.

* Required   Cancel   Previous   Create role

Figure 7-19. *The completed lambda execution role*

Now that we have created the role, we are ready to start working on the lambda function.

Creating the Lambda Function

Still in AWS, we now need to start creating the lambda function itself. Creating a lambda function is done using the following steps:

1.   Select the *Services* menu in the top left.

2.   Search for and select Lambda.

3.   In the top right, select *Create function.*

4. Choose *Author from scratch*.

5. Enter the *Function name*, say, **CalendarLambdaBackend**.

6. For the *Runtime*, select **Python 3.8** or higher under the *Latest Supported* section at the top of the list.

7. Under *Permissions*, expand *Change default execution role*.

8. Select *Use an existing role*.

9. Choose the **CalendarLambdaExecutionRole** role we created previously. (See Figure 7-20.)

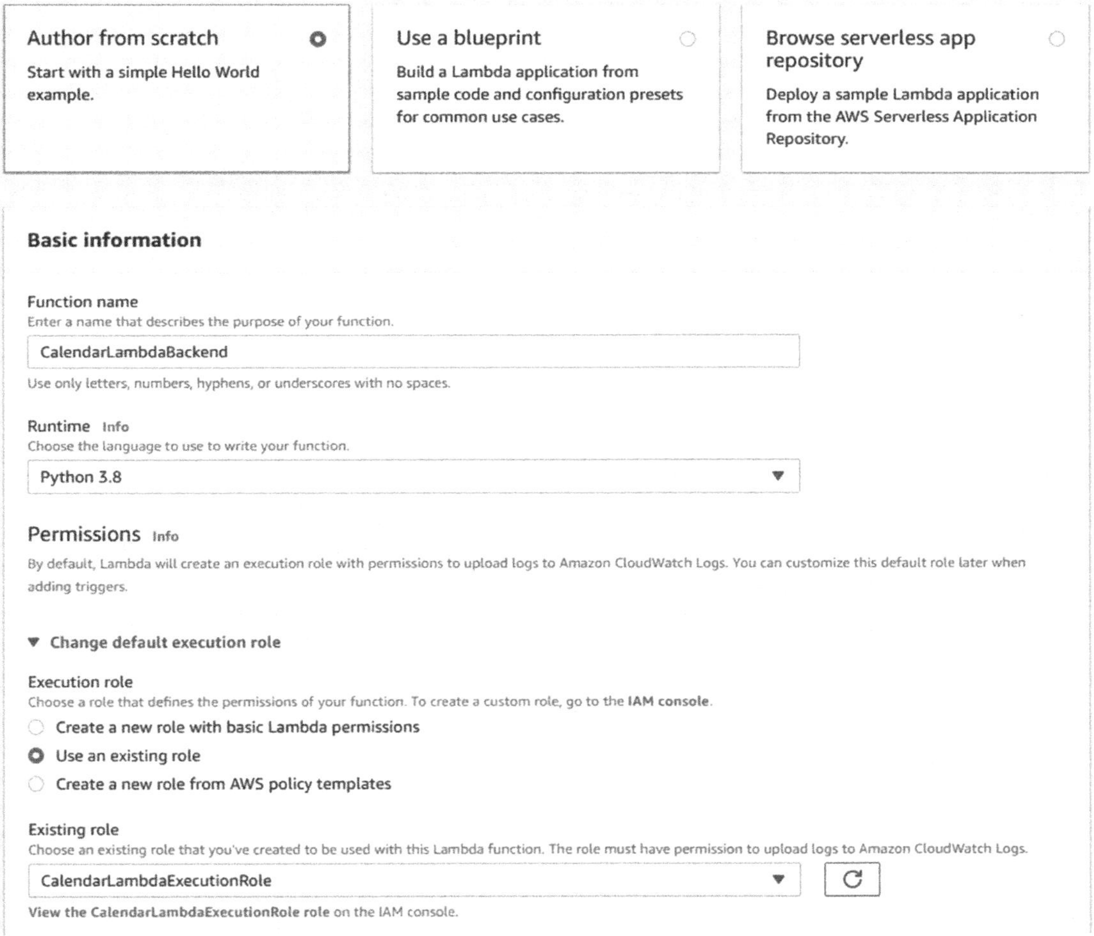

Author from scratch ●	Use a blueprint ○	Browse serverless app repository ○
Start with a simple Hello World example.	Build a Lambda application from sample code and configuration presets for common use cases.	Deploy a sample Lambda application from the AWS Serverless Application Repository.

Basic information

Function name
Enter a name that describes the purpose of your function.

> CalendarLambdaBackend

Use only letters, numbers, hyphens, or underscores with no spaces.

Runtime Info
Choose the language to use to write your function.

> Python 3.8   ▼

Permissions Info

By default, Lambda will create an execution role with permissions to upload logs to Amazon CloudWatch Logs. You can customize this default role later when adding triggers.

▼ Change default execution role

Execution role
Choose a role that defines the permissions of your function. To create a custom role, go to the **IAM console**.
○ Create a new role with basic Lambda permissions
● Use an existing role
○ Create a new role from AWS policy templates

Existing role
Choose an existing role that you've created to be used with this Lambda function. The role must have permission to upload logs to Amazon CloudWatch Logs.

> CalendarLambdaExecutionRole   ▼   │ C │

View the CalendarLambdaExecutionRole role on the IAM console.

Figure 7-20. *The completed Lambda Function Creation dialog*

Now you will be able to configure your lambda function.

10.   On the left, select *Add Trigger* and select the *Alexa Skills Kit* trigger.

11.   In the *Skill ID* box, paste in the *Alexa Skill ID* for your 90-year calendar skill from Notepad++. (See Figure 7-21 for the completed trigger.)

Figure 7-21. *The completed trigger*

Now select the lambda function (the box labeled **CalendarLambdaBackend** in Figure 7-21) to display the function code. You will probably need to scroll down to see the code (see Figure 7-22).

Figure 7-22. *The lambda function code*

At this point, you are ready to write your back-end code, and we've configured all the bits we need to use in our skill.

Summary

In this chapter, we created a skeleton for our new skill. It comprises an Alexa skill, a Botmock project for Skill Design, a DynamoDB database table for capturing user data, an S3 bucket for retrieving pictures, and a lambda function with appropriate security policies for the back-end code.

In the next chapter, we will design the VUI for our 90-year calendar skill.

CHAPTER 8

Beyond Hello World

In the last chapter, you set up all the accounts and services you will need to build the enhanced 90-year calendar skill. This chapter will look at VUI design and how you can work out the dialog flow for more complex skills.

Our skill will come in two styles. As shown in Figure 8-1, the first will be a simple rendering of a 90-year calendar. This will be all that is available to an unauthenticated user.

© Simon A. Kingaby 2022
S. A. Kingaby, *Data-Driven Alexa Skills*, https://doi.org/10.1007/978-1-4842-7449-1_8

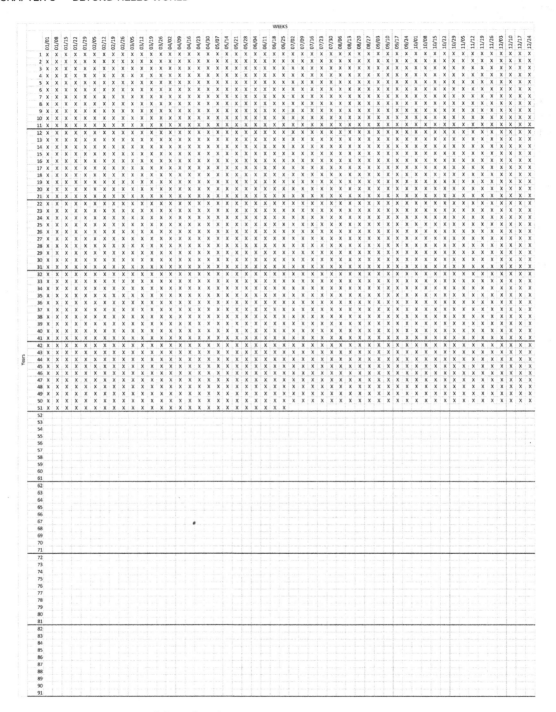

Figure 8-1. *A 90-year life calendar*

Once the user has linked our Alexa skill to their Amazon account, we can ask for and store the significant events of the user's life. This will enable us to render an enhanced version that ends up looking something like Figure 8-2.

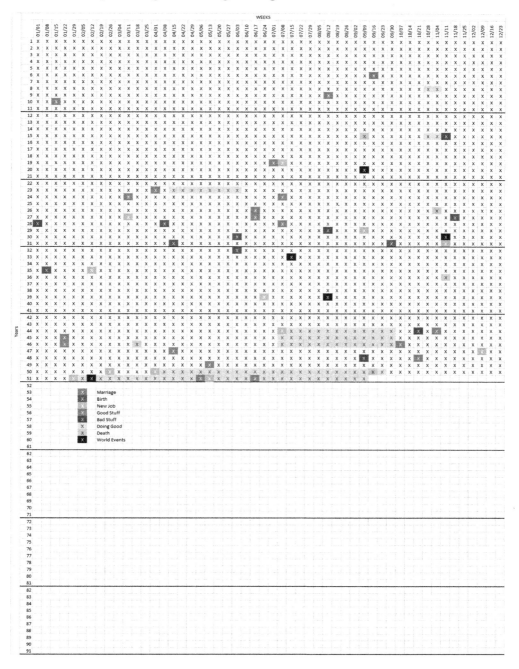

Figure 8-2. *An enhanced 90-year life calendar*

In the next section, we're going to examine some of the considerations for voice-first VUI design.

VUI Design

Voice User Interface design can be a complicated process, especially when contrasted with traditional Graphical User Interface design. When imagining a GUI for an app, you will typically create a menu structure for accessing the various features. Users will then click on a menu option that opens some sort of form to enter data or execute an action. The form will lay out a series of widgets for entering or selecting choices, with a couple of action buttons, like OK and Cancel. None of this translates well to the voice-first user interface. Instead, the "menu" needs to be a wide, flat structure that allows users to say different commands to access all the features of your app. The "form" needs to let the user say things in pretty much any order. VUI also has to allow for a variety of synonyms in a way that GUIs do not.

For example, let's say you want to price an oil change for your car. The process might be the following:

1. You open the app on your phone.

2. You tap the sign up link in the app.

3. You type in an email and password and tap to accept the terms and then tap the sign up button.

4. Then you enter your First Name, Last Name, and Zip Code and tap Done.

5. Then you tap to allow the app to use your location while using the app.

6. Then you tap Don't Allow to the question the app asks about notifications.

7. Then you can tap your local store on the map, search for a store, tap a button to open the main menu, or tap the bottom bar to view your coupons.

8. Tapping the menu button opens a multilevel menu.

9. Tapping on your local store on the map, you are presented with a screen that lets you choose between

   a. Closing the screen.

   b. Favoriting the location.

   c. Seeing the Popular Times chart.

   d. Getting Directions (which launches your default Map/Navigation app).

   e. Looking at the Coupons available.

   f. Checking out the Reviews.

   g. If you scroll down, you can see a brief list of the services available.

10. After all that, you close the app in frustration because this app doesn't provide pricing or the ability to schedule an appointment.

Now, imagine the voice-first experience.

User: Alexa, I need an oil change.

Alexa: I found a few options. 1st Chance Tire 1.3 miles away. Valvoline Instant Oil Change 2.5 miles away.

User: Select Valvoline.

Alexa: Welcome to Valvoline. Would you like to schedule an oil change?

User: Yes.

Alexa: For which car?

User: The 2019 Ford C-Max.

Alexa: When would you like to go?

User: This afternoon, after work.

Alexa: What is the mileage on the 2019 Ford C-Max.?

User: I don't know, maybe 115,000 miles.

> Alexa: OK. I can schedule a high mileage oil change for the 2019 Ford C-Max at Valvoline in Smyrna for 5:30 p.m. tomorrow. You have a coupon for 7 dollars off, so it should cost between 33 and 48 dollars, depending on your oil selection. Shall I schedule the appointment?
>
> User: Yes.
>
> Alexa: OK. I've scheduled the appointment for 5:30 p.m. tomorrow.

What are the most significant differences between these two interactions? Consider how Alexa gets straight to the point, but the GUI has to put everything in menus, screens, and taps. Consider the conversion Alexa did between 115,000 miles and "high mileage" and the transformation from "after work" to "5:30 p.m." Alexa has to be much more flexible to handle the wide variety of things a user could say. Consider what is required of the user in each interaction.

Voice-first design is a strategy that prioritizes the vocal interactions over the screens and taps. While screens can be a component of VUI design, the priority is to model conversations between the user and Alexa. You are looking for ways the user can go through the process to accomplish the desired outcome. Of course, we will model a happy path where the user says the right things in the correct order. But we must also handle curveballs. For example, you're halfway through booking an oil change when you decide you need a tire rotation too. This is where traditional modeling tools, such as Excel, Visio, and Lucidchart, fall down. It is easy to draw the happy path. But listing the synonyms and all the possible utterances becomes increasingly tricky as you expand your model.

Adobe XD has a template for Alexa skills; this is an excellent tool for storyboarding and is familiar to many graphic designers. For a comprehensive guide to XD, check out the My Cactus sample provided by the Alexa Team. (See the Design Assets here: `https://github.com/alexa/skill-sample-nodejs-web-api-my-cactus`. See Alison Atwell and Justin Jeffress explain the process on Twitch here: `www.twitch.tv/collections/S81yydlkRBY-Pw`.)

Tools such as Botmock and Voiceflow were created to address the challenges of VUI design and do not have as steep a learning curve as Adobe XD. In the next section, we will use Botmock to design the dialog for the standard model.

VUI Design with Botmock

To get started with Botmock, log in, and create a new project for the 90-year calendar. After clicking Create New Project

1. Enter 90-Year Calendar for the Project Name.

2. Select Amazon Alexa as the Target Channel.

3. Click Create Project.

This launches the conversation editor, where we can start modeling our dialog.

Lines and boxes represent the dialog model in BotMock. The lines are the user utterances; the boxes are what the Bot (Alexa) says. See Figure 8-3.

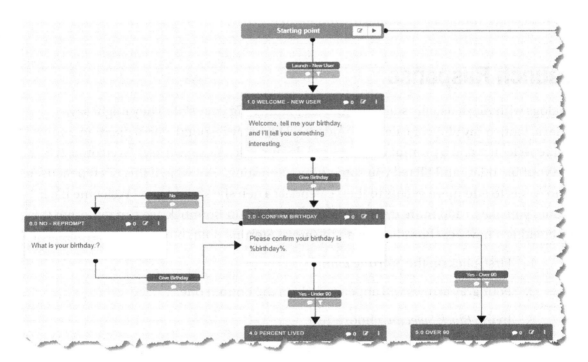

Figure 8-3. *Modeling the dialog in BotMock*

As you can see in Figure 8-3, after the user says the launch phrase, Alexa says, "Welcome, tell me your birthday, and I'll tell you something interesting."

The user then intends to give Alexa their birthday, so they utter something appropriate, perhaps "My birthday is January 1st, 1980." Part of defining the user intents is also to describe all the possible utterances they might say to fulfill that intent. An alternate utterance for the Give Birthday intent might be "I was born on January 1st, 1980."

Alexa then confirms that she decoded the utterance to the right date, "Just to confirm, your birthday is %birthday%." Note the use of percent signs to demarcate the variable for the given birthday.

At this point, you can see in the diagram that the user has two options (Yes or No) and that Alexa differentiates between ages Over 90 and Under 90. If the user says No, they are given another opportunity to provide us with their birthday.

As you can see, so far, the dialog is relatively straightforward. Before we elaborate on the next stage, though, let's create the model so far.

Launch Response

Dialogs with Alexa usually start with the user launching your skill. They might say, "Alexa, launch my 90-year calendar." Alexa will typically respond with a pleasant and polite welcome and a prompt to get started. In our case, Alexa will say, "Welcome, tell me your birthday, and I'll tell you something interesting." But what if this is a repeat user who wants to add more events to their calendar? Then she should say, "Welcome back. Would you like to add more events to your calendar?" In Botmock, we can represent this by creating a new Text box attached to the green Starting point box.

1. First, click on the *Starting point* box.

2. Four gray arrows will appear. Click on the bottom one.

3. In the *Block Selector*, choose *Text*.

4. You can grab the new box with the mouse and line it up with the Starting point if you want to.

5. Double-click on the words *Bot Says*.

6. At the very top of this dialog, change the word *text* to say **1.0 Welcome – New User**. Note that we are numbering each Text box to help keep them organized as we build out our skill.

7. Now, in the Text textbox, enter the words that Alexa will say:
Welcome, tell me your birthday, and I'll tell you something interesting.

8. Lastly, click the Save button in the lower right.

9. Your dialog should now look like Figure 8-4.

Figure 8-4. *The first speech box*

Now that we've got Alexa's Welcome statement, we can add the Launch Intent to the dialog.

Intents

In BotMock, as in Alexa dialogs, the user has intentions. Intents are the things the user wants to accomplish. For the Launch Intent, the user wants our skill to launch. Botmock represents intents as annotations on the lines. First, you define the intent, and then you refer to it in the diagram.

1. To define an intent, select the *Intents* icon on the left menu bar.

2. We are going to define a Launch Intent, so click *Add New Intent*.

3. The *Intent Name* is **Launch**.

4. Click the *Add* button for *Training Phrases.*

5. In the new *Training Phrase* box, type **Alexa, Launch my ninety-year calendar**. (See Figure 8-5.)

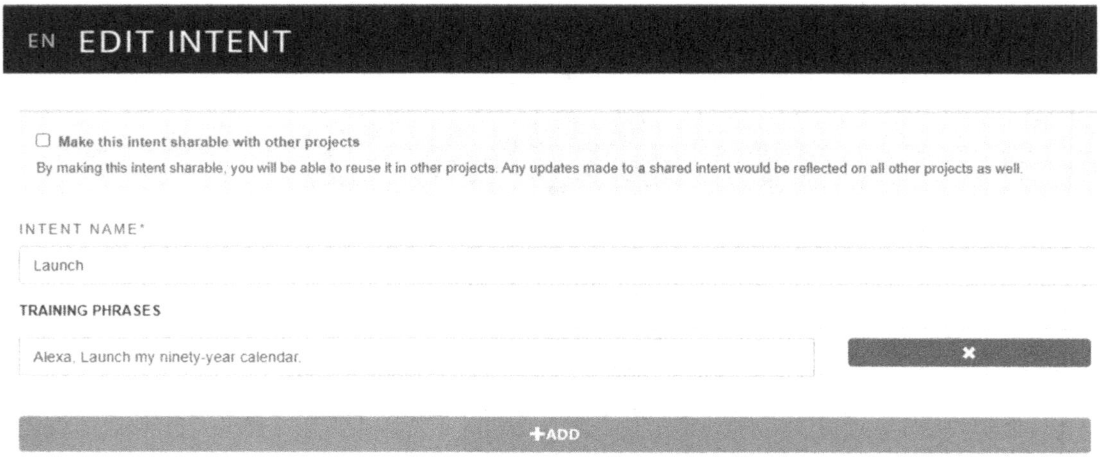

EN **EDIT INTENT**

☐ Make this intent sharable with other projects
By making this intent sharable, you will be able to reuse it in other projects. Any updates made to a shared intent would be reflected on all other projects as well.

INTENT NAME*

Launch

TRAINING PHRASES

Alexa, Launch my ninety-year calendar.   ✖

✚ADD

Figure 8-5. *Creating the Launch Intent*

6. Click the *Save* button in the lower right corner.

7. Then click the arrow at the top of the Intents list to close it.

8. Now, shift-click on the line between the *Starting point* box and the *1.0 Welcome* box we added.

9. In the *Connection Settings* screen, enter **Launch – New User** as the *Connection Label.*

10. Select the **Launch** Intent we just created in the *Check if the User's Utterance matches an intent* box.

11. Next to the *Match all rules below* box in the *Check these Conditions* section, click the *Add Condition* button.

12. In the *Create New Variable* screen that pops up, enter **isNewUser**.

13. Change the condition from Is Empty to *is equal to.*

14. Enter *Yes* in the text box. (See Figure 8-6.)

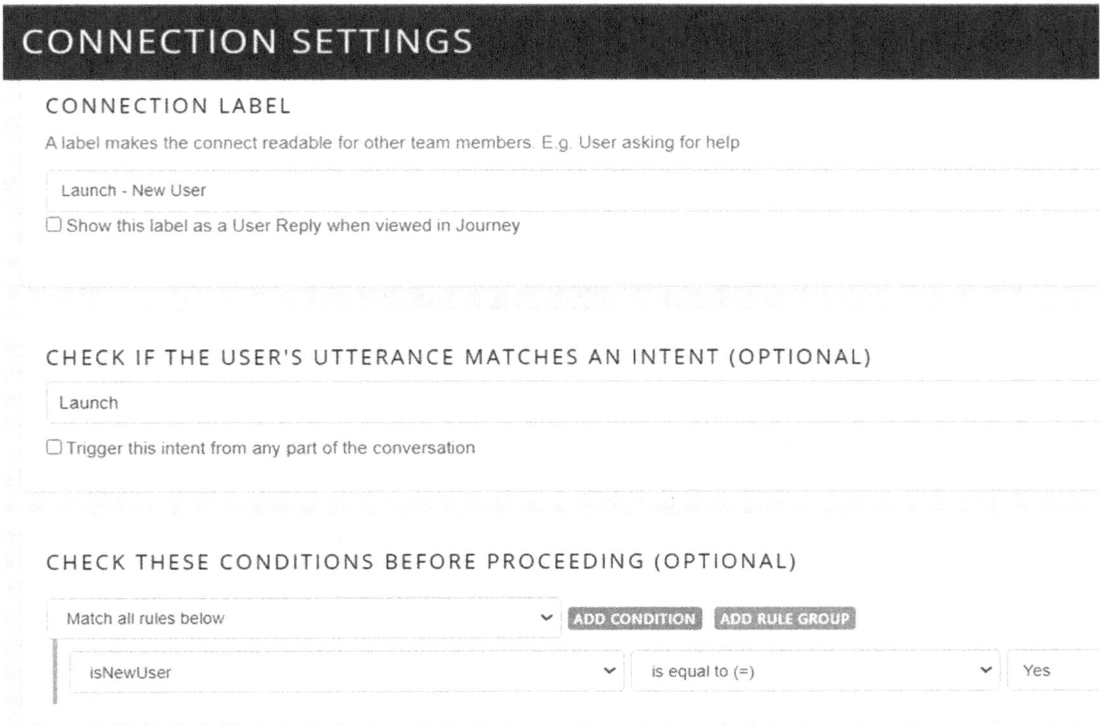

CONNECTION SETTINGS

CONNECTION LABEL

A label makes the connect readable for other team members. E.g. User asking for help

Launch - New User

☐ Show this label as a User Reply when viewed in Journey

CHECK IF THE USER'S UTTERANCE MATCHES AN INTENT (OPTIONAL)

Launch

☐ Trigger this intent from any part of the conversation

CHECK THESE CONDITIONS BEFORE PROCEEDING (OPTIONAL)

| Match all rules below | ⌄ | ADD CONDITION | ADD RULE GROUP |

| isNewUser | ⌄ | is equal to (=) | ⌄ | Yes |

Figure 8-6. *The Connection Settings screen.*

15.   Click the *Save* button in the bottom right corner.

Your diagram should now show the intent, as in Figure 8-7.

Figure 8-7. *The diagram showing the Welcome message and Launch Intent*

Next, we need to add the alternate Launch where this is a returning user. To do this, we'll repeat the previous steps, except the Launch Intent of the user is the same, Alexa's response is different, and the filter criteria change to isNewUser = No. Since we already know the user, we should include their name in the welcome message. To do this, we'll add a variable for the user's name.

1. Click on *Variables* on the left menu bar.

2. Click *Create New Variable.*

3. Enter the variable name: **userName**.

4. Select the entity type: **Name**.

5. Click *Save.*

6. Close the *Manage Variables* flyout screen.

Then, we create Alexa's response, like this:

7. Select the *Starting point* box.

8. Click on the Right arrow and add a new Text box.

9. Double-click the Text box and change the *title* to "**2.0 Welcome – Returning User.**"

10. Change the *Text* from Bot says to "**Welcome %userName%, would you like to add an event to your calendar?**" Note the use of the percent signs to demarcate the variable *userName*.

11. Click *Save*.

12. Shift-click on the line from *Starting point* to **2.0 Welcome**.

13. Enter the label: "**Launch – Returning User**."

14. Select the Launch Intent.

15. Add a condition.

16. Select **isNewUser**, **is equal to**, and enter **No**.

17. Click the *Save* button.

18. Back on the diagram, click the *Save* button on the menu bar in the top right corner.

Your diagram should now look like Figure 8-8.

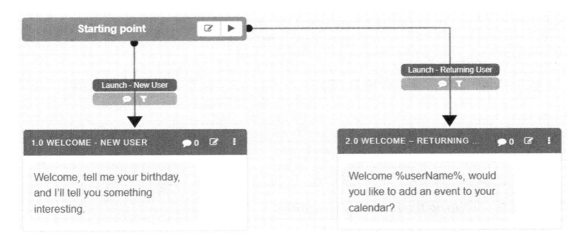

Figure 8-8. *The Launch intents and Welcome messages*

We are now ready to complete the happy path for new users.

Happy Path

What happens when everything goes as planned and all the assumptions are correct? When that happens, you have walked the happy path. In our case, the happy path is when Alexa hears and understands your birthday correctly and then tells you something interesting about it. Deviations from the happy path are exceptions and alternatives. Right now, they are irrelevant. We want to create the happy path.

To do this, create a new variable (Figure 8-9) and a new intent (Figure 8-10) for the user to give us their birthday. Note the use of the `%birthday%` variable in the Training Phrase and the Required flag in the Slot Filling section. Then Alexa will ask to confirm the birthday (Figure 8-11), and we can add the Give Birthday intent to the connection line (Figure 8-12). Then, the user will say the Yes intent (Figure 8-13). Finally, Alexa will tell them something interesting (Figure 8-14), where we can add the Yes intent to the connection line (Figure 8-15).

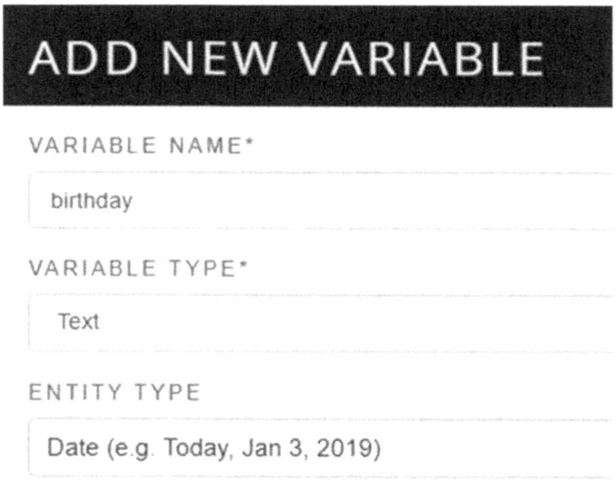

Figure 8-9. *Creating the birthday variable*

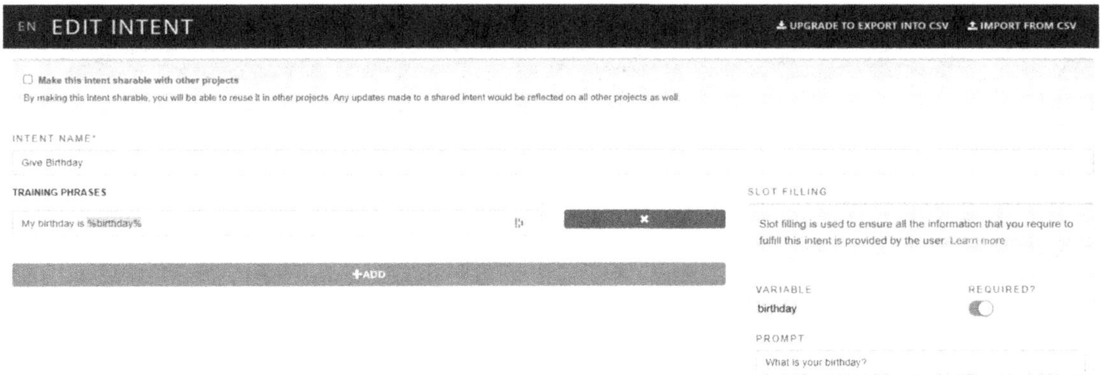

EDIT INTENT

☐ Make this intent sharable with other projects
By making this intent sharable, you will be able to reuse it in other projects. Any updates made to a shared intent would be reflected on all other projects as well.

INTENT NAME*
Give Birthday

TRAINING PHRASES
My birthday is %birthday%

✚ADD

SLOT FILLING
Slot filling is used to ensure all the information that you require to fulfill this intent is provided by the user. Learn more

VARIABLE   REQUIRED?
birthday

PROMPT
What is your birthday?

Figure 8-10. *Creating the Give Birthday intent*

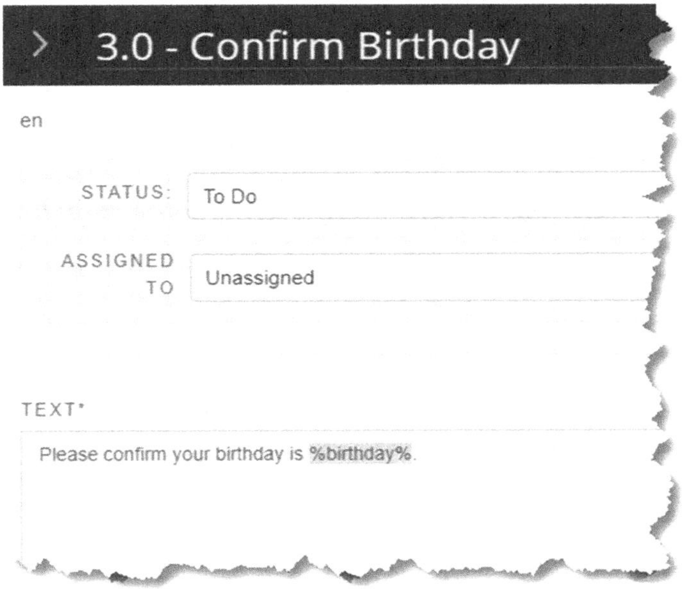

3.0 - Confirm Birthday

en

STATUS: To Do

ASSIGNED
TO   Unassigned

TEXT*
Please confirm your birthday is %birthday%.

Figure 8-11. *Adding the Confirm your birthday Alexa response in the text box*

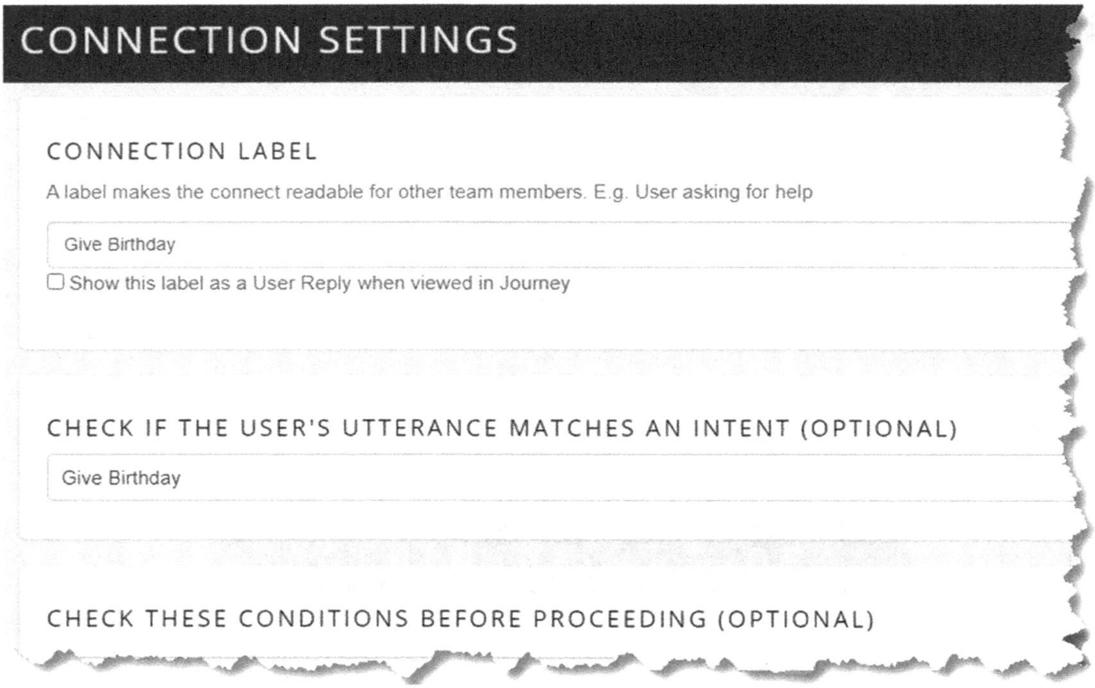

CONNECTION SETTINGS

CONNECTION LABEL

A label makes the connect readable for other team members. E.g. User asking for help

Give Birthday

☐ Show this label as a User Reply when viewed in Journey

CHECK IF THE USER'S UTTERANCE MATCHES AN INTENT (OPTIONAL)

Give Birthday

CHECK THESE CONDITIONS BEFORE PROCEEDING (OPTIONAL)

Figure 8-12. *Adding the Give Birthday intent to the connection line*

INTENT NAME*

Yes

TRAINING PHRASES

Yes

Figure 8-13. *Creating the Yes intent*

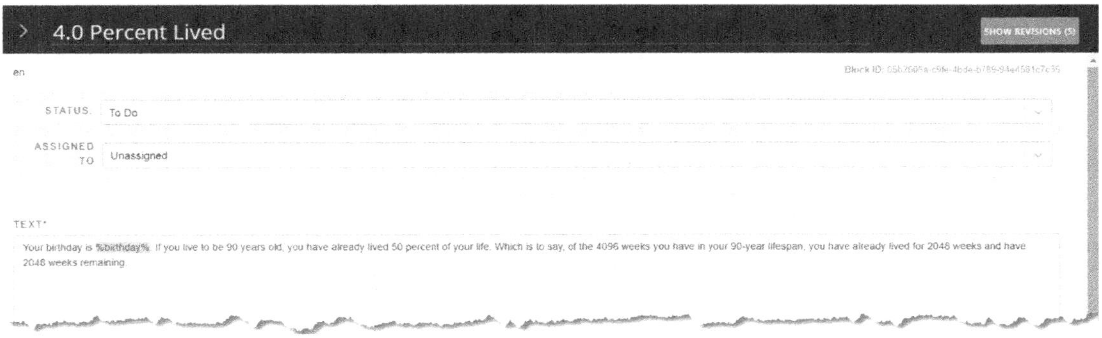

Figure 8-14. *Telling the user something interesting in the text box*

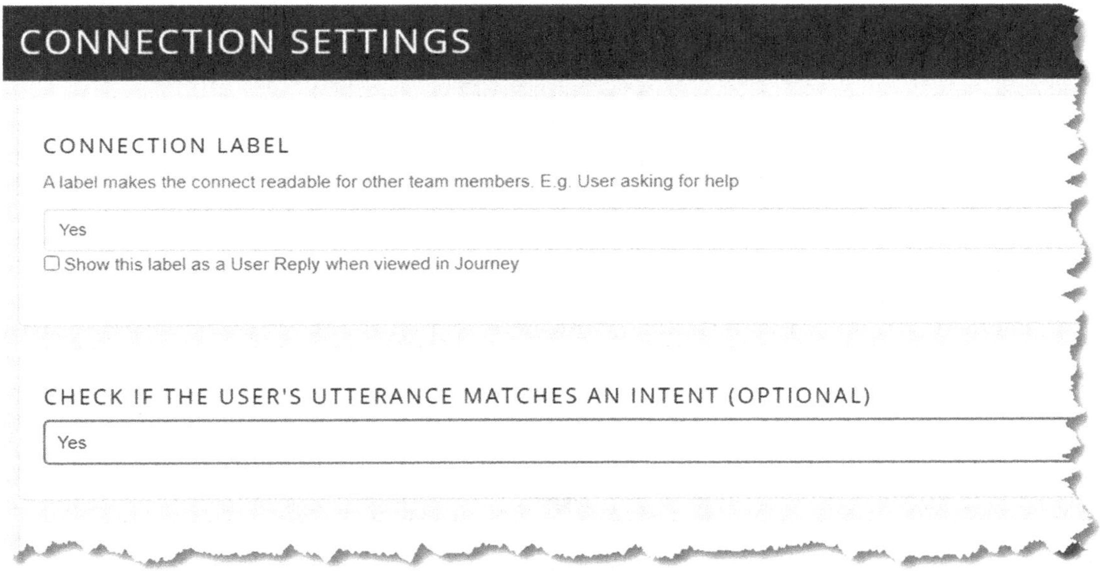

Figure 8-15. *Adding the Yes intent to the connection line*

After adding all the previous steps, the happy path now looks like Figure 8-16.

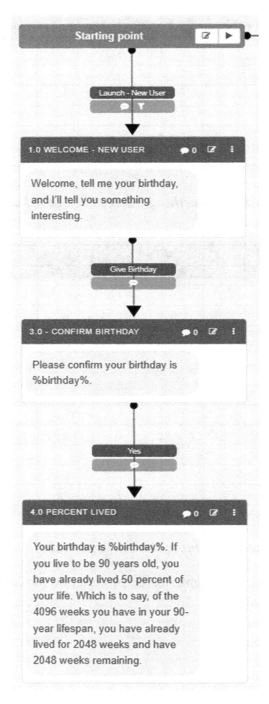

Figure 8-16. *The completed happy path*

What if the user is already over 90 years old? That will complicate things if we're doing all of our math based on a maximum age of 90.

The Over 90 Path

To handle the Over 90 case, we need to split the Yes response into two. The first response is on the happy path and is labeled "Yes – Under 90." The second response is not and is labeled "Yes – Over 90." To add this condition, we need to add a variable for the user's age (see Figure 8-17). Then add a text box for Alexa to respond when the user is over 90 (see Figure 8-18). Lastly, add criteria to the Yes path for (1) age is less than 90 and (2) age is greater than or equal to 90 (see Figure 8-19).

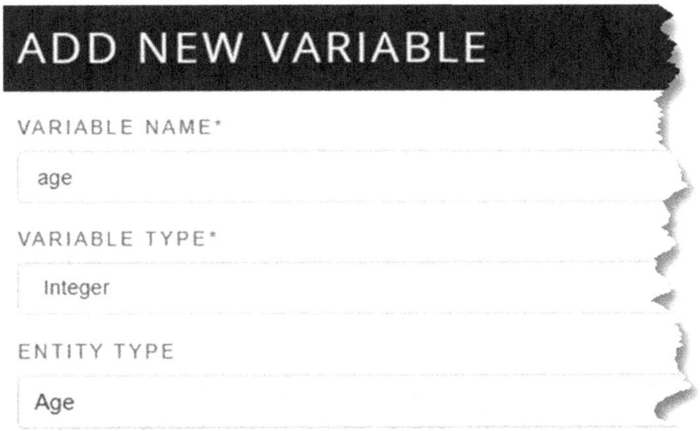

Figure 8-17. *Adding the age variable*

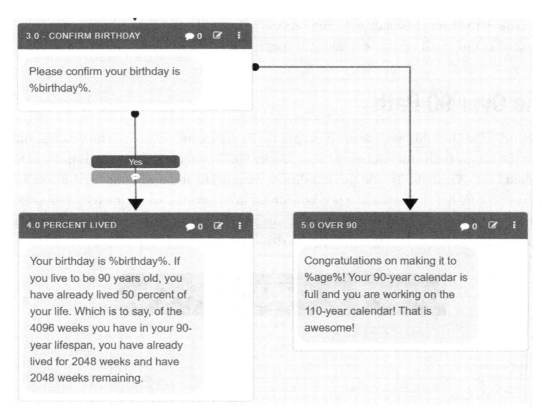

Figure 8-18. *Adding the Over 90 Text box*

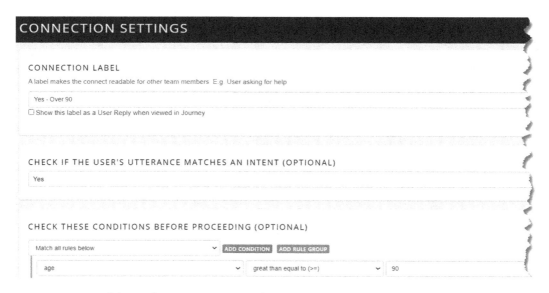

Figure 8-19. *Adding the Yes intent and age criteria to the Over 90 path*

The diagram will now look like Figure 8-20.

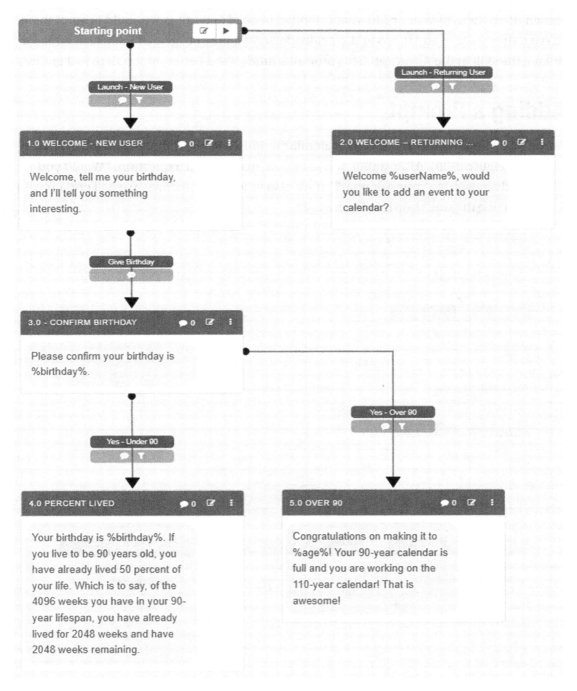

Figure 8-20. *The complete diagram, with the Over 90 path added*

If the user is unauthorized, which is to say they haven't linked their account yet, then the skill ends once we've told them their Percent Lived and, if their device has a screen, shown them their 90-year or 110-year calendar. Instead of ending, we could prompt them to see if they want to add items to their calendar, and if they do, give them instructions for linking the skill in the Alexa app. This prompt sounds like a better option than just ending.

Adding a Prompt

Adding a prompt to add items to the calendar requires us to edit boxes 4.0 and 5.0 in the diagram (Figure 8-20). After stating the result, we need to add a question: "Would you like to add an event to your calendar?" If we also move box 2.0 down, we will end up with a diagram like the one shown in Figure 8-21.

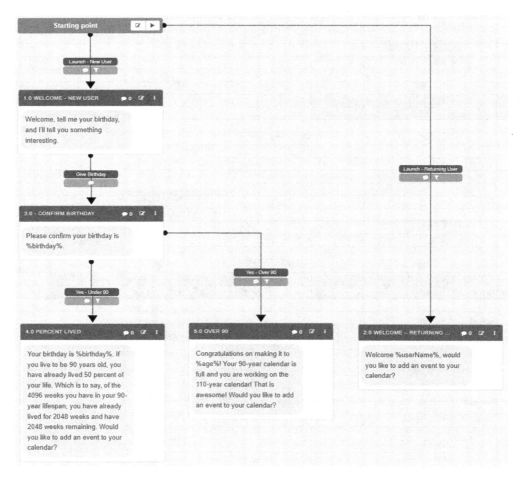

Figure 8-21. *The modified diagram, after adding the prompt to add events*

As you can see in the diagram, we now have a happy path and two variations. What about an exception? How do we handle a mistake? We need to add that to the diagram too. For example, what if Alexa didn't understand the date correctly? So the user says No when confirming the date.

Adding the No Intent

If Alexa didn't get the right birthday, the user would say No when asked to confirm, and Alexa would have to reprompt the user for the correct birthday, as shown in Figure 8-22. This reprompt box implies the addition of a No intent, so add that before editing the line from box 3.0 to box 6.0.

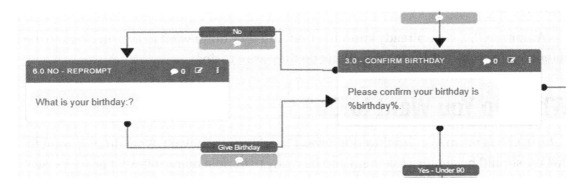

Figure 8-22. *Adding the No intent to the Confirmation box*

Be sure to save your BotMock diagram periodically.

Now we've got the user's birthday and drawn the empty calendar. And we've got as far as asking them if they want to add an event to their calendar. What if they say no?

Saying Goodbye

If the user doesn't want to add an event to their new blank calendar, they are done with the skill, and we should say goodbye. This requires adding a new text box for Alexa to say Goodbye and two uses of the No intent from boxes 4.0 and 5.0, as shown in Figure 8-23. Note, the Goodbye text box is the end of the skill, so scroll down in the editor and select the End Conversation at this Block switch.

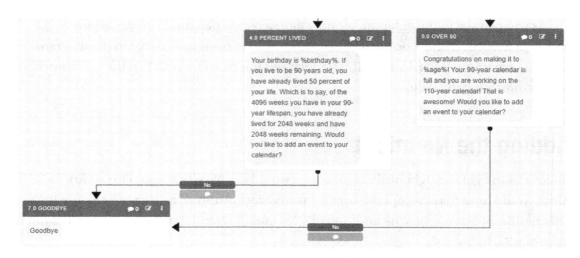

Figure 8-23. *Adding the Goodbye text box*

As for box 2.0, if we already know the user and they don't want to add an event to the calendar, this could be interesting. What do they want to do?

What Do You Want to Do?

If the user has returned, and they don't want to add another event, what do they want to do? We should have Alexa ask them and be ready to handle many different answers. See Figure 8-24 for the additional text box and another use of the No intent.

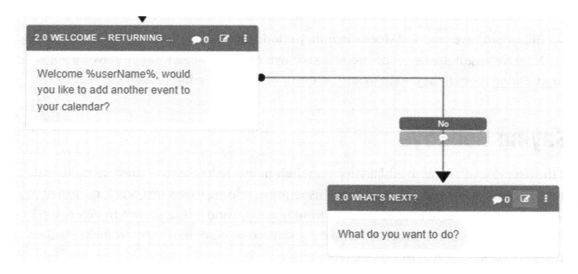

Figure 8-24. *Asking the user what to do next*

Our dialog handles the user telling us they don't want to add an event. Now we are ready to add the Yes path. But...

Linked vs. Unlinked Accounts

Yes, the user wants to add an event to their calendar. However, if their account is not linked, how will we know who is logged in, and how will we store this specific user's data? So we have a diverting path for a user who has not linked our skill yet. Let's add that first. We will need Alexa to instruct the user to link their account. We'll need to know if the account is linked or not, so we'll need a variable for that. We can then use the Yes intent, with a condition based on the new variable, to reroute the user and have Alexa say something like this: "You need to link your account to be able to save your life events. There is no fee for this service. Your data is encrypted and secured. To link your account, please use the Alexa app on your phone." See Figure 8-25 for an example.

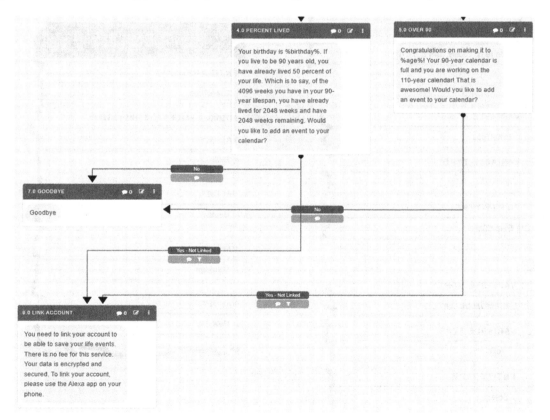

Figure 8-25. *Asking the user to link their account*

If the user has returned and the account is linked, we can get the event.

Getting the Event

Now that we know who the user is, Alexa needs to ask them for the event's details. We can do this sequentially, using the Intent model, or we can be more flexible and use the Conversations model of the dialog. Either way, we need to ask the user for the Event Date, Event Type, and a short Event Description. The Event Type will be a short list to choose from, so when we create the variables, we'll need to add an Entity for the Event Type variable. The three variables are shown in Figure 8-26.

Figure 8-26. *The event variables and the EventType entity*

Next, we need to add the intents for the user to give us the Event Date, Type, and Description, as shown in Figure 8-27. Note how each intent fills a variable.

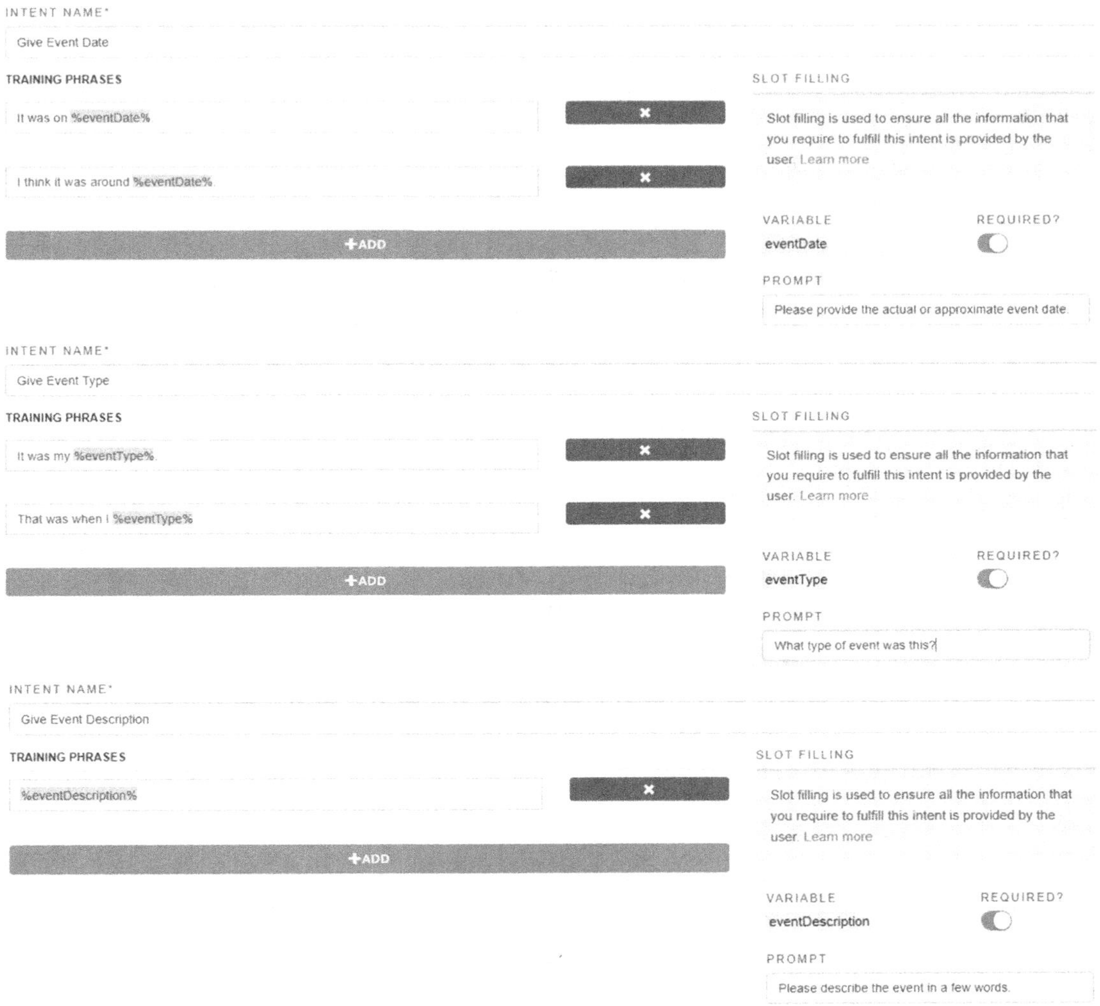

Figure 8-27.   *The event intents*

Now we can add the event dialog that uses the intents to provide us with the event data that we need. Once the user has confirmed the date and type, we can redraw the calendar with the new event added. See Figure 8-28 for the event dialog.

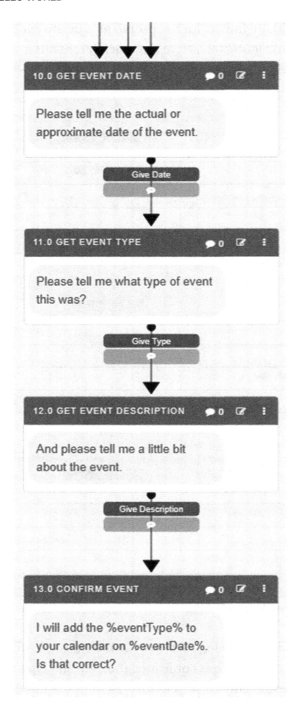

Figure 8-28. *The basic dialog to capture the event details we need*

Once the event is confirmed, we should ask the user if they want to add another event and capture that one too. This would require adding box 14.0 Event Confirmed. You could then loop back to box 10.0 to get the next event. If the user says no, jump up to box 8.0 and determine what the user wants to do next.

Now we've captured the happy path through this part of our skill, what are some other ways this could go?

What Happens Next?

What other things can the user do with our skill? How will you represent that in the dialog? Go back to box 8.0 and fill in the dialog from there as well. (See Figure 8-29.)

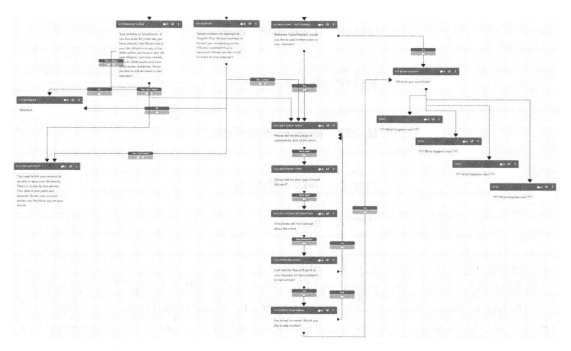

Figure 8-29. *What happens next?*

Some ideas for additional functions from box 8.0 include the following:

- Redraw the calendar with the events added.

- Print the calendar.

- Email an Excel, PDF, or Image version of the calendar.

- Use an API to help the user look up world events.

There is much more to Botmock too. We need to go back through all our intents and add a lot more training phrases. For example, the Give Birthday intent should be trained to accept:

My birthday is %birthday%.

My birthday was %birthday%.

My birthdate is %birthday%.

My birthdate was %birthday%.

I was born on %birthday%.

%birthday%.

And any other variations you can think of.

In Botmock, you can set up journeys (or paths) through the dialog. (See Figure 8-30.) These help you visualize the various paths a user can take through the dialog. You can also run the dialog interactively and see how it flows. You can invite reviewers to examine your dialog and comment on it. You can set up user testing for your flows too.

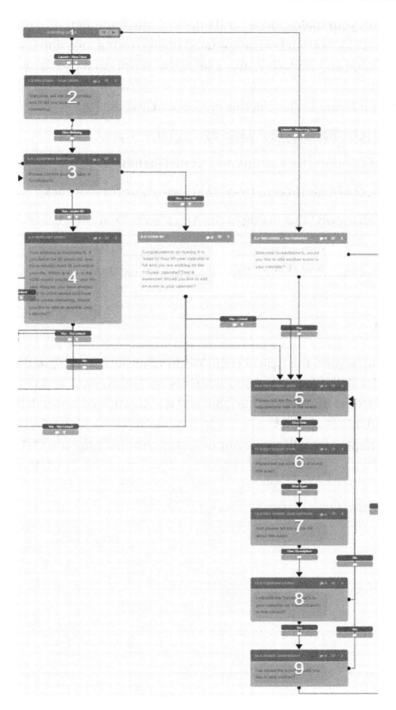

Figure 8-30. *The Happy Path Journey through our dialog*

You can export your dialog model and import it into another tool, called Botium (`https://botium.ai`). Botium is an automated dialog testing tool, and it will take your Botmock dialog and explode it into a set of test scripts that can run as part of an automated build.

To export from Botmock, look at this project on GitHub:

`https://github.com/Botmock/botmock-dialogflow-export`

To import into Botium, look at this project on GitHub:

`https://github.com/codeforequity-at/botium-exporter-botmock`

Lastly, you can export your dialog to the Alexa Skills Kit format using this project on GitHub:

`https://github.com/Botmock/botmock-skills-kit-export`

Summary

This chapter went beyond the typical Hello World example and designed the dialog for a 90-year calendar skill. We learned about intents, variables/slots, and entity types/lists. We learned how to use Botmock to navigate and document a complex dialog model with several paths and lots of options.

In the next chapter, we will create our new skill and configure the VUI.

## CHAPTER 9

Configuring the VUI

In Chapter 8, we created a diagram of the dialog flow for our 90-year calendar skill in Botmock. Now we will convert that diagram into a Voice User Interface in an Alexa skill. In this chapter, we will create intents, slots, and responses based on the diagram.

In this first section, we are going to convert the Botmock diagram into an Alexa skill.

Exporting the Botmock Diagram

To export the Botmock diagram, we need to download and assemble a tool that uses the Botmock API to export the diagram in a format that the Alexa Skills Kit (ASK) can use to build a skill. We'll start by getting the code from GitHub.

1. Navigate your browser to `https://github.com/Botmock/botmock-skills-kit-export`.

2. Click the green Code button and choose the last option to Download ZIP. (See Figure 9-1.)

© Simon A. Kingaby 2022
S. A. Kingaby, *Data-Driven Alexa Skills*, https://doi.org/10.1007/978-1-4842-7449-1_9

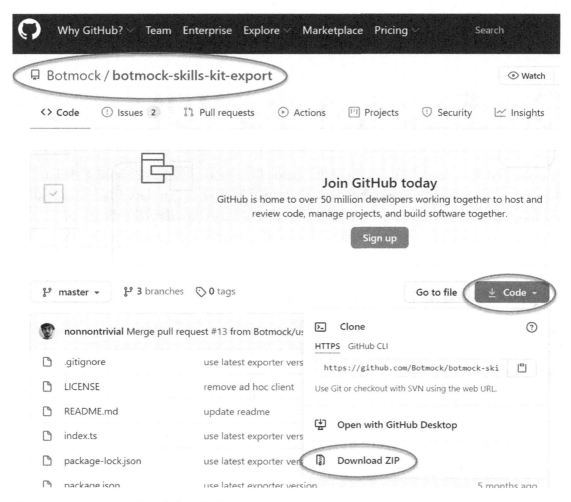

Figure 9-1. *Download the Skills Kit Export Utility from GitHub*

3. Once downloaded, move the file to a new folder in your coding
   directory and unzip it. This will create a folder called *botmock-
   skills-kit-export-master*. (See Figure 9-2.)

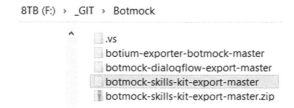

Figure 9-2. *The botmock-skills-kit-export-master folder after unzipping*

4. Open a command line from that folder. To do this, shift-right-click the folder and choose a) Open Command window here, b) Open PowerShell window here, or c) Git Bash here.

5. Type npm -v at the command line. This will report the version of npm you have installed. If you get an error message, then you will need to install npm. If the version is less than 6.14.x, you will need to install the latest version of npm.

6. npm is installed with nodejs. To install nodejs, download the installer from https://nodejs.org/. You will most likely want to install the LTS (Long Term Support) version. See Figure 9-3 for an example.

Figure 9-3. *Downloading the node.js installer*

7. Once node.js is installed, npm will also be installed.

8. From the command line, run `npm install`. (See Figure 9-4.)

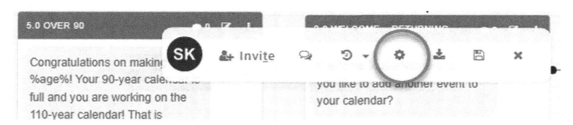

Figure 9-4. *Running npm install*

9. npm will download and install the npm packages needed to run the export.

10. After *npm install*, it is a good idea to run `npm audit fix`

11. Still at the command line, run `mv ./sample.env ./.env`

12. Edit the *.env* file in notepad++.

13. Switch to your browser, open your Botmock project, and click the cog icon to get to Settings. (See Figure 9-5.)

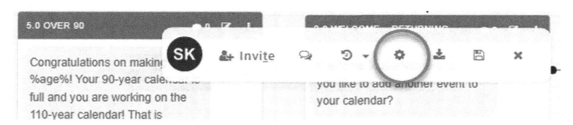

Figure 9-5. *Accessing the Settings menu in Botmock*

14. Click on the API Info tab, and click *Copy .env file for API usage.* (See Figure 9-6.)

15. Paste that into the .env file in Notepad++, pasting over the text already there.

16. Switch back to Botmock and click the link to *generate your API key here*. (Also see Figure 9-6.)

Figure 9-6. *Getting the API info from Botmock*

17. On the *Create API Token* screen, enter a *Token Name*, say, **Botmock Token**.

18. Check the *Access your Teams and Projects* box.

19. Click *Create*. (See Figure 9-7.)

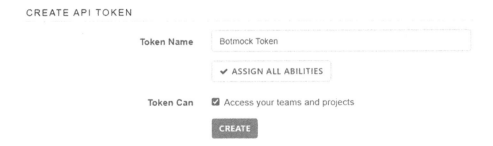

Figure 9-7. *Creating the API Token*

20. Now click the *Copy to Clipboard* button.

21. Paste the entire token between the double quotes in the .env file in Notepad++.

22. I would show you the .env file at this point, but then I'd have to wipe your memory of this event with Agent K's flashy thing.

23. Also, do I need to remind you to save your work at this time?

    With the export utility downloaded, the npm packages installed, and the .env file configured, you are ready to run the export.

24. From the command line, run `npm start`. This will create an *output* folder with a *90-Year Calendar.json* file in it.

At this point, we've exported the dialog file. In the next section, we will put that file to work and create the bones of our skill.

Creating the Skill

To create a skill from the exported Botmock file, we need to launch the Alexa Developer Console. Then we can open the custom skill we created in Chapter 7. Then we will drop in the json from Botmock and spend some time tweaking the results.

To start, open a browser to `https://developer.amazon.com/alexa/console/ask`. Then click on the 90-year calendar skill we created in Chapter 7.

Now we can use the Botmock file to create the initial model for our skill. Even though we will have to tweak and adjust the model afterward, this will save us a ton of time. Expand the interaction model in the left navigation bar. Then follow these instructions:

1. Click on the *JSON Editor*.

2. Click on *Drag and drop a .json file*.

3. Locate and select the 90-Year Calendar.json file from Botmock.

4. Click the *Save Model* button at the top.

5. Now click the Build Model button at the top.

See all the errors. These are where the Botmock model and the Alexa model don't quite line up. Thankfully, they're relatively easy to fix by editing the intents and making sure the slots are correctly defined. No need to edit the JSON, we can fix these through the Alexa Developer Console, as described in the next section.

Cleaning Up the Dialog Model

After importing the model from Botmock, we have a few corrections to make. Before we do, you have a choice to make. To underscore or not to underscore, that is the question. That is, do you want to put underscores in your intent names or remove spaces to go CamelCase instead? My personal preference is CamelCase. But Under_Score is perfectly fine too. Choose now but be consistent.

Start by selecting the Give Birthday intent.

1. Rename the intent from Give Birthday to GiveBirthday, or, if you prefer, Give_Birthday.

2. Then scroll down to the Intent Slots and enter **birthday** in the name space and select the + *button* to add it. Now select *AMAZON.Date* as the Slot Type.

   Select the Give Event Date intent and make the same corrections.

3. Rename the intent.

4. Add the **eventDate** slot and select *AMAZON.Date* as the Slot Type.

   Select the Give Event Description intent and make the corrections.

5. Rename the intent.

6. Add the **eventDescription** slot and select *AMAZON.SearchQuery* as the Slot Type. (The AMAZON.SearchQuery lets the user say a short phrase that we can capture as the event description.)

   Select the Give Event Type intent and correct it. Note: There is no correction to the Slot Type as the Botmock model already had the slot type for eventType.

7. Rename the intent.

Rename each of the Email Calendar, Add an Event, and Print Calendar intents.

Now, we need to delete the Launch Intent. The Launch Intent just needs to be deleted because it isn't really an intent; it's the invocation phrase. Click on the Intents heading in the left navigation bar. Locate the Launch Intent and click Delete to the right of it. Confirm the warning.

Next, we need to convert the Yes and No intents from custom intents to built-in. We can do this by adding the AMAZON.YesIntent and AMAZON.NoIntent to our intents list and by deleting the Yes and No intents we already have.

Also, we should add some of the other built-in intents to control our skill better. Specifically, add the AMAZON.RepeatIntent, AMAZON.StartOverIntent, and AMAZON. StopIntent.

Lastly, as we will have a list of events to manage, we will need to add the AMAZON. MoreIntent, AMAZON.NextIntent, AMAZON.PageDownIntent, AMAZON.PageUpIntent, AMAZON.PreviousIntent, four AMAZON.Scroll*Intents, and AMAZON.SelectIntent.

When you've finished adding the built-in intents, your intents should look like those in Figure 9-8.

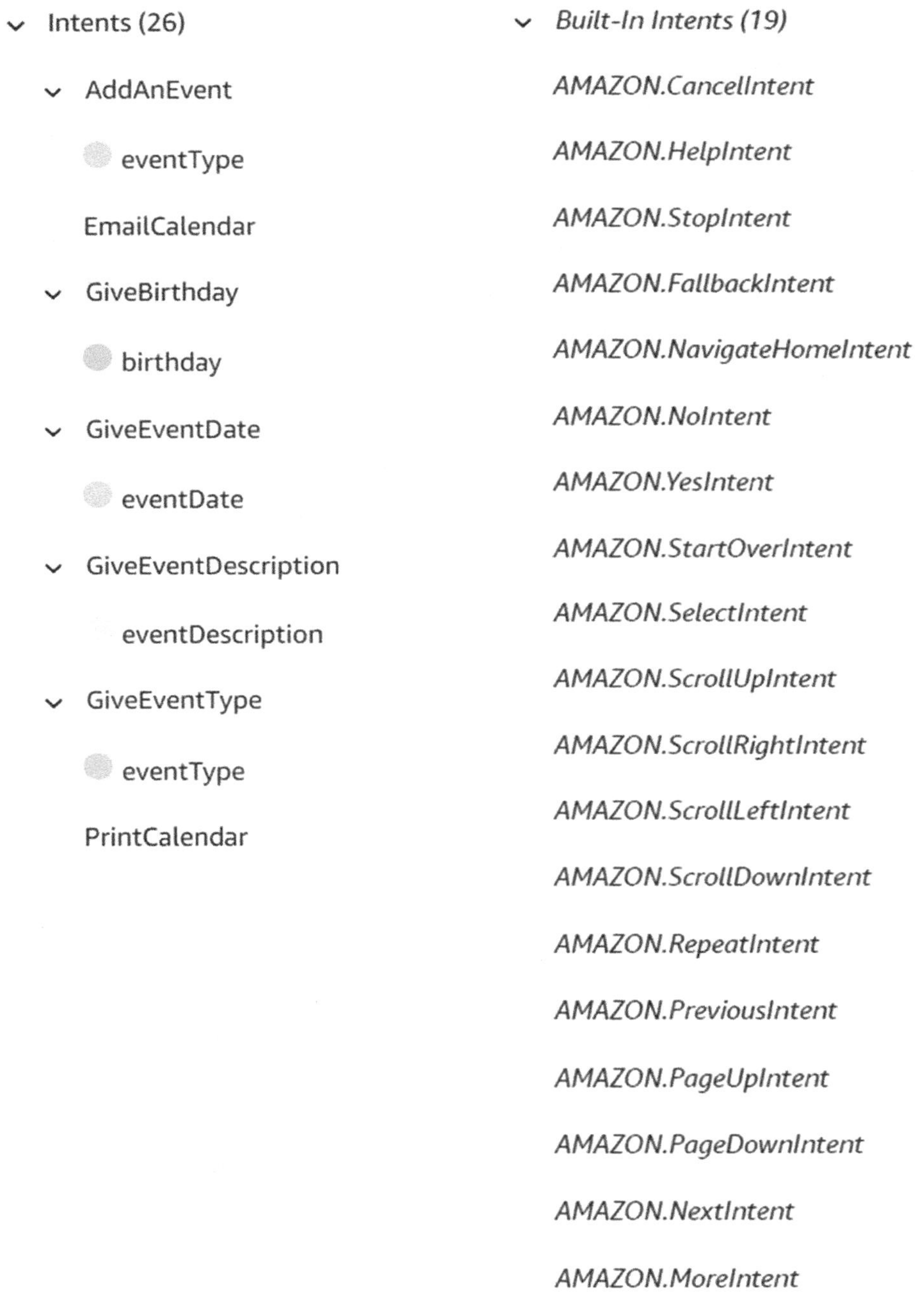

˅ Intents (26)

  ˅ AddAnEvent

    ⬤ eventType

  EmailCalendar

  ˅ GiveBirthday

    ⬤ birthday

  ˅ GiveEventDate

    ⬤ eventDate

  ˅ GiveEventDescription

    eventDescription

  ˅ GiveEventType

    ⬤ eventType

  PrintCalendar

˅ *Built-In Intents (19)*

AMAZON.CancelIntent

AMAZON.HelpIntent

AMAZON.StopIntent

AMAZON.FallbackIntent

AMAZON.NavigateHomeIntent

AMAZON.NoIntent

AMAZON.YesIntent

AMAZON.StartOverIntent

AMAZON.SelectIntent

AMAZON.ScrollUpIntent

AMAZON.ScrollRightIntent

AMAZON.ScrollLeftIntent

AMAZON.ScrollDownIntent

AMAZON.RepeatIntent

AMAZON.PreviousIntent

AMAZON.PageUpIntent

AMAZON.PageDownIntent

AMAZON.NextIntent

AMAZON.MoreIntent

Figure 9-8. *The custom and built-in intents we will be coding*

Now that we've got the intents set up, we can create the visual interface for Alexa devices with a screen in the next chapter.

Summary

In this chapter, we converted our Botmock diagram into an Alexa Skill and configured the VUI. In the next chapter, we'll use the Alexa Presentation Language (APL) to create a visual presentation for Alexa devices with screens.

CHAPTER 10

Using APL to Present on Screens

In Chapter 9, we converted the Botmock diagram into an Alexa skill and configured the VUI. However, the primary purpose of our 90-year calendar skill is to show you your 90-year calendar. To do this, we will need to check if the device has a screen, and if it does, we can create a 90-year calendar presentation with Alexa Presentation Language (APL). "An APL document is a JSON structure that defines a template to display on the viewport. The document controls the overall structure and layout of the visual response."[1] In other words, APL is a JSON file that changes the display on the device. This chapter will look at that file and the data bound to it to draw a simple 90-year calendar on the screen, starting with introducing the APL Editor.

The APL Editor

To get to the APL Editor from the Alexa Developer Console, make sure you are on the Build tab and that you have Assets expanded on the left navigation bar. Then select Interfaces. Scroll down to Alexa Presentation Language, turn the feature on with the toggle switch, and make sure to choose all the Viewport Profiles. Click the Save Interfaces button. Now, select Multimodal Responses from the left navigation bar. See Figure 10-1.

---

[1] Understand Alexa Presentation Language (APL), Amazon, 2020. https://developer.amazon.com/en-US/docs/alexa/alexa-presentation-language/understand-apl.html

© Simon A. Kingaby 2022
S. A. Kingaby, *Data-Driven Alexa Skills*, https://doi.org/10.1007/978-1-4842-7449-1_10

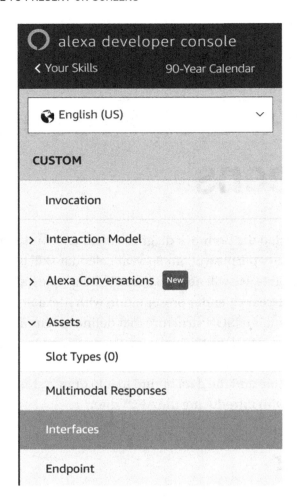

Figure 10-1. *The left navigation bar for Interfaces and Multimodal Responses*

A new tab will open in your browser. Select the Visual responses option. Then click Create Visual Response. Next, select the Start from scratch option. This will open the APL Editor. See Figure 10-2.

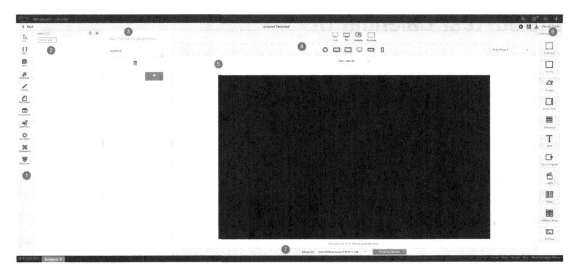

Figure 10-2. *The APL Editor*

Looking at the APL Editor, we see

1. A left navigation bar that we will use to access various parts of the APL document

2. The text panel where we see the components of the APL document or the JSON text

3. The details of the selected component

4. The target screen options

5. The visual preview of the APL document

6. The components toolbar to add components to the APL template

7. The option to view the APL document in the Skill Simulator

8. The main toolbar where we can preview, save, and download the APL

In the next section, we're going to plan some of the components of our UI.

The 90-Year Calendar UI

Unfortunately, we can't just put an Excel spreadsheet on the screen using APL. Instead, we will render our calendar UI using custom code. Specifically, we will use SVG (Scalable Vector Graphics), Alexa style. Suffice to say that with SVG – sometimes referred to as Alexa Vector Graphics (AVG) in the documentation – we can draw anything we want on a device with a screen.

Our 90-year calendar will use SVG to draw a box for each week in the 90-year calendar. We will fill the boxes in for weeks that have passed and leave them open for weeks that have not. For performance reasons, we will need to have three zones. The middle zone will be the current year, where we fill some of the boxes and leave some blank. The top area will be the past, where we fill all the boxes. We will leave all the boxes blank in the bottom zone. See Figure 10-3.

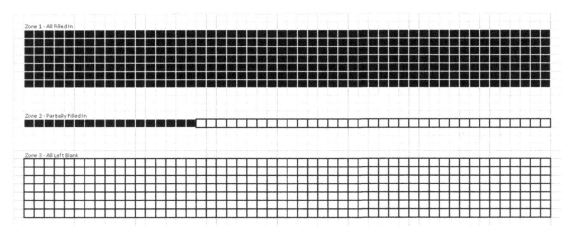

Figure 10-3. *The three zones we'll be drawing*

To achieve this, we will need to define several items in the APL Json format. First, we're going to define some color resources. These allow us to use a color code throughout the APL model without naming the specific color. So we'll start with black and white, but you could easily change it to red and yellow or any other colors if you'd like. Click on the Resources button on the left nav bar, and enter the following Json code:

```
[{
    "colors": {
        "C0": "black",
        "C1": "white"
    }
}]
```

With the colors defined, we can create a dataset that we will bind the APL to so that we can render it dynamically. The dataset will represent Zones 1, 2, and 3, as shown in Figure 10-3. In Zones 1 and 3, a single entry in the dataset will represent the row's background color. In Zone 2, a single entry will be the color of each square in the row. For development, we only need a handful of rows. For testing and in the finished skill, we will need a total of 89 rows (one for each year) for Zones 1 and 3, and 52 columns (one for each week) for the single row in Zone 2. To enter the data, select the Data icon in the left nav bar and enter the following Json code:

```
{
    "data": {
        "type": "object",
        "properties": {
            "zone1": [
                "C1",
                "C1",
                "C1",
                "C1",
                "C1",
                "C1",
                "C1"
            ],
            "zone2": [
                "C0",
                "C0",
                "C0",
                "C0",
                "C0",
                "C0",
```

```
                    "C0",
                    "C0",
                    "C0",
                    "C1",
                    "C0",
                    "C0",
                    "C0",
                    "C0",
                    "C0",
                    "C0",
                    "C0",
                    "C0",
                    "C0",
                    "C1",
                    "C0",
                    "C0",
                    "C0",
                    "C0",
                    "C0",
                    "C0",
                    "C0",
                    "C0",
                    "C0",
                    "C1",
                    "C0",
                    "C0",
                    "C0",
                    "C0",
                    "C0",
                    "C0",
                    "C0",
                    "C0",
                    "C1",
                    "C0",
```

```
                    "C0",
                    "C0",
                    "C0",
                    "C0",
                    "C0",
                    "C0",
                    "C0",
                    "C0",
                    "C1",
                    "C0",
                    "C0"
                ],
                "zone3": [
                    "C0",
                    "C0",
                    "C0",
                    "C0",
                    "C0"
                ]
            }
        }
    }
}
```

There is another dynamic parameter we need to know for each zone – its height in pixels. Eventually, the height will get calculated in our skill code, but we can hard-code it for the sample data. In Figure 10-3, each box has a 2-pixel border and is 32 pixels square, including the border. For Zone 1, our sample data has seven rows. Zone 2 has one row. Zone 3 has five rows. The zone heights are therefore

Zone 1: $7 \times 32 = 224$.

Zone 2: $1 \times 32 = 32$.

Zone 3: $5 \times 32 = 160$.

Total width: $52 \times 32 = 1664$.

Total height: $90 \times 32 = 2880$.

After Zone 3's data in the dataset, we need to add the following Json code:

```
"zone1Height": 224,
"zone2Height": 32,
"zone3Height": 160,
"totalWidth": 1664,
"totalHeight": 2880
```

After adding these items, the Json code will look like Figure 10-4.

```
{
    "data": {
        "type": "object",
        "properties": {
            "zone1": [...],
            "zone2": [...],
            "zone3": [...],
            "zone1Height": 224,
            "zone2Height": 32,
            "zone3Height": 160,
            "totalWidth": 1664,
            "totalHeight": 2880
        }
    }
}
```

Figure 10-4. *The Data Json entries (with the zones collapsed)*

At this point, we can configure the imports for the document.

Configuring the Imports for the Document

We need to import the `alexa-styles` module and the `alexa-layouts` module. Click on the Document icon on the left nav bar and enter the following Json code:

```
{
    "type": "APL",
    "version": "1.5",
    "theme": "dark",
    "import": [{
            "name": "alexa-styles",
            "version": "1.1.0"
        },
```

```
    {
        "name": "alexa-layouts",
        "version": "1.2.0"
    }
  ]
}
```

Next, we need to define three shapes for our 90-year calendar – one for each zone.

Drawing the Three Zones

The Zone 2 shape is a simple box. Zones 1 and 3 are complex rows of boxes. In SVG, you draw a simple square by moving a pen to one vertice and then drawing a line to each of the vertices, forming the sides of a square. Like this:

M0,0 L0,6 L6,6 L6,0 L0,0 (see Figure 10-5).

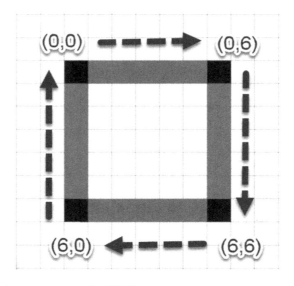

Figure 10-5. *Drawing a square in SVG*

In our case, for Zone 2, we want to draw a box that is 32 × 32 with a 2-pixel border. The SVG command will be

M0,0 L0,31 L31,31 L31,0 L0,0 M1,1 L1,30 L30,30 L30,1 L1,1

With this command, we can create the graphics we need to draw the boxes in Zone 2. Click on the Graphics icon on the left nav bar and enter the following Json code:

```
{
    "blackBox": {
        "type": "AVG",
        "version": "1.0",
        "height": 32,
        "width": 32,
        "items": [{
            "type": "path",
            "stroke": "@C1",
            "pathData": "M0,0 L0,31 L31,31 L31,0 L0,0 M1,1 L1,30 L30,30
            L30,1 L1,1",
            "fill": "@C0"
        }]
    },
    "whiteBox": {
        "type": "AVG",
        "version": "1.0",
        "height": 32,
        "width": 32,
        "items": [{
            "type": "path",
            "stroke": "@C0",
            "pathData": "M0,0 L0,31 L31,31 L31,0 L0,0 M1,1 L1,30 L30,30
            L30,1 L1,1",
            "fill": "@C1"
        }]
    }
}
```

Tip   Save early, save often. Make sure you save your work often. (The first time you save, you will need to name your template.)

With these building blocks in place, we can start to put together the APL document's main template. The `mainTemplate` section takes a parameter, called `payload`, that binds to the data we entered earlier in the template. Our data object has properties that we can access using APL variable substitution like this: `"${payload.data.properties.propertyname}"`.

We have three zones, and we will use an APL `GridSequence` object for each zone. These will all be in an APL `Container` object. Click on the APL icon on the left nav bar. Scroll down to find the following code block:

```
"mainTemplate": {
    "parameters": [
        "payload"
    ],
    "items": []
}
```

Then change that code by adding the `Container` and three `GridSequences`, like this:

```
"mainTemplate": {
    "parameters": [
        "payload"
    ],
    "items": [{
        "type": "Container",
        "width": "${payload.data.properties.totalWidth}",
        "height": "${payload.data.properties.totalHeight}",
        "paddingLeft": "10",
        "paddingTop": "10",
        "paddingRight": "10",
        "paddingBottom": "10",
        "items": [{
                "type": "GridSequence",
                "width": "${payload.data.properties.totalWidth}",
                "height": "${payload.data.properties.zone1Height}",
                "childHeight": "32",
                "childWidth": "32",
                "data": "${payload.data.properties.zone1}",
```

225

```
            "items": [{
                "type": "VectorGraphic",
                "source": "blackBox"
            }]
        },
        {

            "type": "GridSequence",
            "width": "${payload.data.properties.totalWidth}",
            "height": "${payload.data.properties.zone2Height}",
            "childHeight": "32",
            "childWidth": "32",
            "data": "${payload.data.properties.zone2}",
            "items": [{
                "type": "VectorGraphic",
                "source": "blackBox"
            }]
        },
        {

            "type": "GridSequence",
            "width": "${payload.data.properties.totalWidth}",
            "height": "${payload.data.properties.zone3Height}",
            "childHeight": "32",
            "childWidth": "32",
            "data": "${payload.data.properties.zone3}",
            "items": [{
                "type": "VectorGraphic",
                "source": "whiteBox"
            }]
        }
    ]
}]
}
```

With this code in place, the sample rendered to the right should look like Figure 10-6.

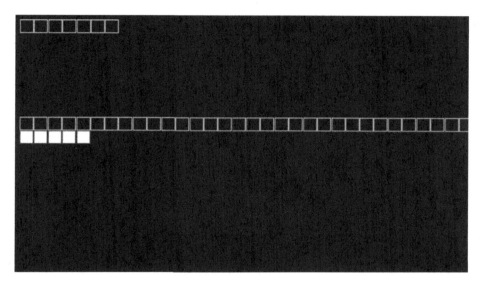

Figure 10-6. *The example rendered after we blocked in the three zones*

Next, we can add a when clause to the Zone 2 boxes so that they change color based on the data value. Change Zone 2's code as shown here:

```
"data": "${payload.data.properties.zone2}",
"items": [{
        "when": "${data == 'C1'}",
        "type": "VectorGraphic",
        "source": "whiteBox"
    },
    {
        "when": "${data == 'C0'}",
        "type": "VectorGraphic",
        "source": "blackBox"
    }
]
```

Notice how the term data is declared before items so that we get one item for each element in the data array. In the items themselves, we refer to the data term, not the properties.zone2 term.

Now comes the tricky part. If we draw the other rows like we have drawn the single row in Zone 2, the entire drawing takes forever to render. To improve performance, we need to draw the whole row in one go. This requires quite a bit of math, so it's easiest to compose the SVG expression in Excel. To start with, we can create a map of where the cursor/pen needs to move to to draw the lines, something like Figure 10-7.

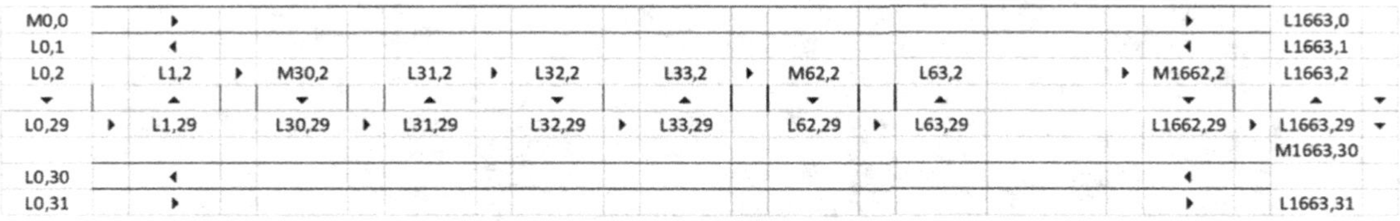

M0,0	▶									▶		L1663,0
L0,1	◀									◀		L1663,1
L0,2	L1,2	▶	M30,2	L31,2	▶	L32,2	L33,2	▶	M62,2	L63,2	▶ M1662,2	L1663,2
▼		▲		▼		▲		▼		▲		
L0,29	▶	L1,29	L30,29	▶	L31,29	L32,29	▶	L33,29	L62,29	▶	L63,29	L1662,29 ▶ L1663,29 ▼
												M1663,30
L0,30	◀									◀		
L0,31	▶									▶		L1663,31

Figure 10-7. *A map of the cursor movements to draw the lines in a row*

The finished SVG expression will therefore look like this:

```
M0,0 L1663,0 L1663,1 L0,1 L0,2 L0,29 L1,29 L1,2 M30,2 L30,29 L31,29 L31,2
L32,2 L32,29 L33,29 L33,2 M62,2 L62,29 L63,29 L63,2 M1662,2 L1662,29
L1663,29 L1663,2 M1663,30 L0,30 L0,31 L1663,31
```

We need to figure out what goes in the middle, where the arrow is in the preceding code. Back in Excel, we're going to enter the SVG expression's seed values by looking at the vertices for the vertical lines. In Figure 10-7, these vertices start at L0,2, then down to L0,29, then right to L1,29, then L1,2, then M30,2, and so on. The pattern repeats after the eighth entry. In a new worksheet, in column A, enter the values for the first number in each vertice, numbers 0, 0, 1, 1, 30, 30, 31, 31. In column B, enter the second number in each vertice, 2, 29, 29, 2, 2, 29, 29, 2. In column C, enter the letter for the pen movement in each vertice, L, L, L, L, M, L, L, L, as shown in Figure 10-8.

0	2	L
0	29	L
1	29	L
1	2	L
30	2	M
30	29	L
31	29	L
31	2	L

Figure 10-8. *The seed values for the SVG expression*

Now we can enter the formulae in the ninth row as shown here:

	A	B	C
9	=A1+32	=B1	=C1

Also, in columns E and F, in rows 1 and 2, enter the formulae to concatenate the values generated in columns A, B, and C:

	E	F
1	=CONCAT(C1,A1,",",B1," ")	=E1
2	=CONCAT(C2,A2,",",B2," ")	=CONCAT(F1, E2)

Now copy the formulae for E2:F2 down to rows 3:9. Then carefully copy the formulae from A9:F9 down to rows 10:416. The final worksheet will look like Figure 10-9.

	A	B	C	D	E	F	G	H	I	J	K	L
1	0	2	L		L0,2	L0,2						
2	0	29	L		L0,29	L0,2 L0,29						
3	1	29	L		L1,29	L0,2 L0,29 L1,29						
4	1	2	L		L1,2	L0,2 L0,29 L1,29 L1,2						
5	30	2	M		M30,2	L0,2 L0,29 L1,29 L1,2 M30,2						
6	30	29	L		L30,29	L0,2 L0,29 L1,29 L1,2 M30,2 L30,29						
7	31	29	L		L31,29	L0,2 L0,29 L1,29 L1,2 M30,2 L30,29 L31,29						
8	31	2	L		L31,2	L0,2 L0,29 L1,29 L1,2 M30,2 L30,29 L31,29 L31,2						
9	32	2	L		L32,2	L0,2 L0,29 L1,29 L1,2 M30,2 L30,29 L31,29 L31,2 L32,2						
10	32	29	L		L32,29	L0,2 L0,29 L1,29 L1,2 M30,2 L30,29 L31,29 L31,2 L32,2 L32,29						
11	33	29	L		L33,29	L0,2 L0,29 L1,29 L1,2 M30,2 L30,29 L31,29 L31,2 L32,2 L32,29 L33,29						
12	33	2	L		L33,2	L0,2 L0,29 L1,29 L1,2 M30,2 L30,29 L31,29 L31,2 L32,2 L32,29 L33,29 L33,2						
13	62	2	M		M62,2	L0,2 L0,29 L1,29 L1,2 M30,2 L30,29 L31,29 L31,2 L32,2 L32,29 L33,29 L33,2 ...						
14	62	29	L		L62,29	L0,2 L0,29 L1,29 L1,2 M30,2 L30,29 L31,29 L31,2 L32,2 L32,29 L33,29 L33,2 M						
15	63	29	L		L63,29	L0,2 L0,29 L1,29 L1,2 M30,2 L30,29 L31,29 L31,2 L32,2 L32,29 L33,29 L33,2 N...						
16	63	2	L		L63,2	L0,2 L0,29 L1,29 L1,2 M30,2 L30,29 L31,29 L31,2 L32,2 L32,29 L33,29 L33,2 M6						
17	64	2	L		L64,2	L0,2 L0,29 L1,29 L1,2 M30,2 L30,29 L31,29 L31,2 L32,2 L32,29 L33,29 L33,2 M						
18	64	29	L		L64,29	L0,2 L0,29 L1,29 L1,2 M30,2 L30,29 L31,29 L31,2 L32,2 L32,29 L33,29 L33,2 N						
19	65	29	L		L65,29	L0,2 L0,29 L1,29 L1,2 M30,2 L30,29 L31,29 L31,2 L32,2 L32,29 L33,29 L33,2...						
20	65	2	L		L65,2	L0,2 L0,29 L1,29 L1,2 M30,2 L30,29 L31,29 L31,2 L32,2 L32,29 L33,29 L33,2 M..						
21	94	2	M		M94,2	L0,2 L0,29 L1,29 L1,2 M30,2 L30,29 L31,29 L31,2 L32,2 L32,29 L33,29 L33,2						
22	94	29	L		L94,29	L0,2 L0,29 L1,29 L1,2 M30,2 L30,29 L31,29 L31,2 L32,2 L32,29 L33,29 L33,2						
23	95	29	L		L95,29	L0,2 L0,29 L1,29 L1,2 M30,2 L30,29 L31,29 L31,2 L32,2 L32,29 L33,29 L33,2 N						
24	95	2	L		L95,2	L0,2 L0,29 L1,29 L1,2 M30,2 L30,29 L31,29 L31,2 L32,2 L32,29 L33,29 L33,2 M6						
25	96	2	L		L96,2	L0,2 L0,29 L1,29 L1,2 M30,2 L30,29 L31,29 L31,2 L32,2 L32,29 L33,29 L33,2 M8						
26	96	29	L		L96,29	L0,2 L0,29 L1,29 L1,2 M30,2 L30,29 L31,29 L31,2 L32,2 L32,29 L33,29 L33,2						
27	97	29	L		L97,29	L0,2 L0,29 L1,29 L1,2 M30,2 L30,29 L31,29 L31,2 L32,2 L32,29 L33,29 L33,2 Mr						
28	97	2	L		L97,2	L0,2 L0,29 L1,29 L1,2 M30,2 L30,29 L31,29 L31,2 L32,2 L32,29 L33,29 L33,2 M						
29	126	2	M		M126,2	L0,2 L0,29 L1,29 L1,2 M30,2 L30,29 L31,29 L31,2 L32,2 L32,29 L33,29 L33,2 N						
30	126	29	L		L126,29	L0,2 L0,29 L1,29 L1,2 M30,2 L30,29 L31,29 L31,2 L32,2 L32,29 L33,29 L33,2						
31	127	29	L		L1...9	L0,2 L0,29 L1,29 L1,2 M30,2 ...29 L31,29 L31,2 L32... L33,29 L32...						

Figure 10-9. *The finished worksheet with the completed SVG expression*

The finished SVG expression will therefore comprise the top two lines:

```
M0,0 L1663,0 L1663,1 L0,1
```

Followed by the big string from Excel cell F416:

```
L0,2 L0,29 L1,29 L1,2 M30,2 L30,29 L31,29 L31,2 L32,2 L32,29 L33,29 L33,
2 M62,2 L62,29 L63,29 L63,2 L64,2 L64,29 L65,29 L65,2 L1601,2 M1630,
2 L1630,29 L1631,29 L1631,2 L1632,2 L1632,29 L1633,29 L1633,2 M1662,
2 L1662,29 L1663,29 L1663,2
```

Followed by the last two lines:

```
M1663,30 L0,30 L0,31 L1663,31
```

Back in the Alexa Developer Console, we will copy and paste the blackBox and whiteBox graphic code to create a blackRow and whiteRow graphic. To do this, click on the Graphics icon on the left nav bar and duplicate the blackBox and whiteBox code, renaming each to blackRow and whiteRow, respectively. Then change the width to 1664 and change the pathData to match the giant SVG expression previously shown. We can remove the fill for the row because we're not drawing a closed shape, so the fill is irrelevant. But we need to add a white background to the Zone 3 rows, so we'll add a plain, filled rectangle that does that. Here's the code:

```
"blackRow": {
    "type": "AVG",
    "version": "1.2",
    "height": 32,
    "width": 1664,
    "viewportHeight": 32,
    "viewportWidth": 1664,
    "items": [{
        "type": "path",
        "stroke": "@C1",
        "pathData": "M0,0 L1663,0 L1663,1 L0,1 L0,2 L0,29 L1,29 L1,2 M30,
            2 L30,29 L31,29 L31,2 L32,2 L32,29 L33,29 L33,2 M62,2
L1630,29 L1631,29 L1631,2 L1632,2 L1632,29 L1633,29 L1633,2 M1662,
2 L1662,29 L1663,29 L1663,2 M1663,30 L0,30 L0,31 L1663,31"
    }]
},
```

```
"whiteRow": {
    "type": "AVG",
    "version": "1.2",
    "height": 32,
    "width": 1664,
    "viewportHeight": 32,
    "viewportWidth": 1664,
    "items": [{
            "type": "path",
            "stroke": "@C1",
            "pathData": "M0,0 L1663,0 L1663,31 L0,31",
            "fill": "@C1"
        },
        {
            "type": "path",
            "stroke": "@C0",
            "pathData": "M0,0 L1663,0 L1663,1 L0,1 L0,2 L0,29 L1,29 L1,
            2 M30,2 L30,29 L31,29 L31,2 L32,2 L32,29 L33,29 L33,2
L1630,29 L1631,29 L1631,2 L1632,2 L1632,29 L1633,29 L1633,2 M1662,
2 L1662,29 L1663,29 L1663,2 M1663,30 L0,30 L0,31 L1663,31"
        }
    ]
}
```

When it's complete, you should see code like that in Figure 10-10.

```
58        },
59 ▾      "blackRow": {
60            "type": "AVG",
61            "version": "1.2",
62            "height": 32,
63            "width": 1664,
64            "viewportHeight": 32,
65            "viewportWidth": 1664,
66 ▾          "items": [
67 ▾              {
68                    "type": "path",
69                    "stroke": "@C1",
70                    "pathData": "M0,0 L1663,0 L1663,1 L0,1 L0,2 L0,29 L1,29 L1,2 M30,2
71                }
72            ]
73        },
74 ▾      "whiteRow": {
75            "type": "AVG",
76            "version": "1.2",
77            "height": 32,
78            "width": 1664,
79            "viewportHeight": 32,
80            "viewportWidth": 1664,
81 ▾          "items": [
82 ▾              {
83                    "type": "path",
84                    "stroke": "@C1",
85                    "pathData": "M0,0 L1663,0 L1663,31 L0,31",
86                    "fill": "@C1"
87                },
88 ▾              {
89                    "type": "path",
90                    "stroke": "@C0",
91                    "pathData": "M0,0 L1663,0 L1663,1 L0,1 L0,2 L0,29 L1,29 L1,2 M30,2
92                }
93            ]
94        }
95    },
```

Figure 10-10. *The Graphic definition for the blackRow and whiteRow*

Notice the addition of the viewportHeight and viewportWidth. These properties are the full size of the graphic (32 × 1664). The height and width properties will be the scaled versions.

We will now parameterize the height and width so the graphics will scale correctly for the different Echo devices.

Parameterizing the Height and Width

Flip back to the APL template (click on the APL icon on the left nav bar). Here, we will change the childHeight and childWidth for Zone 1 and Zone 3 to ${payload.data. properties.boxHeight} and ${payload.data.properties.rowWidth}, respectively.

And we will change the blackBox/whiteBox sources to blackRow/whiteRow for Zones 1 and 3. You will end up with the code in Figure 10-11.

```
111 ▾        "items": [
112 ▾            {
113                  "type": "GridSequence",
114                  "height": "${payload.data.properties.zone1Height}",
115                  "childHeight": "${payload.data.properties.boxHeight}",
116                  "childWidth": "${payload.data.properties.rowWidth}",
117                  "data": "${payload.data.properties.zone1}",
118 ▾                "items": [
119 ▾                    {
120                          "type": "VectorGraphic",
121                          "source": "blackRow",
122                          "height": "${payload.data.properties.boxHeight}",
123                          "width": "${payload.data.properties.rowWidth}"
124                      }
125                  ]
126              },
127 ▾            {
128                  "type": "GridSequence",
129                  "width": "${payload.data.properties.totalWidth}",
130                  "height": "${payload.data.properties.zone2Height}",
131                  "childHeight": "${payload.data.properties.boxHeight}",
132                  "childWidth": "${payload.data.properties.boxWidth}",
133                  "data": "${payload.data.properties.zone2}",
134 ▸                "items": [▢]
150              },
151 ▾            {
152                  "type": "GridSequence",
153                  "height": "${payload.data.properties.zone3Height}",
154                  "childHeight": "${payload.data.properties.boxHeight}",
155                  "childWidth": "${payload.data.properties.rowWidth}",
156                  "data": "${payload.data.properties.zone3}",
157 ▾                "items": [
158 ▾                    {
159                          "type": "VectorGraphic",
160                          "source": "whiteRow",
161                          "height": "${payload.data.properties.boxHeight}",
162                          "width": "${payload.data.properties.rowWidth}"
163                      }
164                  ]
165              }
166          ]
```

Figure 10-11. *The code for Zones 1 and 3 after switching to row graphics*

Lastly, we need to add the properties from the code in Figure 10-10 to the sample data by clicking on the Data icon in the left nav bar and adding the following Json to the bottom of the data:

```
"zone1Height": 1600,
"zone2Height": 32,
"zone3Height": 1248,
"totalWidth": 1664,
"totalHeight": 2880,
"boxHeight": 32,
"boxWidth": 32,
"rowWidth": 1664
```

With all this in place, the finished preview should now look like Figure 10-12.

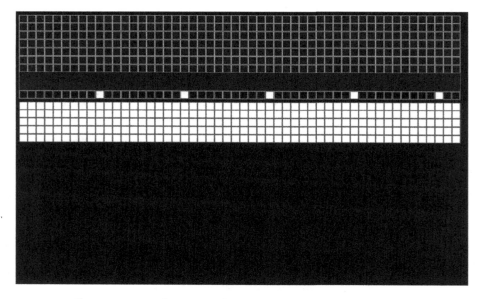

Figure 10-12. *The preview after switching to row graphics*

Now we need to change the data to deal with scaling.

Scaling the Boxes and Rows to Fit

First, we'll add the rest of the sample data, and then we'll scale the Zone Heights to fit the Echo Show 2 screen.

Click the Data icon in the left nav bar. Update the code so that there are 50 rows in Zone 1 and 39 rows in Zone 3. Adding the existing 52 columns (one row) for Zone 2, we get $50 + 1 + 39 = 90$ years worth of weekly data. The completed Data Json is therefore

```
{
    "data": {
        "type": "object",
        "properties": {
            "zone1": [
                "C1",
                "C1",
                "C1",
                ...
                "C1",
                "C1",
                "C1"
            ],
            "zone2": [
                "C1",
                "C1",
                ...
                "C0",
                "C0"
            ],
            "zone3": [
                "C0",
                "C0",
                "C0",
                ...
                "C0",
                "C0",
                "C0"
            ],
            "zone1Height": 1600,
            "zone2Height": 32,
            "zone3Height": 1248,
```

```
            "totalWidth": 1664,
            "totalHeight": 2880,
            "boxHeight": 32,
            "boxWidth": 32,
            "rowWidth": 1664
        }
    }
}
```

To scale the boxes to fit on an Echo Show 2, which is 1280 x 800 pixels, we need to decrease the box height as follows:

$$800 \text{ pixels over } 90 \text{ rows} = 800 / 90 = 8.889 \sim 8$$

And decrease the box width as follows:

$$1280 \text{ pixels over } 52 \text{ rows} = 1280 / 52 = 24.231 \sim 24$$

The net width of a row is therefore

$$24 \times 52 = 1248.$$

The zone heights are then

$$\text{Zone 1: } 8 \times 50 = 400$$

$$\text{Zone 2: } 8$$

$$\text{Zone 3: } 8 \times 39 = 312$$

Plugging those values into the data properties changes it as follows:

```
            "zone1Height": 400,
            "zone2Height": 8,
            "zone3Height": 312,
            "totalWidth": 1664,
            "totalHeight": 2880,
            "boxHeight": 8,
            "boxWidth": 24,
            "rowWidth": 1248
```

Now that we've entered the data and configured the parameters, you should have a diagram that looks like Figure 10-13.

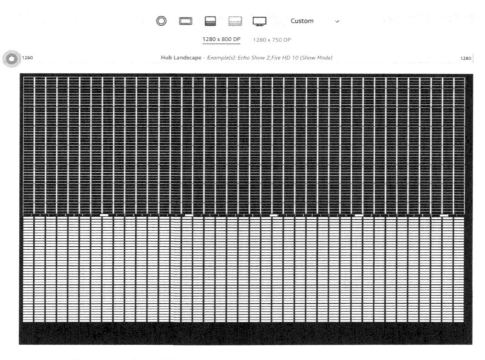

Figure 10-13. *The completed 90-year calendar*

The Finished APL Code

The final APL template is

```
{
    "type": "APL",
    "version": "1.5",
    "theme": "dark",
    "import": [{
            "name": "alexa-styles",
            "version": "1.1.0"
        },
        {
            "name": "alexa-layouts",
            "version": "1.2.0"
        }
    ],
```

```
"settings": {},
"resources": [{
    "colors": {
        "C0": "black",
        "C1": "white"
    }
}],
"styles": {},
"onMount": [],
"graphics": {
    "blackBox": {
        "type": "AVG",
        "version": "1.2",
        "height": 32,
        "width": 32,
        "viewportHeight": 32,
        "viewportWidth": 32,
        "items": [{
            "type": "path",
            "stroke": "@C1",
            "pathData": "M0,0 L0,31 L31,31 L31,0 L0,0 M1,1 L1,30 L30,30
            L30,1 L1,1",
            "fill": "@C0"
        }]
    },
    "whiteBox": {
        "type": "AVG",
        "version": "1.2",
        "height": 32,
        "width": 32,
        "viewportHeight": 32,
        "viewportWidth": 32,
        "items": [{
            "type": "path",
            "stroke": "@C0",
```

```
                "pathData": "M0,0 L0,31 L31,31 L31,0 L0,0 M1,1 L1,30 L30,30
                L30,1 L1,1",
                "fill": "@C1"
        }]
    },
    "blackRow": {
        "type": "AVG",
        "version": "1.2",
        "height": 32,
        "width": 1664,
        "viewportHeight": 32,
        "viewportWidth": 1664,
        "items": [{
            "type": "path",
            "stroke": "@C1",
            "pathData": "M0,0 L1663,0 L1663,1 L0,1 L0,2 L0,29 L1,29
            L1,2 M30,2 L30,29 L31,29 L31,2 L32,2 L32,29 L33,29 L33,
            2M1662,2 L1662,29 L1663,29 L1663,2 M1663,30 L0,30 L0,
            31 L1663,31"
        }]
    },
    "whiteRow": {
        "type": "AVG",
        "version": "1.2",
        "height": 32,
        "width": 1664,
        "viewportHeight": 32,
        "viewportWidth": 1664,
        "items": [{
                "type": "path",
                "stroke": "@C1",
                "pathData": "M0,0 L1663,0 L1663,31 L0,31",
                "fill": "@C1"
            },
```

```
                {
                    "type": "path",
                    "stroke": "@C0",
                    "pathData": "M0,0 L1663,0 L1663,1 L0,1 L0,2 L0,29 L1,
                    29 L1,2 M30,2 L30,29 L31,29 L31,2 L32,2 L32,29 L33,
                    29 M1662,2 L1662,29 L1663,29 L1663,2 M1663,30 L0,
                    30 L0,31 L1663,31"
                }
            ]
        }
    },
    "commands": {},
    "layouts": {},
    "mainTemplate": {
        "parameters": [
            "payload"
        ],
        "items": [{
            "type": "Container",
            "height": "${payload.data.properties.totalHeight}",
            "width": "${payload.data.properties.totalWidth}",
            "paddingLeft": "10",
            "paddingTop": "10",
            "paddingRight": "10",
            "paddingBottom": "10",
            "items": [{
                    "type": "GridSequence",
                    "height": "${payload.data.properties.zone1Height}",
                    "childHeight": "${payload.data.properties.boxHeight}",
                    "childWidth": "${payload.data.properties.rowWidth}",
                    "data": "${payload.data.properties.zone1}",
                    "items": [{
                        "type": "VectorGraphic",
                        "source": "blackRow",
```

```
            "height": "${payload.data.properties.boxHeight}",
            "width": "${payload.data.properties.rowWidth}"
        }]
    },
    {

        "type": "GridSequence",
        "width": "${payload.data.properties.totalWidth}",
        "height": "${payload.data.properties.zone2Height}",
        "childHeight": "${payload.data.properties.boxHeight}",
        "childWidth": "${payload.data.properties.boxWidth}",
        "data": "${payload.data.properties.zone2}",
        "items": [{
                "when": "${data == 'C1'}",
                "type": "VectorGraphic",
                "source": "whiteBox",
                "height": "${payload.data.properties.boxHeight}",
                "width": "${payload.data.properties.boxWidth}"
            },
            {

                "when": "${data == 'C0'}",
                "type": "VectorGraphic",
                "source": "blackBox",
                "height": "${payload.data.properties.boxHeight}",
                "width": "${payload.data.properties.boxWidth}"
            }
        ]
    },
    {

        "type": "GridSequence",
        "height": "${payload.data.properties.zone3Height}",
        "childHeight": "${payload.data.properties.boxHeight}",
        "childWidth": "${payload.data.properties.rowWidth}",
        "data": "${payload.data.properties.zone3}",
```

```
                "items": [{
                    "type": "VectorGraphic",
                    "source": "whiteRow",
                    "height": "${payload.data.properties.boxHeight}",
                    "width": "${payload.data.properties.rowWidth}"
                }]
            }
        ]
    }]
  }
}
```

Summary

In the previous chapters, you designed and implemented the VUI for the 90-year calendar skill. In this chapter, you built the visual presentation for Alexa devices with screens using APL, SVG, and Json. In the next chapter, we'll create the back-end lambda function that puts the code behind the VUI and connects the VUI to the APL.

CHAPTER 11

Coding the Lambda Function

In Chapter 9, we converted the Botmock diagram into an Alexa Skill and configured the VUI. In Chapter 10, we added the APL presentation for our 90-year calendar visual display. In this chapter, we'll create the back-end lambda function that puts the code behind the VUI and connects the VUI to the APL. Since we're not using an Alexa-hosted skill, in Chapter 7, we provisioned the lambda function as an Amazon Web Service.

To get started

1. First, log in to the AWS Developer Console as your admin user, not as the root user. The AWS console is here: `https://console.aws.amazon.com`.

2. Select Services | Compute | Lambda.

3. Select the **CalendarLambdaBackend** we created in Chapter 7.

You should see the little snippet of code in the `lambda_function.py` file:

```python
import json

def lambda_handler(event, context): #TODO implement
return {
    'statusCode': 200,
    'body': json.dumps('Hello from Lambda!')
}
```

At this point, we need to do several things:

1. Hook up the VUI to the lambda function.

2. Create all the functions that will handle the intents.

© Simon A. Kingaby 2022
S. A. Kingaby, *Data-Driven Alexa Skills*, https://doi.org/10.1007/978-1-4842-7449-1_11

3. Do the math to calculate the 90-year calendar values.

4. Define the dataset for the 90-year calendar visual to bind to.

5. Do the math to scale the visual to the current device's screen.

6. Return the rendered APL and speech output as a response object.

7. Define the Skill Builder object at the bottom of the lambda function.

Hook Up the VUI to the Lambda Function

To hook up the VUI to the lambda function, we need to copy the Skill ID from the Alexa skill to the lambda function and the ARN (Amazon Resource Name) from the lambda function to the Alexa skill.

1. In the top right corner of the lambda function, you can see the ARN. (See Figure 11-1.) Click the icon to Copy the ARN.

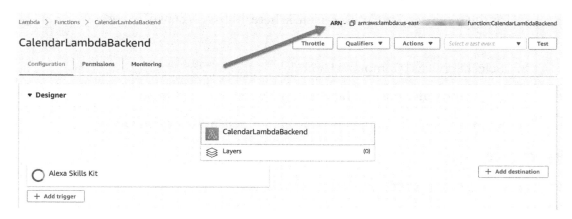

Figure 11-1. *The ARN of the lambda function*

2. Switch over to the 90-Year Calendar Alexa Skill. The Alexa Developer Console is here: `https://developer.amazon.com/alexa/console/ask`

3. Select Endpoint from the left navigation bar.

4. Paste the ARN into the Default Region box.

5. Click the Save Endpoints button at the top. You should see a green success message.

6. Switch back to the lambda function in AWS.

In the next section, we're going to create the intent handlers.

Creating the Intent Handlers

Our interaction model in the Alexa skill has a lot of intents. Each of these needs to be handled in the lambda function. To create the intent handlers, we will need the following Python imports:

```python
import json
import logging
import ask_sdk_core.utils as ask_utils
from ask_sdk_core.skill_builder import SkillBuilder
from ask_sdk_core.dispatch_components import AbstractRequestHandler
from ask_sdk_core.dispatch_components import AbstractExceptionHandler
from ask_sdk_core.handler_input import HandlerInput
from ask_sdk_model import Response
```

Just completely replace the snippet of code that is already there with these import statements. Then turn on logging with the following lines of code:

```python
logger = logging.getLogger(__name__)
logger.setLevel(logging.INFO)
```

Then we can look at the structure of an intent handler.

The Structure of an Intent Handler

The structure of an intent handler is as follows:

```python
class xxxIntentHandler(AbstractRequestHandler):
    """Handler for xxx Intent."""

    # Section A - The Can Handle Declaration
    def can_handle(self, handler_input):
        return ask_utils.is_intent_name("AMAZON.HelpIntent")(handler_input)
```

```
# Section B - The Handle Function
def handle(self, handler_input):
    speak_output = """Speech."""
    handler_input.attributes_manager.session_attributes["last_speech"]
    = speak_output

    #Section C - Return a Response
    return (
        handler_input.response_builder
        .speak(speak_output)
        .ask(speak_output)
        .response
    )
```

As shown previously, there are three sections, which are described as follows.

Section A – The Can Handle Declaration

Each handler declares which Intent it is to handle. For example, the handler for the built-in Help intent looks like this:

```
def can_handle(self, handler_input):
    return ask_utils.is_intent_name("AMAZON.HelpIntent")(handler_input)
```

While the handler for the custom Get Percent Done Intent looks like this:

```
def can_handle(self, handler_input):
    return ask_utils.is_intent_name("GetPercentDone")(handler_input)
```

Alexa's AI will look through all the declared intent handlers and call the one that matches the Intent the user has uttered. Once the correct handler class is identified, Alexa will invoke the Handle Function for that class.

Section B – The Handle Function

Each intent handler class declares a Handle Function that does the work of figuring out what Alexa will say to handle the user's intention. For example, the built-in Help intent handler for the 90-year calendar looks like this:

```
def handle(self, handler_input):
    speak_output = """Try saying your birthday in month, day, year
    format. For example, January first, nineteen-eighty.
    Tell me your birthday, and I'll tell you something interesting."""
    handler_input.attributes_manager.session_attributes["last_speech"]
    = speak_output
```

In this handler, there are two lines of code. The first defines the speech that Alexa will make in response to the user asking for Help. The second is a helper function that stores this response in the session attributes as the last thing Alexa said. There are some circumstances where we will want to know what Alexa said last.

After defining the speech, we return it as a Response object.

Section C – Return a Response

Once we have created the speech to output, we need to convert it into a Response object. This is done by the Response Builder, as shown here:

```
return (
    handler_input.response_builder
    .speak(speak_output)
    .ask(speak_output)
    .response
)
```

The first line calls the response_builder. The second defines the speech we created previously as the words that Alexa will say. The third defines that same speech as the question she asks the user to move on in the dialog (she won't say it twice, though). And the fourth is the created response object that is being returned.

Now that we have an intent handler structure, we can make the intent handlers that we will be using.

Building Out the Intent Handlers

When we imported the project from Botmock, we ended up with 26 intents. We will not be creating intent handlers for all of those at this time. The ones that render the basic 90-year calendar, and some of the built-in intents, we will handle now. We will build out some of the others over the following few chapters. Some we will leave as an exercise for you to complete.

We will need to put quite a bit of code into the GiveBirthday intent handler, which we need to render the calendar. So we'll leave that alone for now and focus on the built-in intents. The ones we need are

- Help

- Fallback

- Cancel

- Stop

- Repeat

- Start Over

The Help Intent

The Help intent handler for our skill starts pretty simply. As we add Calendar Events to the skill in later chapters, the Help intent handler should become more helpful by responding in a context-specific way. For now, we'll limit the Help response to the birthdate prompt. First, we apply the template previously shown. Then we change the class and Intent name. Then we define the speech response. Here's the code:

```
class HelpIntentHandler(AbstractRequestHandler):
    """Handler for Help Intent."""

    def can_handle(self, handler_input):
        return ask_utils.is_intent_name("AMAZON.HelpIntent")(handler_input)

    def handle(self, handler_input):
        speak_output = """Try saying your birthday in month, day, year
        format. For example, January first, nineteen-eighty.
        Tell me your birthday and I'll tell you something interesting."""
        handler_input.attributes_manager.session_attributes["last_speech"]
        = speak_output

        return (
            handler_input.response_builder
            .speak(speak_output)
```

```
        .ask(speak_output)
        .response
)
```

The Fallback Intent

If the user makes an utterance that doesn't resolve to any of the other intent handlers, then Alexa will call the Fallback Intent Handler if there is one defined. You should always define one. Like the previous Help intent, there could be more elaborate versions of this intent handler, but we'll keep it simple in this first pass. Here's the code:

```
class FallbackIntentHandler(AbstractRequestHandler):
    """Handler for Fallback Intent."""

    def can_handle(self, handler_input):
        return ask_utils.is_intent_name("AMAZON.FallbackIntent")
        (handler_input)

    def handle(self, handler_input):
        speak_output = """The ninety-year calendar can't help with that,
        but I can help you learn something interesting about your life.
        Tell me your birthday and I'll tell you something interesting."""
        handler_input.attributes_manager.session_attributes["last_speech"]
        = speak_output

        return (
            handler_input.response_builder
            .speak(speak_output)
            .ask(speak_output)
            .response
)
```

The Cancel and Stop Intents

There may be some difference between the Cancel and Stop intents when our skill gets more advanced, but for now, they serve the same purpose, which is to end the skill. Here, we combine the handlers by OR'ing the conditionals. Here's the code:

```
class CancelOrStopIntentHandler(AbstractRequestHandler):
    """Single handler for Cancel and Stop Intent."""

    def can_handle(self, handler_input):
        return (ask_utils.is_intent_name("AMAZON.CancelIntent")
        (handler_input) or
                ask_utils.is_intent_name("AMAZON.StopIntent")
                (handler_input))

    def handle(self, handler_input):
        speak_output = "Goodbye!"

        return (
            handler_input.response_builder
            .speak(speak_output)
            .response
        )
```

The last_speech session attribute is irrelevant because we're ending the skill here.

The Repeat Intent

When the user doesn't hear or mishears Alexa, they may ask her to repeat what was said. This is why we've been collecting the last_speech session attribute in the other handlers. In this intent handler, we will say the same thing that we last said or prompt the user if last_speech has not been set yet. Here's the code:

```
class RepeatIntentHandler(AbstractRequestHandler):
    """Handler for Repeat Intent."""

    def can_handle(self, handler_input):
        return ask_utils.is_intent_name("AMAZON.RepeatIntent")
        (handler_input)

    def handle(self, handler_input):
        if "last_speech" in handler_input.attributes_manager.session_
        attributes:
            speak_output = handler_input.attributes_manager.session_
            attributes["last_speech"]
```

```
    else:
        speak_output = """Tell me your birthday and I'll tell you
        something interesting."""
        handler_input.attributes_manager.session_attributes["last_
        speech"] = speak_output

    return (
        handler_input.response_builder
        .speak(speak_output)
        .ask(speak_output)
        .response
    )
```

The Start Over Intent

```
class StartOverIntentHandler(AbstractRequestHandler):
    """Handler for Start Over Intent."""

    def can_handle(self, handler_input):
        return ask_utils.is_request_type("AMAZON.StartOverIntent")
        (handler_input)

    def handle(self, handler_input):
        speak_output = "Welcome, tell me your birthday and I'll tell you
        something interesting."
        handler_input.attributes_manager.session_attributes["last_speech"]
        = speak_output

        return (
            handler_input.response_builder
            .speak(speak_output)
            .ask(speak_output)
            .response
        )
```

Great! We've defined the necessary intent handlers for the basic calendar. In addition to these, we need some system defined handlers:

- Launch Request handler

- Session Ended Request handler

- Intent Reflector handler for debugging

- Catch-All Exception handler in case anything goes wrong

The Launch Request Handler

When the skill launches, Alexa calls the Launch Request handler. This will return the initial prompt that starts our skill. In our case, we need to ask for the user's birthday. Here's the code:

```python
class LaunchRequestHandler(AbstractRequestHandler):
    """Handler for Skill Launch."""

    def can_handle(self, handler_input):
        return ask_utils.is_request_type("LaunchRequest")(handler_input)

    def handle(self, handler_input):
        speak_output = "Welcome, tell me your birthday, and I'll tell you
        something interesting."
        handler_input.attributes_manager.session_attributes["last_speech"]
        = speak_output

        return (
            handler_input.response_builder
            .speak(speak_output)
            .ask(speak_output)
            .response
        )
```

The Session Ended Request Handler

When the user stops or cancels the session or the code exits the session, the Session Ended Request handler is called. It is responsible for any cleanup logic, such as closing open database connections. We don't have any cleanup logic yet. We'll stub out the Session Ended Request handler for now. Here's the code:

```python
class SessionEndedRequestHandler(AbstractRequestHandler):
    """Handler for Session End."""

    def can_handle(self, handler_input):
        return ask_utils.is_request_type("SessionEndedRequest")
        (handler_input)

    def handle(self, handler_input):
        # Any cleanup logic goes here.
        return handler_input.response_builder.response
```

The Intent Reflector Handler

When testing, you may want to know which intents are firing. The Intent Reflector handler is specified to do this. Simply 'OR' in the intents you want to announce in the can_handle logic, as we did with the Cancel and Stop intents. Here's the code:

```python
class IntentReflectorHandler(AbstractRequestHandler):
    """The intent reflector is used for interaction model testing and
    debugging.
    It will simply repeat the intent the user said. You can create custom
    handlers
    for your intents by defining them above, then also adding them to the
    request
    handler chain below.
    """

    def can_handle(self, handler_input):
        return ask_utils.is_request_type("IntentRequest")(handler_input)

    def handle(self, handler_input):
        intent_name = ask_utils.get_intent_name(handler_input)
        speak_output = "You just triggered " + intent_name + "."
```

```
    return (
        handler_input.response_builder
        .speak(speak_output)
        # .ask("add a reprompt if you want to keep the session open for
        the user to respond")
        .response
    )
```

To reflect (announce) the Help intent, you would add it to the can_handle by OR'ing it in, like this:

```
def can_handle(self, handler_input):
    return (ask_utils.is_request_type("IntentRequest")(handler_input) or
            ask_utils.is_intent_name("AMAZON.HelpIntent")(handler_
            input))
```

To add another intent, chain them together with OR's.

The Catch-All Exception Handler

If anything goes wrong, Alexa will just stop and say, "Sorry, I don't know that." To avoid this and say something more helpful, we need a Catch-All Exception handler. Notice the addition of logger.error() to log the exception. Depending on the exception being handled, you can have Alexa say different things. In our example, we'll just elaborate on the default message. Here's the code:

```
class CatchAllExceptionHandler(AbstractExceptionHandler):
    """Generic error handling to capture any syntax or routing errors. If
    you receive an error
    stating the request handler chain is not found, you have not
    implemented a handler for
    the intent being invoked or included it in the skill builder below.
    """

    def can_handle(self, handler_input, exception):
        return True
```

```
def handle(self, handler_input, exception):
    logger.error(exception, exc_info=True)

    speak_output = "Sorry, I had trouble doing what you asked. Please
    try again."
    handler_input.attributes_manager.session_attributes["last_speech"]
    = speak_output

    return (
        handler_input.response_builder
        .speak(speak_output)
        .ask(speak_output)
        .response
    )
```

And that's it. Those are the built-in intent handlers that we need. In the next few sections, we will add the GiveBirthday intent handler and flesh it out.

The GiveBirthday Intent Handler

First, we'll stub out the GiveBirthday intent handler:

```
class GiveBirthdayIntentHandler(AbstractRequestHandler):
    """Handler for GiveBirthday Intent."""

    def can_handle(self, handler_input):
        return ask_utils.is_intent_name("GiveBirthday")(handler_input)

    def handle(self, handler_input):
        speak_output = """Speech."""
        handler_input.attributes_manager.session_attributes["last_speech"]
        = speak_output

        return (
            handler_input.response_builder
            .speak(speak_output)
            .ask(speak_output)
            .response
        )
```

Remember, in the Launch Request handler, we prompt the user, "Welcome, tell me your birthday, and I'll tell you something interesting". The GiveBirthday intent handler accepts the user's birthdate and returns the "something interesting," which is the amount of their 90-year lifetime that has elapsed. In the next section, we calculate that amount.

Calculate 90-Year Calendar Values

To start with, we'll be working with dates, so we need a few more imports. Add these at the top of the module:

```
from datetime import datetime, timedelta
import calendar
import regex as re
```

And then, add the following utility functions at the bottom of the module. These will come in handy when doing date manipulations:

```
def addYears(d, years):
    try:
        # Return same day of the current year
        return d.replace(year=d.year + years)
    except ValueError:
        # If not same day, it will return some other date, i.e., February
        29 to March 1, etc.
        return d + (datetime.date(d.year + years, 1, 1) - datetime.date(d.
        year, 1, 1))

def days_between(d1, d2):
    return abs((d2 - d1).days)

def period_from_amazon_date[ii](iso):
    logger.info("Converting AMAZON.DATE: {}".format(iso))
```

[ii] period_from_amazon_date function was posted by Andre Ploszaj on the Amazon Developer Forums, June 6, 2020. https://forums.developer.amazon.com/questions/227584/python-get-start-and-end-dates-from-amazondate-202.html

```python
def no_future(date):
    dnow = datetime.now()
    today = datetime(dnow.year, dnow.month, dnow.day)
    if date > today:
        return datetime(date.year-1, date.month, date.day)
    else:
        return date

def week_to_start_date(week_wanted):
    now = datetime.now()
    year, week, day = now.isocalendar()
    this_week_start = datetime(
        now.year, now.month, now.day) - timedelta(days=day)
    wanted_week_start = this_week_start - \
        timedelta(days=(week - week_wanted) * 7)
    return wanted_week_start

period = None
start = None
end = None
wutterance = None
if re.match("\\d{4}-\\d{2}-\\d{2}", iso):
    # single day
    start = datetime.fromisoformat(iso)
    end = datetime(start.year, start.month, start.day) + timedelta(days=1)
    period = "day"
    utterance = "{} of {}".format(
        start.day, calendar.month_name[start.month])

elif re.match("\\d{4}-W\\d{2}", iso) or re.match("\\d{4}-W\\d{2}-XX", iso):
    # week
    # start = datetime.fromisocalendar(int(iso[0:4]), int(iso[6:8]), 1)
    # ^python 3.7 doesn't have fromisocalendar
    start = week_to_start_date(int(iso[6:8]))
    end = datetime(start.year, start.month, start.day) +
    timedelta(days=7)
```

```
        period = "week"
        utterance = "the week number {} of {}".format(iso[6:8], start.year)

    elif re.match("\\d{4}-\\d{2}", iso) or re.match("\\d{4}-\\d{2}-XX", iso):
        # month
        start = datetime(int(iso[0:4]), int(iso[5:7]), 1)
        start = no_future(start)
        end = datetime(start.year, start.month+1, start.day)
        period = "month"
        utterance = "{}".format(calendar.month_name[start.month])

    elif re.match("\\d{4}", iso) or re.match("\\d{4}-XX-XX", iso) or
    re.match("\\d{4}-XX", iso):
        # year
        start = datetime(int(iso[0:4]), 1, 1)
        start = no_future(start)
        end = datetime(start.year+1, start.month, start.day)
        period = "year"
        utterance = "{}".format(start.year)

    if not start:
        logger.error("Failed to get date.")
        return None

    logger.info("{} - {} - {} - {}".format(period, start, end, utterance))

    now = datetime.now()
    if start > now:
        logger.info("Future")
        return None
    if end > now:
        end = datetime(now.year, now.month, now.day)

    return start, end, period, utterance
```

Now, we're ready to do the date manipulation to find the boundaries of our 90-year calendar. Specifically, we need to know the following:

Variable	Meaning	Calculation
bday	Birthday	In the Intent Slot
today	Today	datetime.today()
dday	End of 90-year lifespan	bday + 90 years
lived	Days lived	days_between(bday, today)
weeksLived	Weeks lived	lived / 7
life	Days in 90-year lifespan	days_between(bday, dday)
weeksLife	Weeks in life	life / 7
remain	Days remaining in life	days_between(today, dday)
weeksRemain	Weeks remaining	remain / 7
livedPercent	Percentage of life lived	lived / life
yearsLived	Years lived	weeksLived / 52
weeksInYear	Weeks elapsed in current year	weeksLived modulus 52

The code for this is placed in the GiveBirthdayIntentHandler in the handle function, like this:

```
def handle(self, handler_input):
    bday_str = handler_input.request_envelope.request.intent.
    slots["birthday"].value
    logger.info(f"Birthday: {bday_str}")
    bday, _, _, _ = period_from_amazon_date(bday_str)
    today = datetime.today()
    dday = addYears(bday, 90)
    lived = days_between(bday, today)
    weeksLived = round(lived / 7.0, 1)
    life = days_between(bday, dday)
    weeksLife = round(life / 7.0, 1)
    remain = days_between(today, dday)
    weeksRemain = round(remain / 7.0, 1)
```

```
livedPercent = round(lived / life * 100.0, 1)
yearsLived = int(weeksLived / 52)
weeksInYear = int(weeksLived % 52)
```

With all the dates sorted out, we can make a statement about the user's 90-year calendar. For example:

```
speak_output = f"""Your birthday is: {bday}.
    If you live to be 90 years old, you have already
    lived {livedPercent} percent of your life.
    Which is to say, of the {weeksLife} weeks you have in
    your 90-year lifespan, you have already lived for
    {weeksLived} weeks and have {weeksRemain} weeks
    remaining."""
logger.info(f"Speech: {speak_output}")
handler_input.attributes_manager.session_attributes["last_speech"]
= speak_output
```

At this point, we are ready to build the data source for the APL template.

Define the Dataset for the 90-Year Calendar

Knowing all the week and year values from the previous section, we can readily build the 90-year calendar APL dataset. Based on the work we did in Chapter 10, the dataset has three zones. Zone 1 has an @C1 for each year already lived. Zone 3 has an @C0 for each year yet to be lived. And Zone 2 has a @C1 for each week before today and an @C0 for each week after. The code to generate these data might look like this:

```
zone1 = []
for z1 in range(0, yearsLived):
    zone1.append("@C1")

zone2 = []
for z2 in range(0, 52):
    if z2 <= weeksInYear:
        zone2.append("@C1")
```

```
        else:
            zone2.append("@C0")

    zone3 = []
    for z3 in range(yearsLived + 1, 90):
        zone3.append("@C0")
```

With these zones defined, we can scale the zones and boxes to fit the Alexa screen, if there is one.

Scale the Visuals to the Current Screen

Now, we need to determine the final size of the zones and boxes so they fit the current Alexa device's screen, known as the viewport. If the Alexa device has a screen, we can get the viewport state and determine the final box height and width. From these values, we can determine the final row width and zone heights. The code to do this wraps the previous zone code, as there is no point in building the zones if there is no screen. The final code to build the scaled dataset is as follows:

```
if ask_utils.get_supported_interfaces(handler_input) \
        .alexa_presentation_apl is not None:
    logger.info("APL is Enabled")

    viewportWidth = 0
    viewportHeight = 0
    viewport_state = handler_input.request_envelope.context.viewport
    if viewport_state:
        viewportWidth = int(viewport_state.current_pixel_width)
        viewportHeight = int(viewport_state.current_pixel_height)

    boxHeight = int(viewportHeight / 90)
    boxWidth = int(viewportWidth / 52)

    zone1 = []
    for z1 in range(0, yearsLived):
        zone1.append("@C1")
```

```python
    zone2 = []
    for z2 in range(0, 52):
        if z2 <= weeksInYear:
            zone2.append("@C1")
        else:
            zone2.append("@C0")

    zone3 = []
    for z3 in range(yearsLived + 1, 90):
        zone3.append("@C0")

    dataset = {
        "data": {
            "type": "object",
            "properties": {
                    "zone1": zone1,
                    "zone2": zone2,
                    "zone3": zone3,
                    "zone1Height": boxHeight * yearsLived,
                    "zone2Height": boxHeight,
                    "zone3Height": boxHeight * (90 - yearsLived - 1),
                    "totalWidth": 32 * 52,
                    "totalHeight": 32 * 90,
                    "boxHeight": boxHeight,
                    "boxWidth": boxWidth,
                    "rowWidth": boxWidth * 52
            }
        }
    }
    logger.info(f"Data: {dataset}")
```

Now that we've created the final dataset, we need to wrap it in a Response Builder and return a Response object.

Return the Rendered APL and Response

In our standard intent handler, the Response object is created by this line of code:

```
return (
    handler_input.response_builder
    .speak(speak_output)
    .ask(speak_output)
    .response
)
```

We can split this up and move the `response_builder` to its own line, as follows:

```
rb = handler_input.response_builder

...

return (
    rb
    .speak(speak_output)
    .ask(speak_output)
    .response
)
```

This allows us to add the RenderApl directive to the Response Builder, if there is a screen. So before the `if ask_utils.get_supported_interfaces(handler_input)` we need to place the `rb = handler_input.response_builder`. Then after the `logger.info(f"Data: {dataset}")`line, we need to add the following:

```
 rb.add_directive(
    RenderApl(
        token = CALENDAR_TOKEN,
        document = load_apl_document(calendarPath),
        datasources = dataset
    )
)
```

This directive needs a couple of lines to be inserted at the top of the module after the imports.

```
calendarPath = "90-year week calendar APL.json"
CALENDAR_TOKEN = "CalendarToken"
```

It needs a new import:

```
from ask_sdk_model.interfaces.alexa.presentation.apl import
RenderDocumentDirective as RenderApl
```

And it needs this utility function:

```
def load_apl_document(file_path):
    """Load the apl json document at the path into a dict object."""
    c = os.getcwd()
    logger.info(f"CWD: {c}")
    with open(file_path) as f:
        return json.load(f)
```

Finally, we need to return the response object from the response builder, like this:

```
return (
    rb
    .speak(speak_output)
    #.ask("Would you like to personalize your calendar?")
    .set_should_end_session(True)
    .response
)
```

Notice that for now, we are setting the set_should_end_session to True instead of asking the user if they want to personalize their calendar. In a later chapter, we will switch these.

The finished GiveBirthday Intent Handler will look like this:

```
class GiveBirthdayIntentHandler(AbstractRequestHandler):
    """Handler for GiveBirthday Intent."""

    def can_handle(self, handler_input):
        return ask_utils.is_intent_name("GiveBirthday")(handler_input)
```

```python
def handle(self, handler_input):
    bday_str = handler_input.request_envelope.request.intent.
    slots["birthday"].value
    logger.info(f"Birthday: {bday_str}")
    bday, _, _, _ = period_from_amazon_date(bday_str)
    today = datetime.today()
    dday = addYears(bday, 90)
    lived = days_between(bday, today)
    weeksLived = round(lived / 7.0, 1)
    life = days_between(bday, dday)
    weeksLife = round(life / 7.0, 1)
    remain = days_between(today, dday)
    weeksRemain = round(remain / 7.0, 1)
    livedPercent = round(lived / life * 100.0, 1)
    yearsLived = int(weeksLived / 52)
    weeksInYear = int(weeksLived % 52)

    speak_output = f"""Your birthday is: {bday}. If you live to be 90
years old,
        you have already lived {livedPercent} percent of your life.
        Which is to say, of the {weeksLife} weeks you have in your 90
        year lifespan, you have already lived for {weeksLived} weeks
        and have {weeksRemain} weeks remaining."""
    logger.info(f"Speech: {speak_output}")
    handler_input.attributes_manager.session_attributes["last_speech"]
    = speak_output

    rb = handler_input.response_builder

    if ask_utils.get_supported_interfaces(handler_input) \
            .alexa_presentation_apl is not None:
        logger.info("APL is Enabled")

        viewportWidth = 0
        viewportHeight = 0
        viewport_state = handler_input.request_envelope.context.
        viewport
```

```
if viewport_state:
    viewportWidth = int(viewport_state.current_pixel_width)
    viewportHeight = int(viewport_state.current_pixel_height)

boxHeight = int(viewportHeight / 90)
boxWidth = int(viewportWidth / 52)

zone1 = []
for z1 in range(0, yearsLived):
    zone1.append("@C1")

zone2 = []
for z2 in range(0, 52):
    if z2 <= weeksInYear:
        zone2.append("@C1")
    else:
        zone2.append("@C0")

zone3 = []
for z3 in range(yearsLived + 1, 90):
    zone3.append("@C0")

dataset = {
    "data": {
        "type": "object",
        "properties": {
                "zone1": zone1,
                "zone2": zone2,
                "zone3": zone3,
                "zone1Height": boxHeight * yearsLived,
                "zone2Height": boxHeight,
                "zone3Height": boxHeight * (90 - yearsLived - 1),
                "totalWidth": 32 * 52,
                "totalHeight": 32 * 90,
                "boxHeight": boxHeight,
                "boxWidth": boxWidth,
                "rowWidth": boxWidth * 52
        }
```

```
            }
        }
        logger.info(f"Data: {dataset}")

        rb.add_directive(
            RenderApl(
                token = CALENDAR_TOKEN,
                document = load_apl_document(calendarPath),
                datasources = dataset
            )
        )
    return (
        rb
        .speak(speak_output)
        #.ask("Would you like to personalize your calendar?")
        .set_should_end_session(True)
        .response
    )
```

There is one last activity required to finish the lambda function. We need to define
the Skill Builder object.

Defining the Skill Builder

Now that we've defined the imports, utility functions, constants, and intent handler classes,
we have one more required piece of code to write. We need to define the Skill Builder. The
Skill Builder is the entry point for your skill and manages routing intents and requests to the
correct handler(s). Each intent/request handler is added to the Skill Builder, ending with
the Intent Reflector and Catch-All Exception handlers. The finished Skill Builder is then
bound to the AWS Lambda Handler. The code for the Skill Builder looks like this:

```
# The SkillBuilder object acts as the entry point for your skill, routing
all request and response
# payloads to the handlers above. Make sure any new handlers or
interceptors you've
# defined are included below. The order matters - they're processed top to
bottom.
```

```
sb = SkillBuilder()
sb.add_request_handler(LaunchRequestHandler())
sb.add_request_handler(GiveBirthdayIntentHandler())
sb.add_request_handler(StartOverIntentHandler())
sb.add_request_handler(HelpIntentHandler())
sb.add_request_handler(CancelOrStopIntentHandler())
sb.add_request_handler(SessionEndedRequestHandler())
sb.add_request_handler(RepeatIntentHandler())
sb.add_request_handler(FallbackIntentHandler())
# make sure the IntentReflectorHandler and CatchAllExceptionHandler
# are last so they don't override your custom intent handlers
sb.add_request_handler(IntentReflectorHandler())
sb.add_exception_handler(CatchAllExceptionHandler())

lambda_handler = sb.lambda_handler()
```

And that, my friends, is a lot of code. For the completed module, see the attached code for this chapter.

Summary

In this chapter, we wrote the code to bind the VUI intents and APL visuals to the data we use to represent the weeks of the years in a 90-year calendar. We defined the lambda function in AWS, and we added the intent handlers and skill builder to make the Alexa skill work. We are ready to do some Unit Testing to validate our code and make sure it is working correctly. In the next chapter, we will be manually and programmatically testing our Alexa skill.

## CHAPTER 12

Unit Testing an Alexa Skill

In the previous chapter, we wrote the lambda function code that serves as our skill's back end. In this chapter, we will learn some ways to unit test that code to ensure that it works as expected.

For a small skill, the primary method for Unit Testing will likely be manual testing. As your skill grows, though, you will want to automate some of the testing. There are several stages of manual testing. First, make sure the lambda function compiles and works. Second, make sure the user utterances resolve to the correct intents. Third, make sure your skill works as you interact with it.

Unit Testing the Lambda Function

Something we should probably have been doing while we created our lambda function was unit testing it as we developed it. This technique is called Test-Driven Development (TDD). TDD is about creating unit tests as you create code. Like too many programmers, we've saved testing to last. But all is not lost. With lambda functions, we can still add unit tests to our code.

Unit Testing the Launch Intent

First, you need to locate the Test button in the Lambda console.

1. Launch the AWS Console (`https://console.aws.amazon.com`) and log in as your admin account (not your root user).

2. Select the *Lambda* service.

3. Select your **CalendarLambda**

4. Above the code window, click the *Deploy* button if it is enabled.

5. There are two *Test* buttons, as shown in Figure 12-1.

© Simon A. Kingaby 2022
S. A. Kingaby, *Data-Driven Alexa Skills*, https://doi.org/10.1007/978-1-4842-7449-1_12

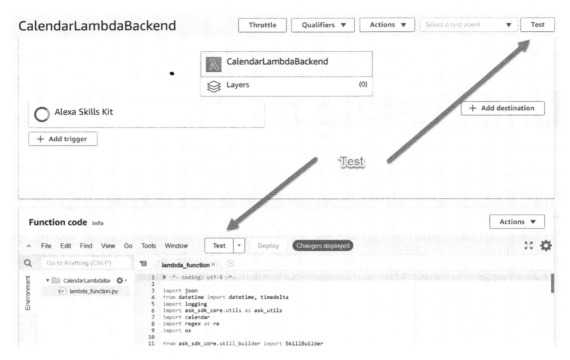

Figure 12-1. *Locating the Test buttons*

Clicking either of the *Test* buttons will open the *Configure Test Event* dialog. This is where you create the unit tests, as follows:

6. Make sure the *Create new test event* button is selected at the top of the Configure Test Event dialog.

7. In the *Event template* drop-down, scroll down until you find the Alexa templates, and then pick **Amazon Alexa Start Session**.

8. Give your unit test event a name, such as **LaunchCalendar**. See Figure 12-2.

Configure test event   ✕

A function can have up to 10 test events. The events are persisted so you can switch to another computer or web browser and test your function with the same events.

◉ Create new test event
◉ Edit saved test events

Event template

alexa-skills-kit-start-session	▼

Event name

LaunchCalendar

```json
 1 ▾ {
 2     "version": "1.0",
 3 ▾   "session": {
 4       "new": true,
 5       "sessionId": "amzn1.echo-api.session.123456789012",
 6 ▾     "application": {
 7         "applicationId": "amzn1.ask.skill.987654321"
 8       },
 9 ▾     "user": {
10         "userId": "amzn1.ask.account.testUser"
11       },
12       "attributes": {}
13     },
14 ▾   "context": {
15 ▾     "AudioPlayer": {
16         "playerActivity": "IDLE"
17       },
18 ▾     "System": {
19 ▾       "application": {
20           "applicationId": "amzn1.ask.skill.987654321"
21         },
22 ▾       "user": {
23           "userId": "amzn1.ask.account.testUser"
24         },
25 ▾       "device": {
26 ▾         "supportedInterfaces": {
27             "AudioPlayer": {}
28           }
29         }
30       }
31     },
```

Cancel   Format JSON   Create

Figure 12-2. *The completed LaunchCalendar test event*

9.   Click *Create*.

You now have a Unit Test for the Launch Intent.

10.   Click the *Test* button again to run the test.

You will get an error message telling you we are missing a library. See Figure 12-3.

```
▼ Execution results                                          Status: Failed   Max memory used: 52 MB   Time: 1.59 ms
Response
{
  "errorMessage": "Unable to import module 'lambda_function': No module named 'ask_sdk_core'",
  "errorType": "Runtime.ImportModuleError"
}

Function Logs
START RequestId: 32cd655a-c199-424f-8bb6-661f0c189856 Version: $LATEST
[ERROR] Runtime.ImportModuleError: Unable to import module 'lambda_function': No module named 'ask_sdk_core'END RequestId: 32cd655a-c
REPORT RequestId: 32cd655a-c199-424f-8bb6-661f0c189856  Duration: 1.59 ms   Billed Duration: 2 ms   Memory Size: 128 MB Max Memory Us
```

Figure 12-3. *The first of many errors we will see when running Unit Tests*

To fix this error (No Module named 'ask_sdk_core'), we need to configure the lambda function with the Python libraries we need. This is best done by adding a layer and uploading a zip file of the libraries to the layer. First, to create the zip file, follow these steps:

1. Create a folder on your local machine.

2. Pip install the packages we need into that folder.

3. Zip the folder up.

4. Upload it to a new layer in the lambda function.

You can execute these steps at a command line with the following code:

```
md package\python\lib\python3.8\site-packages
cd package\python\lib\python3.8\site-packages
pip install --target . datetime
pip install --target . ask_sdk_core
```

Notice the pip install lines. Those work fine for most modules, but some modules, like regex, are distributed as binary files, and you can't just pip install them. Instead, you need to follow these steps:

5. Open a browser to https://pypi.org/project/regex.

6. Click the Download Files link.

7. Locate the correct file. Ours is the Python **3.8** file, with the phrase manylinux1_x86_64 in the name. So the full name of the file is

    regex-2021.08.21-cp38-cp38-manylinux1_x86_64.whl

8. Once downloaded, unzip the file and copy the two unzipped
    folders from your download to the `package\python\lib\`
    `python3.8\site-packages` folder.

Back at the command line, you can run the following:

```
zip -r .\deployment-package.zip .\package
```

Note   You may not have a zip utility on your path, so you may need to modify the last line accordingly. For example, I use 7-Zip, which is installed on my E: drive, so my command line needed to be

```
"E:\Program Files\7-Zip\7z.exe" a -r ./deployment-package.zip ./package
```

Once you have the `deployment-package.zip` sorted out, you will need to create the layer:

9. From the lambda function screen, open the left navigation bar and
    select *Layers*. See Figure 12-4.

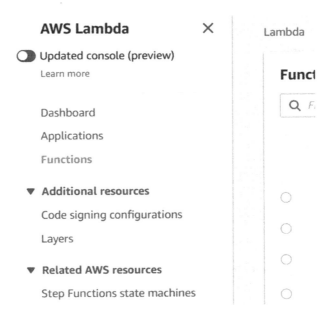

Figure 12-4. *From the left nav bar, select Layers*

10.   Now select *Create Layer*.

11.   Give the layer a name, say, **CalendarDependencies**.

12.   Select to *Upload a .zip file* and upload the `deployment-package.zip`.

13.   Select *Python 3.8* as the compatible runtime. See Figure 12-5.

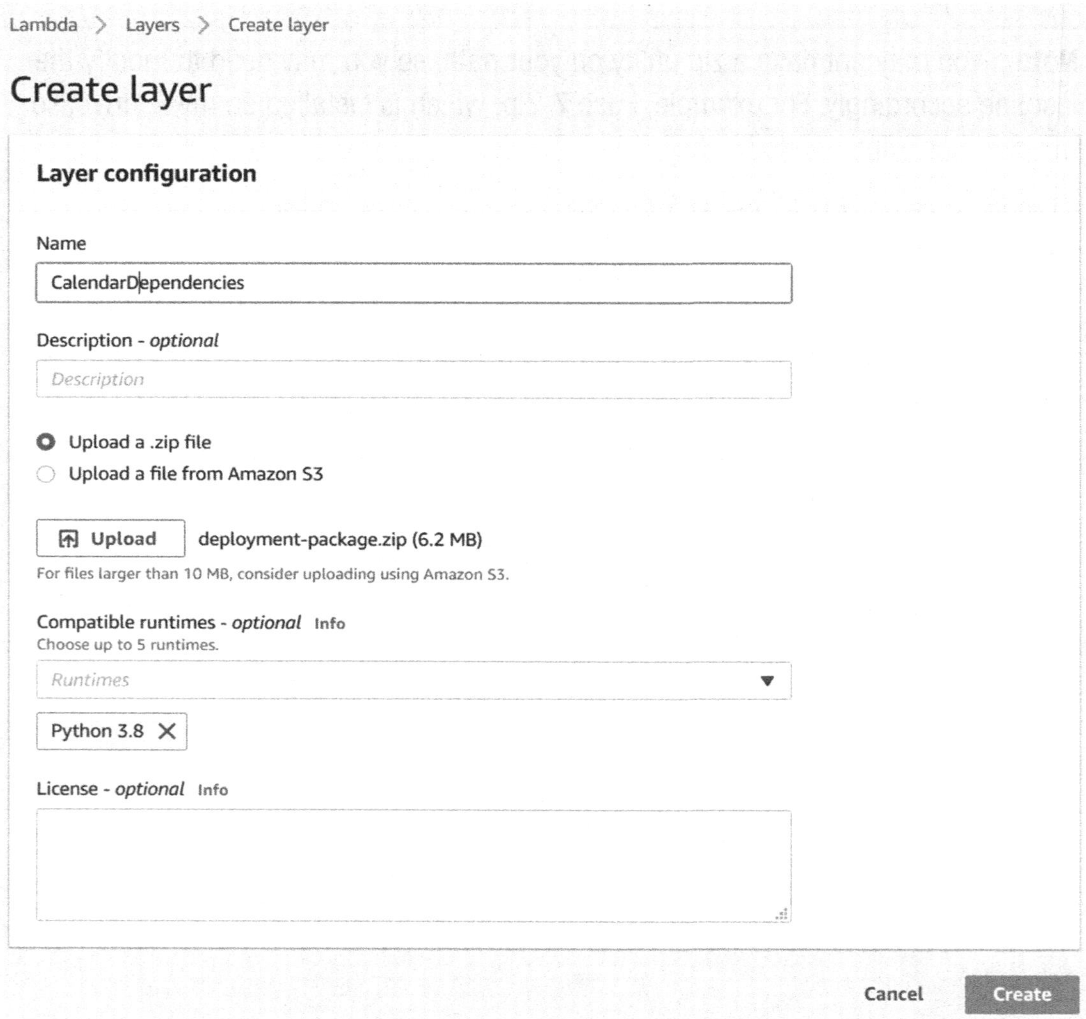

Figure 12-5. *The completed Create Layer dialog*

14.   Now select *Create* in the bottom right.

With the Layer created, we have to add it to the lambda function.

15.   Navigate back to the **CalendarLambdaBackend** function.

16.   Click on the *Layers* box in the middle of the *Designer*. (See Figure 12-6.)

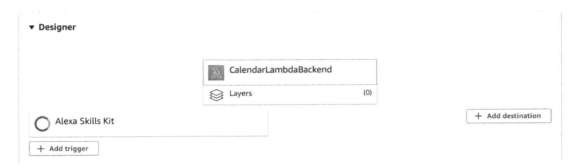

Figure 12-6. *Select the Layers box*

17.   In the *Layers* list that appears (below the *Designer*), click *Add a layer*.

18.   Then choose *Custom Layers*.

19.   Pick the **CalendarDependencies** custom layer.

20.   Pick Version **1**.

21.   Click *Add* in the bottom right.

Now click the *Test* button again. This time you should get a warm welcome from your skill. See Figure 12-7.

```
⊟        lambda_function ✕        Execution result: ✕   ⊕
  ▼ Execution results
Response
{
  "version": "1.0",
  "sessionAttributes": {
    "last_speech": "Welcome, tell me your birthday, and I'll tell you something interesting."
  },
  "userAgent": "ask-python/1.15.0 Python/3.8.6",
  "response": {
    "outputSpeech": {
      "type": "SSML",
      "ssml": "<speak>Welcome, tell me your birthday, and I'll tell you something interesting.</speak>"
    },
    "reprompt": {
      "outputSpeech": {
        "type": "SSML",
        "ssml": "<speak>Welcome, tell me your birthday, and I'll tell you something interesting.</speak>"
      }
    },
    "shouldEndSession": false
  }
}
```

Figure 12-7. *The Welcome message from the Launch Intent*

Now we can create Unit Tests for the other intents, starting with the Give Birthday intent.

Unit Testing the Give Birthday Intent

With the Launch Intent successfully tested, we test the secondary intents, such as the Give Birthday intent. The first step in doing this is opening the skill in the Alexa Developer Console. Once there, click on the Test tab and change the **Off** drop-down to **Development**. You can now use the Alexa Simulator.

Testing in the Alexa Simulator

Click or type your launch phrase (90 kilo) into the simulator. (See Figure 12-8.)

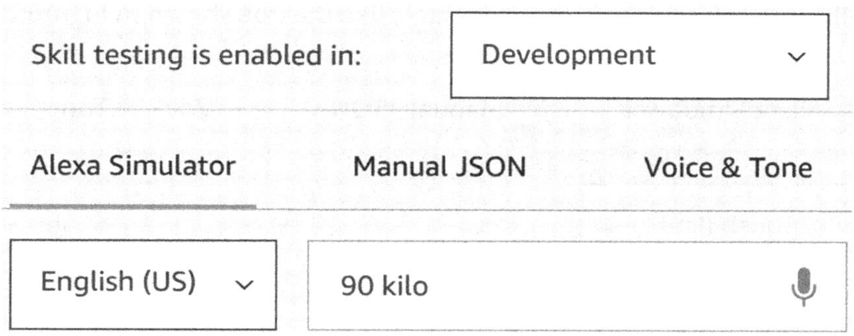

Skill testing is enabled in:
Development
Alexa Simulator
Manual JSON
Voice & Tone
English (US)
90 kilo

Figure 12-8. *Type your launch phrase into the simulator*

When you press enter, Alexa will respond. If Alexa immediately says, "There was a problem with the requested skill's response," you probably have a compile error in the lambda function. (See Figure 12-9.)

Skill testing is enabled in:
Development
Alexa Simulator
Manual JSON
Voice & Tone
English (US)
Type or click and hold the mic
ninety kilo
There was a problem with the requested skill's response

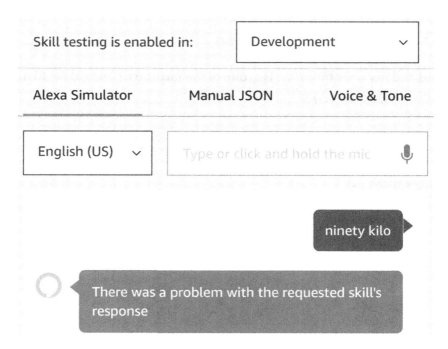

Figure 12-9. *This indicates a problem with the lambda function*

Hopefully, you will see a welcome message, like the one shown in Figure 12-10.

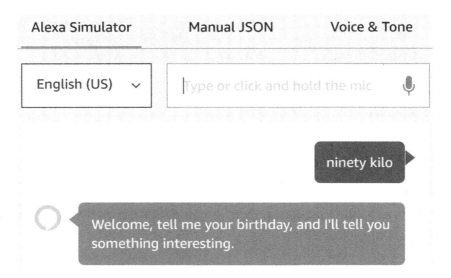

Figure 12-10. *The Launch Intent in action*

Go ahead, tell her your birthday. Use one of the forms we planned for in the utterances. (See Figure 12-11.)

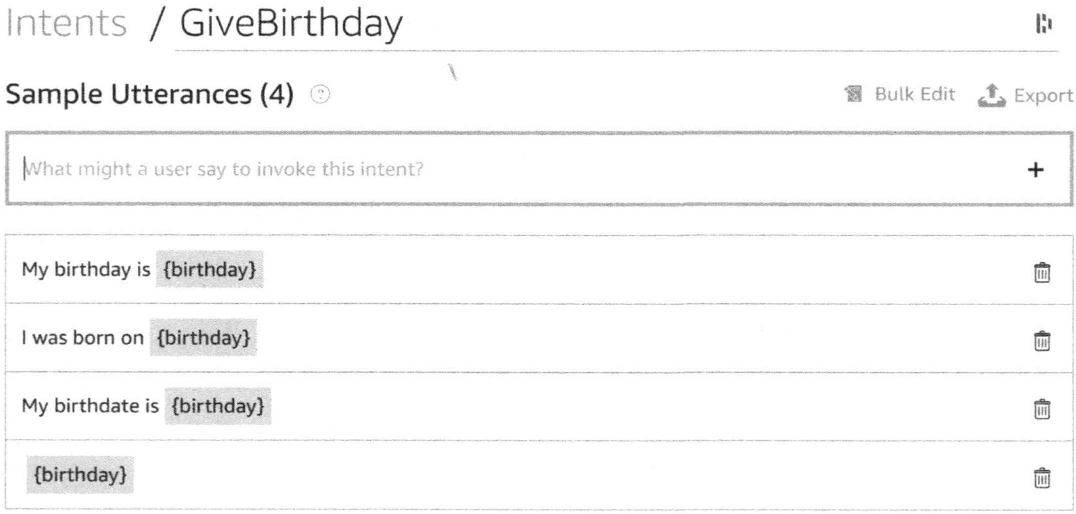

Intents / GiveBirthday

Sample Utterances (4) ☺   🗟 Bulk Edit   ⬆ Export

What might a user say to invoke this intent?   +

| My birthday is {birthday}   🗑 |
| I was born on {birthday}   🗑 |
| My birthdate is {birthday}   🗑 |
| {birthday}   🗑 |

Figure 12-11. *The Give Birthday intent's utterances*

We can test the intent with this phrase:

```
I was born on Jan 1, 1975
```

See Figure 12-12.

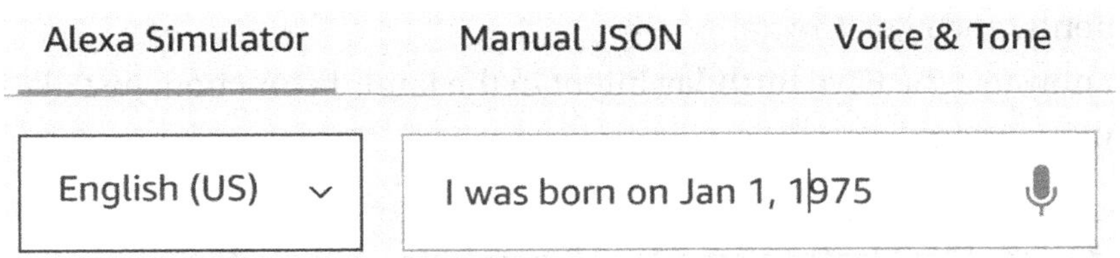

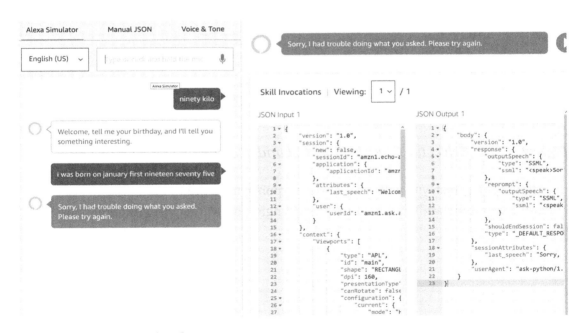

Figure 12-12. *Entering your birthday in an Alexa-friendly way*

Alexa will probably say, "Sorry, I had trouble doing what you asked." (See Figure 12-13.)

Figure 12-13. *Uh-oh. There was an error*

Notice all that Json on the right-hand side? The first panel is the Input that resulted from us telling Alexa our birthday. The second panel is the Json Output from our CatchAllExceptionHandler in the lambda function. The Json for the Input is precisely what we need for Unit Testing the Give Birthday intent. The other thing to note is that because the CatchAllExceptionHandler handled the exception, the actual error was logged for us.

First, let's copy the Json from the Input box and paste it into a text editor. (Notepad++ or VS Code will do.) Second, switch over to AWS, to the lambda function, and pull down the *Test* drop-down. Select *Configure test event*. Then select to *Create new test event*. Third, give the new test event a name, such as **GiveBirthday01011975**. (It can only be letters and numbers.) Finally, paste the Json code from the first step in place of the current contents, and click *Create*.

You can now test the Give Birthday intent in the lambda function, just like we did with the Launch Intent.

Testing Give Birthday in the Lambda Function

Back in the lambda function, test the Give Birthday intent by ensuring it is the currently selected test and clicking the Test button. See Figure 12-14.

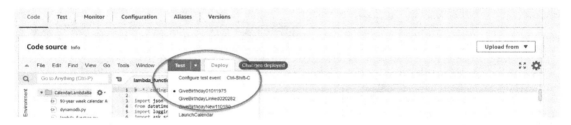

Figure 12-14. *Select the GiveBirthday test and click Test*

After clicking Test, you will see the Json response from the CatchAllExceptionHandler. But, more interestingly, you will see the Function Logs. See Figure 12-15.

```
🗐      lambda_function ×     Execution result ×    ⊕
▼ Execution results
              type   JSON ,
          "ssml": "<speak>Sorry, I had trouble doing what you asked. Please try again.</speak>"
        }
      },
      "shouldEndSession": false
    }
}

Function Logs
START RequestId: 1daf0bc4-3300-4588-9c4e-4f3edc598211 Version: $LATEST
[INFO] 2021-02-13T20:40:54.785Z    1daf0bc4-3300-4588-9c4e-4f3edc598211    Birthday: 1975-01-01
[INFO] 2021-02-13T20:40:54.785Z    1daf0bc4-3300-4588-9c4e-4f3edc598211    Converting AMAZON.DATE: 1975-01-01
[INFO] 2021-02-13T20:40:54.824Z    1daf0bc4-3300-4588-9c4e-4f3edc598211    day - 1975-01-01 00:00:00 - 1975-01-02 00:00:00 - 1 of January
[INFO] 2021-02-13T20:40:54.824Z    1daf0bc4-3300-4588-9c4e-4f3edc598211    Speech: Your birthday is: 1975-01-01. If you live to be 90 years old,
              you have already lived 51.2 percent of your life.
              Which is to say, of the 4696.1 weeks you have in your 90 year lifespan, you have already lived for 2406.4 weeks and have 2289.6 weeks remainin
[INFO] 2021-02-13T20:40:54.824Z    1daf0bc4-3300-4588-9c4e-4f3edc598211    APL is Enabled
[INFO] 2021-02-13T20:40:54.824Z    1daf0bc4-3300-4588-9c4e-4f3edc598211    Data: {'data': {'type': 'object', 'properties': {'zone1': ['@C1', '@C1', '@C1'
[INFO] 2021-02-13T20:40:54.824Z    1daf0bc4-3300-4588-9c4e-4f3edc598211    CWD: /var/task
[ERROR] 2021-02-13T20:40:54.824Z    1daf0bc4-3300-4588-9c4e-4f3edc598211    [Errno 2] No such file or directory: '90-year week calendar APL.json'
Traceback (most recent call last):
  File "/opt/python/lib/python3.8/site-packages/ask_sdk_runtime/dispatch.py", line 118, in dispatch
    output = self.__dispatch_request(handler_input)  # type: Union[Output, None]
  File "/opt/python/lib/python3.8/site-packages/ask_sdk_runtime/dispatch.py", line 182, in __dispatch_request
    output = supported_handler_adapter.execute(
  File "/opt/python/lib/python3.8/site-packages/ask_sdk_runtime/dispatch_components/request_components.py", line 437, in execute
    return handler.handle(handler_input)
  File "/var/task/lambda_function.py", line 132, in handle
    document=load_apl_document(calendarPath),
  File "/var/task/lambda_function.py", line 317, in load_apl_document
    with open(file_path) as f:
FileNotFoundError: [Errno 2] No such file or directory: '90-year week calendar APL.json'END RequestId: 1daf0bc4-3300-4588-9c4e-4f3edc598211
REPORT RequestId: 1daf0bc4-3300-4588-9c4e-4f3edc598211  Duration: 348.95 ms Billed Duration: 349 ms Memory Size: 128 MB Max Memory Used: 69 MB
```

Figure 12-15. *The Function Logs showing the error that occurred*

That error is in the line that looks like this:

[ERROR] 2021-02-13T20:40:54.824Z 1daf0bc4-3300-4588-9c4e-4f3edc598211
[Errno 2] No such file or directory: '90-year week calendar APL.json'

That error means that the lambda function can't find all that lovely APL we wrote in Chapter 10. Because we're using AWS to host our lambda function, we also need to put the APL here. To do this, follow these instructions.

Copying the APL Over to the Lambda Function

Start by switching back to the Alexa Developer Console and selecting the *Build* tab. Then click on *Multimodal Responses* on the left nav bar. Now select *Visual*. Then select *Download*. (See Figure 12-16.)

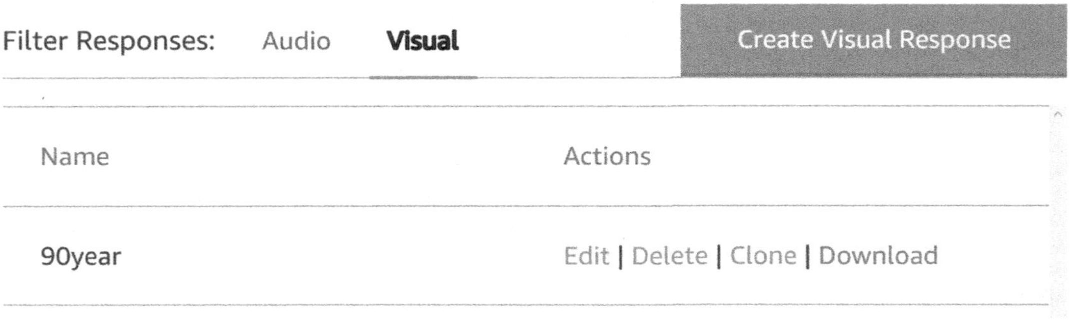

Filter Responses:	Audio	**Visual**	Create Visual Response

Name	Actions
90year	Edit | Delete | Clone | Download

Figure 12-16. *Download the 90year.json file*

With the Json file downloaded, locate it in your *Downloads* folder and open the file with VS Code.

Next, switch back to the lambda function and follow these steps.

1. In the *Function code* pane, select the *File* menu.

2. Select *New*.

3. Click *File | Save As*.

4. Remember the name of the APL file in the lambda function (90-year week calendar APL.json - see Figure 12-17).

```
19   logger = logging.getLogger(__name__)
20   logger.setLevel(logging.INFO)
21
22   calendarPath = "90-year week calendar APL.json"
23   CALENDAR_TOKEN = "CalendarToken"
24
25
26   class LaunchRequestHandler(AbstractRequestHandler):
```

Figure 12-17. *The Lambda code showing the APL file name in line 22*

5. Enter that name in the *Save As* dialog (see Figure 12-18) and click *Save*.

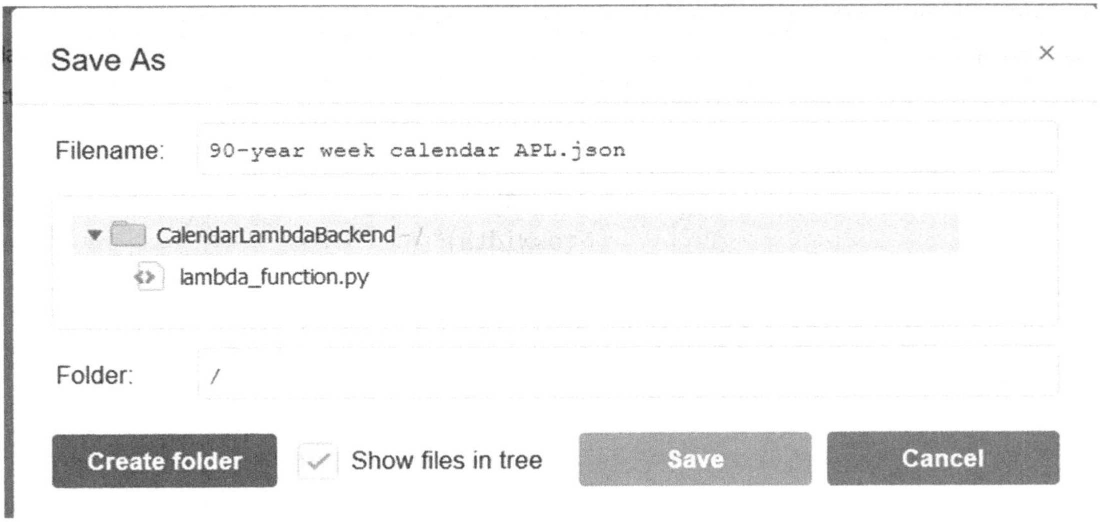

Save As   ×

Filename: `90-year week calendar APL.json`

▼ 📁 CalendarLambdaBackend – /
   `<>` lambda_function.py

Folder: /

Create folder   ✓ Show files in tree   **Save**   **Cancel**

Figure 12-18. *Completing the Save As dialog*

6. Edit the APL in VS Code, scroll down, and remove the entire
   datasources section. So delete this code from the brace and the
   comma before `"datasources"` to the two closing braces near the
   bottom. You should leave just two closing braces at the bottom:

```
},
"datasources": {
    "data": {
        "type": "object",
        "properties": {
            "zone1": [
                "C1",
                "C1",
                ...
            "boxWidth": 24,
            "rowWidth": 1248
        }
    }
```

You will have a square bracket followed by three closing braces at the bottom of the Json file, like so:

```
                                    "height": "${payload.data.properties.
                                    boxHeight}",
                                    "width": "${payload.data.properties.
                                    rowWidth}"
                                }
                            ]
                        }
                    ]
                }
            ]
        }
    }
}
```

7. Now go to the top of the APL and remove the document tag, so delete the opening brace through the colon after "document", so that this

```
{
    "document": {
        "type": "APL",
        "version": "1.5",
        "theme": "dark",
        "import": [
```

becomes this:

```
{
        "type": "APL",
        "version": "1.5",
        "theme": "dark",
        "import": [
```

8. Now delete the last closing brace at the bottom of the file so that
    this

```
                ]
              }
           ]
         }
      }
}
```

becomes this:

```
                ]
              }
           ]
         }
      }
```

9. Copy and paste the remaining APL code from VS Code to the new
    file in the lambda function.

10. *Save* the changes.

11. *Deploy* the changes.

Now click the *Test* button again! You should see a ton of Json, starting with

```
{
  "version": "1.0",
  "sessionAttributes": {
    "last_speech": "Your birthday is: 1975-01-01. If you live to be
    90 years old,\n            you have already lived 51.2 percent of your
    life.\n          Which is to say, of the 4696.1 weeks you have in
    your 90 year lifespan, you have already lived for 2406.4 weeks and have
    2289.6 weeks remaining."
  },
```

```
    "userAgent": "ask-python/1.15.0 Python/3.8.6",
    "response": {
      "outputSpeech": {
        "type": "SSML",
        "ssml": "<speak>Your birthday is: 1975-01-01. If you live to be 90
        years old,\n          you have already lived 51.2 percent of your
        life.\n          Which is to say, of the 4696.1 weeks you have in
        your 90 year lifespan, you have already lived for 2406.4 weeks and
        have 2289.6 weeks remaining.</speak>"
      },
```

As you scroll down, you will find the entire APL document and the generated datasources, all the way down to

```
              "totalHeight": 2880,
              "boxHeight": 6,
              "boxWidth": 19,
              "rowWidth": 988
            }
          }
        }
      }
    ],
    "shouldEndSession": true
  }
}
```

One last test, click over to the Alexa Developer Console again. Click on the Test tab. Enter your Launch phrase, 90 kilo. Then enter your birthday: I was born on 1/1/1975. You should see and hear Alexa tell you something interesting. (See Figure 12-19.)

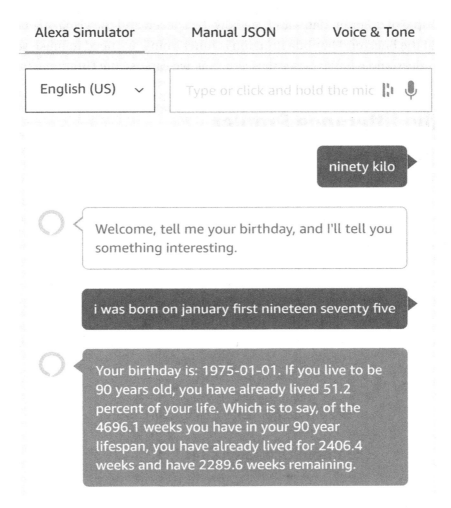

Figure 12-19. *The Alexa dialog with the Give Birthday intent and response*

There's more; scroll to the right and scroll down to see the rendered APL in the default Alexa Device Display. See Figure 12-20.

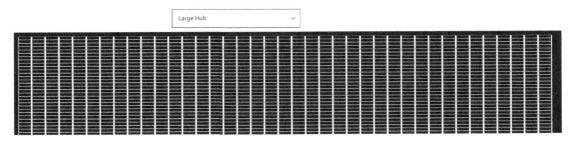

Figure 12-20. *The rendered APL in the Alexa viewer*

Try a couple of different dates and see how the speech and the visual are changed.

Now that the back-end lambda function is functioning, we need to make sure that Alexa will understand what the user says. For that, we can use the Utterance Profiler.

Using the Utterance Profiler

Another tool for Unit Testing is the Utterance Profiler. It's on the Build tab in the Alexa Developer Console, and it allows you to create tests to see which intent various utterances will match. It is important to understand that the Utterance Profiler only tests Alexa's ability to interpret the utterance, match to an intent, and fill the slot values. None of this requires calling the lambda function. However, many of the utterance results will need you to rethink how the lambda function takes its input and how it handles misunderstandings.

When you design your skill intents, the more sample utterances you have, within reason, the better Alexa will be able to match them and find the right intent. For example, in the Give Birthday intent, we listed four sample utterances, as shown in Figure 12-21.

Figure 12-21. *The sample utterances for the Give Birthday intent*

By clicking the *Evaluate Model* button in the top right, you can test your utterances to see how Alexa will interpret the words a user says. For example, if a user says, "I was born on 1/1/75," Alexa will hear, "I was born on 1 1 75." Notice how Alexa does not interpret the date "1/1/75" as a date at all, but instead, she hears a series of three numbers: one, one, and seventy-five. See Figure 12-22.

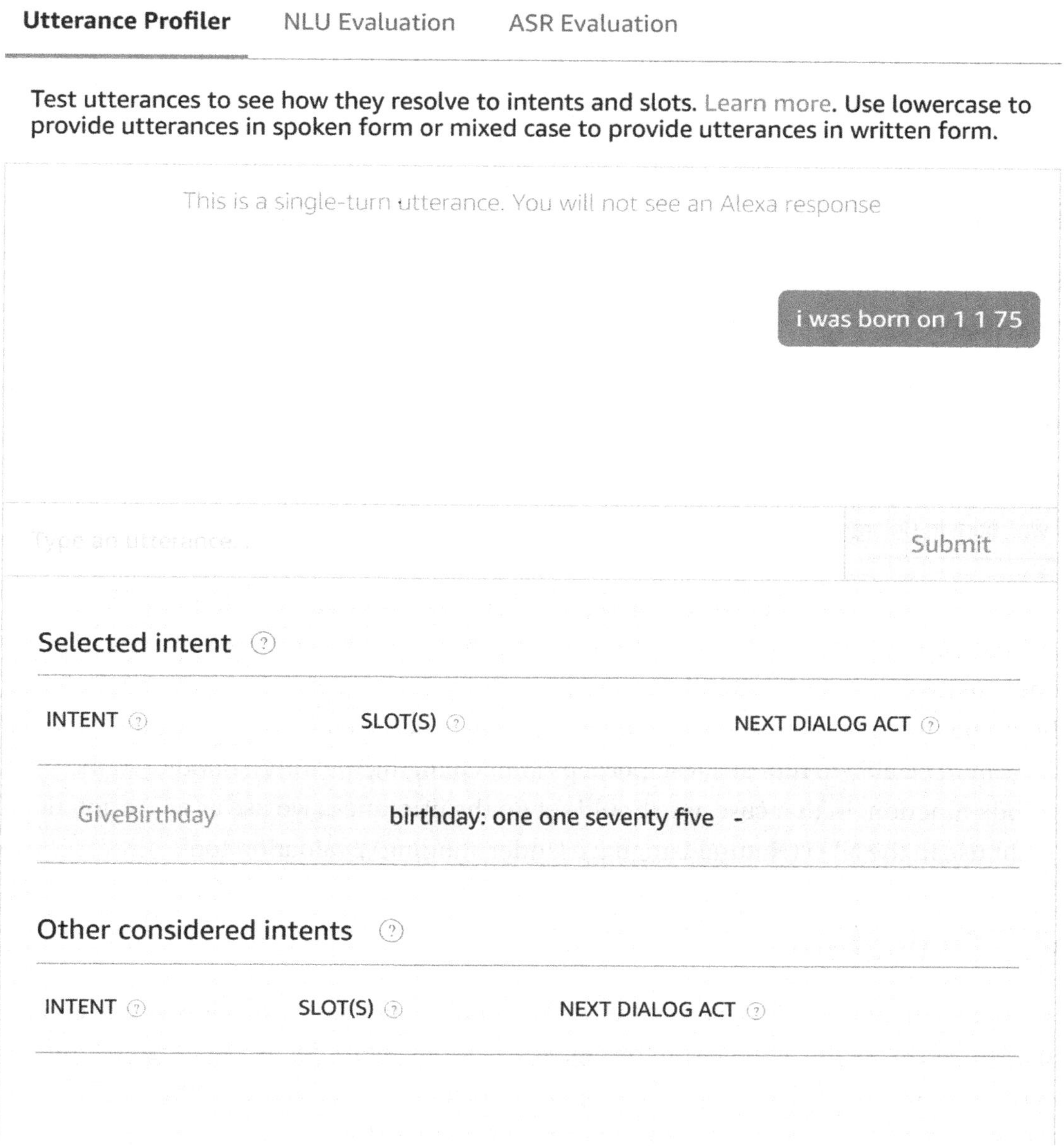

Utterance Profiler   NLU Evaluation   ASR Evaluation

Test utterances to see how they resolve to intents and slots. Learn more. Use lowercase to provide utterances in spoken form or mixed case to provide utterances in written form.

This is a single-turn utterance. You will not see an Alexa response

i was born on 1 1 75

Type an utterance...   Submit

Selected intent ⓘ

INTENT ⓘ	SLOT(S) ⓘ	NEXT DIALOG ACT ⓘ
GiveBirthday	birthday: one one seventy five	-

Other considered intents ⓘ

INTENT ⓘ	SLOT(S) ⓘ	NEXT DIALOG ACT ⓘ

Figure 12-22. *The Utterance Profiler and a sample utterance*

Those numbers are all included in the slot value for {birthday}, but they would probably break our existing code because we require the slot value to be a date:

```
bday_str = handler_input.request_envelope.request.intent.slots
["birthday"].value
logger.info(f"Birthday: {bday_str}")
bday, _, _, _ = period_from_amazon_date(bday_str)
```

This indicates that we should change our code in the period_from_amazon_date function to be able to understand a series of three numbers as a date.

Try some other dates in the Utterance Profiler:

Utterance	Slot Value
I was born on 1 1 75	one one seventy-five
I was born on Jan 1 75	2022-01-01
I was born on Jan 1 1975	1975-01-01
I was born on 1 1 2000	2000
I was born in 1975. January the first 1975.	1975-01-01
I was born in Colorado Springs Colorado on June fifth 1962	1962-06-05

Notice how sometimes Alexa can figure out the correct date from the utterance, and sometimes she can't. Notice the fourth utterance, which you'd expect to result in "one one two thousand," actually resulted in a slot value of "2000." So our intent handler should be coded to handle a partial date and reprompt the user for the full date. Suppose we want to be able to repeat a test, perhaps after changing the intent handler in the lambda function. In that case, we should set up the utterances we use as an Annotation Set for use in the NLU (Natural Language Understanding) Evaluation tool.

NLU Evaluation

From the Utterance Profiler, select the *NLU Evaluation* tab. This will allow you to create an Annotation Set that can be run through the Utterance Profiler as a set, significantly increasing your productivity as a developer. For example, we can put all the utterances from the last section into an Annotation Set. See Figure 12-23.

NLU Annotation Set / GiveBirthdayDateSet

Create annotation sets on your intent mappings that will be used for model evaluation. Learn more. Use lowercase to provide utterances in spoken form or mixed case to provide utterances in written form.

#	UTTERANCE	EXPECTED INTENT	EXPECTED SLOTS (OPTIONAL)		REFERENCE TIMESTAMP (UTC, OPTIONAL)
1	I was born 24 years ago today	GiveBirthday	birthday	1997-02-14	2021-02-14T12:00:00.000Z
2	I was born in Colorado Springs Colorado on June fifth 1962	GiveBirthday	birthday	1962-06-05	
3	I was born in 1975. January the first 1975.	GiveBirthday	birthday	1975-01-01	
4	I was born on 1 1 2000	GiveBirthday	birthday	2000-01-01	
5	I was born on Jan 1 1975	GiveBirthday	birthday	1975-01-01	
6	I was born on Jan 1 75	GiveBirthday	birthday	1975-01-01	
7	I was born on 1 1 75	GiveBirthday	birthday	1975-01-01	

Figure 12-23. *The Utterances added to an Annotation Set*

The optional *Reference Timestamp* column is for use with Date slots. It provides the Date and Time that is to be used when the Utterance includes relative date terms, such as Yesterday, Six Months Ago, and Twenty-four Years ago today.

Once you've entered your Annotation Set, click the *Save Annotation Set* button at the top of the screen. After saving, click the Evaluate Model button and then click the Run An Evaluation button. The Model will fail because several of the utterances do not yield the slot value we want. (See Figure 12-24.)

Utterance Profiler   **NLU Evaluation**   ASR Evaluation

Evaluate batches of utterances to improve your Skill's model accuracy. Learn more.

Run an Evaluation

Stage	Development ∨	Annotation Source view all	GiveBirthdayDateS... ∨	Run an Evaluation

NLU Evaluation Results   Create Annotation Set

EVALUATION ID	STATUS	RESULTS	ANNOTATION SET	STAGE	START TIME
ae281ff2-8c38-4bf8-bbb3-c8886eab82a6	Complete	Failed	GiveBirthdayDateSet (f78de9df-c4f...)	Development	6 minutes ago

Figure 12-24. *The NLU Evaluation, showing that the test failed*

By clicking on the Evaluation ID, you can drill down to see the test run's details and the utterances that failed, as shown in Figure 12-25.

NLU Evaluation / ae281ff2-8c3...   Source: GiveBirthdayDateSet (f78de9df-c4f6-4177-b09b-8bf41fdbace9)

57% Passed (4)   ASK_SAA_EVALUATION_RESULTS_ENDED_LABEL
      Failed (3)   8 minutes ago in **DEVELOPMENT**   ⬆ Export JSON
      Total Test Cases: 7   Feb 14, 2021 4:16 AM

#	UTTERANCE	EXPECTED [E] VS ACTUAL [A] INTENT	EXPECTED [E] VS ACTUAL [A] SLOT NAMES	EXPECTED [E] VS ACTUAL [A] SLOT VALUES	PASS/FAIL
1	I was born 24 years ago today	⊘ GiveBirthday	⊘ birthday	E: 1997-02-14, A: [ ]	FAIL
2	I was born in Colorado Springs Colorado on June fifth 1962	⊘ GiveBirthday	⊘ birthday	⊘ 1962-06-05	PASS
3	I was born in 1975. January the first 1975.	⊘ GiveBirthday	⊘ birthday	⊘ 1975-01-01	PASS
4	I was born on Jan 1 1975	⊘ GiveBirthday	⊘ birthday	⊘ 1975-01-01	PASS
5	I was born on 1 1 2000	⊘ GiveBirthday	⊘ birthday	E: 2000-01-01, A: 2000	FAIL
6	I was born on Jan 1 75	⊘ GiveBirthday	⊘ birthday	⊘ 1975-01-01	PASS
7	I was born on 1 1 75	⊘ GiveBirthday	⊘ birthday	E: 1975-01-01, A: [ ]	FAIL

‹ 1 – 7 of 7 ›

Figure 12-25. *The NLU test details*

Notice how in Figure 12-25 test #7 failed because the Expected value is 1975-01-01 and the Actual value is [ ], or blank. Blank is not a valid value in the NLU Annotation Set, and the Utterance Profiler said the Actual value should be "one one seventy-five." Neither of these works. However, we want Alexa to understand "1 1 75" as a date. To do this, we might need to create a new intent that accepts a multivalue slot that can hear "1 1 75" and interpret it as three numbers. There would be a new intent handler in the lambda function to deal with this new intent and the new slot values.

Once you've created your Annotation Sets, you need to start asking your friends to "tell me your birthday" and see what they say. See how it fits into your utterances. If you ask and a friend says, "On Jan 1 1975 I was born," consider adding that as an Utterance in your NLU Annotation Set and see whether Alexa understands it. If not, change the intent utterances accordingly or possibly create a new intent with different slots entirely.

The next step in testing is to throw voice recordings at Alexa and see how she does.

ASR Evaluation

ASR (Automatic Speech Recognition) Evaluation is a potent testing tool. It allows you to create a set of voice recordings (as MP3, WAV, OGG, or AIFF files) and upload them as an Annotation Set. Or you can record the utterances directly into the test. Either way, Alexa will listen to the recordings and interpret them, matching them against your expected transcriptions. This is a great way to test a wide variety of voices – male, female, from different cultures, with different accents, etc., and then see how the Alexa ASR Evaluator hears them.

To create a simple ASR Annotation Set, select the ASR Evaluation tab, give the Annotation Set a name, and press and hold the button to record some of the preceding utterances. Assign a Weight from 1 to 10. Higher numbers are more important utterances. (See Figure 12-26.) Don't forget to Save the Annotation Set often.

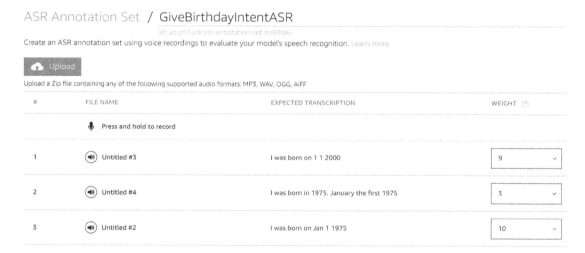

Figure 12-26. *The Recorded Utterances for the ASR Test*

Then click the Evaluate Model button and select the ASR tab to test the recorded utterances. (See Figure 12-27.)

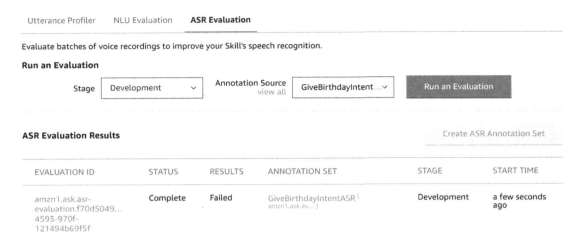

Figure 12-27. *The ASR Evaluation*

Then review the details by clicking the Evaluation ID. (See Figure 12-28.)

ASR Evaluation / amzn1.ask.as...

Source: GiveBirthdayIntentASR (amzn1.ask.asr-annotation-set.db88fa64-dc68-41ad-8c52-9248fcef183c)

0% Passed (0)
Failed (3)
Total Test Cases: 3

Evaluation Started:
3 minutes ago in **DEVELOPMENT**
Feb 14, 2021 8:32 AM

Export to an annotation set to batch test the model's Natural Language Understanding(NLU) ⓘ

Select export location: | Select an option ⌄ | Export and go

#	FILE NAME	[E] EXPECTED VS [A] ACTUAL TRANSCRIPTION	WEIGHT	PASS / FAIL
1	🔊 Untitled #3	[E] I was born on 1 1 2000 [A] i was born on 11 2000	9	FAIL
2	🔊 Untitled #4	[E] I was born in 1975. January the first 1975 [A] i was born in 1975 january the 1st 1975	3	FAIL
3	🔊 Untitled #2	[E] I was born on Jan 1 1975 [A] i was born on jan one 1975	10	FAIL

Figure 12-28. *The Failed ASR Tests*

It looks like we need to tweak our speech syntax a little. Let's change the Annotation Set text to be lowercase, no punctuation, etc. (See Figure 12-29.)

1	🔊 Untitled #3	i was born on 11 2000
2	🔊 Untitled #4	i was born in 1975 january the 1st 1975
3	🔊 Untitled #2	i was born on jan one 1975

Figure 12-29. *The Revised Annotation Set*

Yay! The ASR Test passes now. (See Figures 12-30 and 12-31.)

EVALUATION ID	STATUS	RESULTS	ANNOTATION SET	STAGE	START TIME
amzn1.ask.asr-evaluation.301daf98-f068-4d3f-a57a-ac054e9d3368	Complete	Passed	GiveBirthdayIntentASR (amzn1.ask.as...)	Development	a few seconds ago

Figure 12-30. *The Passing ASR Test*

ASR Evaluation / amzn1.ask.as...

Source: GiveBirthdayIntentASR (amzn1.ask.asr-annotation-set.db88fa64-dc68-41ad-8c52-9248fcef183c)

100%   Passed (3)   Evaluation Started:
Failed (0)   a minute ago in **DEVELOPMENT**
Total Test Cases: 3   Feb 14, 2021 8:38 AM

Export to an annotation set to batch test the model's Natural Language Understanding(NLU) ⓘ

Select export location: Select an option ⌄   Export and go

#	FILE NAME	[E] EXPECTED VS [A] ACTUAL TRANSCRIPTION	WEIGHT	PASS / FAIL
1	🔊 Untitled #3	⊙ i was born on 11 2000	9	PASS
2	🔊 Untitled #4	⊙ i was born in 1975 january the 1st 1975	3	PASS
3	🔊 Untitled #2	⊙ i was born on jan one 1975	10	PASS

Figure 12-31. *The test details for the Passing ASR Test*

Once you have recorded the ASR tests and the evaluation passes, you can export the ASR text to an NLU Annotation Set and automatically test the utterances there too.

So send a short script to your friends and relatives, asking them to record a bunch of utterances. Edit and split the files they send you so that you have one utterance per file. Zip it all up and upload it to an ASR Annotation Set. Save and Run the tests. Tweak the text until your happy. Then Export those to an NLU Annotation Set. Fill in the expected values. Save and Run those tests. Now change and add the Lambda intent handlers to handle the NLU Annotations.

When your skill is live, you can use the utterances shown in the intent history (on the Build tab) as a source for your test annotations. This lets you test the accuracy of the real-world utterances your users are speaking. Use the utterances where the Interaction type is MODAL, and the Dialog Act column is blank. (Note: For your skill to show an Intent History, you need to have at least ten active users in a day.)

With that, we'll take a break from Unit Testing and move on to manipulating event data as we track our 90-year calendar users' life events.

Summary

In this chapter, we learned several different ways of Unit Testing our Alexa skill. First, we used the built-in testing in the lambda function to make sure our code compiles, runs, and launches our skill. Then we used the Alexa Simulator to test our skill further and get into the intent handlers. Next, we combined these two approaches by taking the Json from the Alexa Simulator and using it in the lambda function test to find and fix the errors that occurred. Lastly, we learned about utterance testing by creating Annotation Sets for NLU and ASR testing evaluations. In the next chapter, we will look at creating and storing life events to augment our 90-year calendar.

CHAPTER 13

Storing the Data

So far, we've created a working Alexa skill that asks you for your birthdate, tells you something interesting about it, and draws a 90-year calendar on devices with a screen. Now we're going to take that skill and create the ability for the user to add personal events in their lives – things like births, deaths, marriages, divorces, education, and job changes. We already created the intents and some sample utterances for the life events. (See Figure 13-1.)

S. A. Kingaby, *Data-Driven Alexa Skills*, https://doi.org/10.1007/978-1-4842-7449-1_13

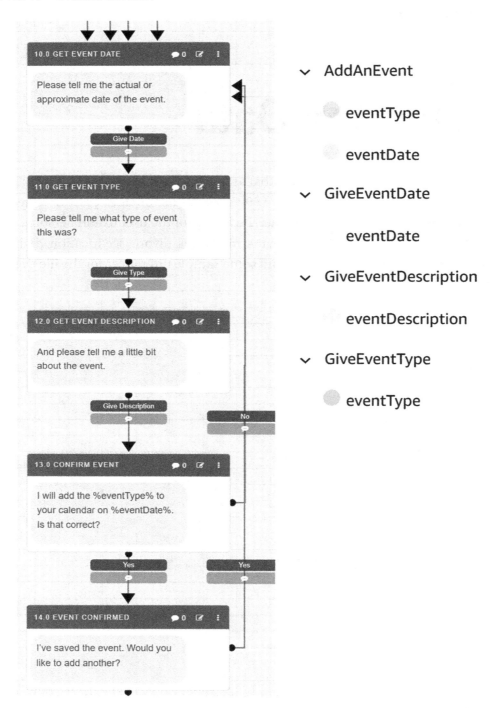

Figure 13-1. *The Botmock diagram and generated intents for life events*

In this chapter, we will write some of the code that will bring those intents to life, but the focus will be on storing the users' responses in a database.

Account Linking and Access Tokens

To store user responses, we need to know who the user is, which is why we turned on account linking in Chapter 7. At this point, we need to do the following:

1. Check if an account is linked.

2. If it is, ask if they want to add an event to their calendar.

3. If not, let them create a standard 90-year calendar.

First, we need to link our development account to our skill.

Linking Your Development Account

To test account linking, you will need to link and unlink your development account several times. You want to link the account you log into the Alexa Developer Console with, not the account with which you log into AWS Lambda. Linking your account is done in the Alexa app on your phone, as follows:

1. Open the Alexa app on your phone and select the *More* tab (Figure 13-2).

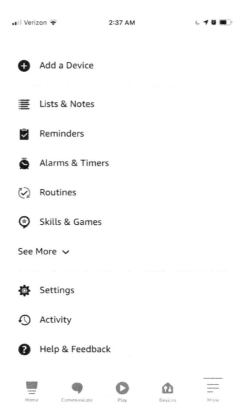

Figure 13-2. *Select More*

2. Select *Skills & Games*.

3. Select *Your Skills*.

4. Scroll sideways to get to *Dev* skills (Figure 13-3).

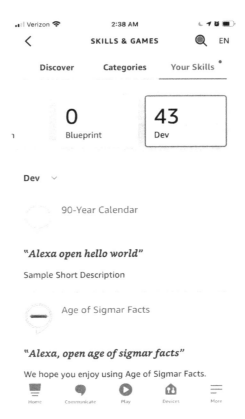

Figure 13-3. *Select Dev Skills*

5. Pick the **90-Year Calendar** skill.

6. Select *Settings* (Figure 13-4).

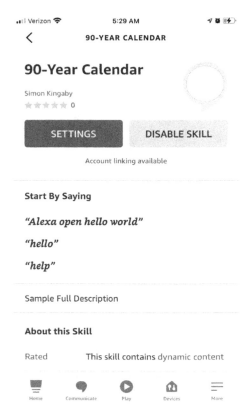

Figure 13-4. *Select Settings*

7.   Select *Link Account* (Figure 13-5).

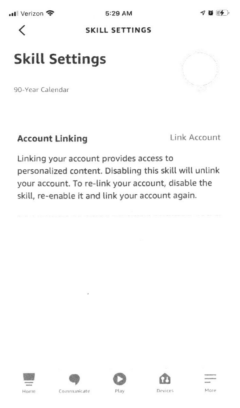

Figure 13-5. *Select Link Account*

8. Log in with your Alexa Developer Console account.

9. Select *Done* (Figure 13-6).

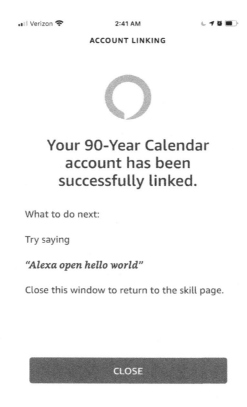

Figure 13-6. *Click Done*

To unlink the account, Disable the skill. Then Enable the skill so you can continue testing.

After linking the account, you can see the Access Token.

Checking If an Account Is Linked

When the account is not linked, the Launch request Json will include a userId. If the account is linked, you will get both a userId and an accessToken. You can see the Launch request Json from the Alexa Developer Console | Test tab. (See Figure 13-7.) Just launch the skill by typing 90 kilo into the Alexa Simulator.

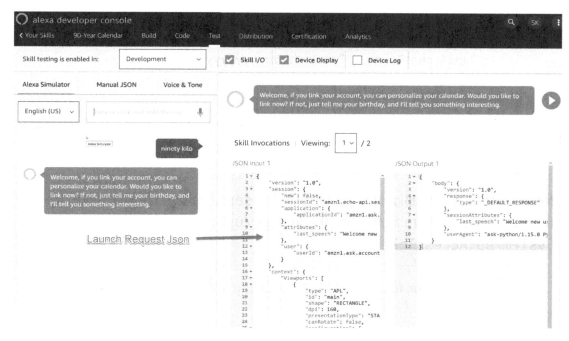

Figure 13-7. *Getting the Launch Request Json*

There are a lot of configuration options in the Launch Request Json, but it is the context/System/user/accessToken that we are looking for:

```
{
    "version": "1.0",
    "session": { },
    "context": {
        "Viewports": [ ],
        "System": {
            "application": {
                "applicationId": "amzn1.ask.ski
                ll.1111111-2222-3333-4444-5555555"
            },
            "user": {
                "userId": "amzn1.ask.account.XXXXXXXXXX",
                "accessToken": "Atza|AAAAAABBBBBCCCCCC"
            },
```

```
        "device": { },
        "apiEndpoint": "https://api.amazonalexa.com",
        "apiAccessToken": "zzzzzzzzzz.yyyyyyyyyy.xxxxxxxxxx"
      }
    },
    "request": { }
}
```

Note   There's an additional user block in the session tag too. That's not the one we need. We're looking for the System/user/accessToken, not the System/apiAccessToken.

Now we can write the function in the lambda that will get the Access Token.

Getting the Access Token

Getting the Access Token out of the handler input should be in a function so that we only have the expression in one place. (This is a coding principle called DRY – Don't Repeat Yourself.) To keep things organized, place the Get Access Token function in a new module, along with all the other persistence code from this chapter. To do this, create a new file in the lambda function called **dynamodb.py**. (See Figure 13-8.)

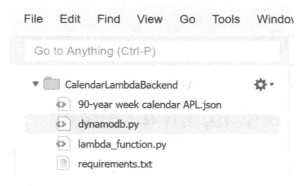

Figure 13-8.   *Adding the dynamodb.py file to the lambda function project*

The function to check if we have an Access Token is

```
def has_access_token(handler_input):
  reqEnv = handler_input.request_envelope
  if reqEnv.context.system.user.access_token:
    return True
  else:
    return False
```

There are several places where we need to check if the account is linked, i.e., has an accessToken. The first is in the Launch Intent handler. Since we're offering the basic calendar to everyone and only need the account to be linked to store additional calendar events, we will need to provide the user the option to link their account. This sets up three possible Launch Intent handlers:

1. The Account is not Linked (a guest user).

2. The Account has just been Linked (a new user).

3. The Account was already Linked, and we have stored the user's profile (an established user).

Not only do we need to know if the account is linked, i.e., has_access_token() is True, but we need to know if we've already stored the user profile or not. This entails checking if the user exists in our database. If it doesn't, then this is a new user account, freshly linked. If it does, then this is a returning user. To test the token for validity, we need to return one of four states: No Token, New Token, Valid Token, or an Error state. In the **dynamodb.py** file, add the following enumeration:

```
from enum import Enum

class AccessTokenValidity(Enum):
    NONE = 1
    VALID = 2
    NEW = 3
    ERROR = 4
```

After adding this code, *Save* both modules and *Deploy* them. Then run the Launch test we created in Chapter 12. You should see your welcome response. If you do not, then fix the bugs before moving on. This is one of the benefits of Unit Tests; you can run them often to make sure your changes are not buggy.

In the next section, we'll use the Alexa Persistence Adapter to access our database.

Getting the User Profile from DynamoDB

In Chapter 7, we set up a DynamoDB table to use for the user profile. Before we write the code to access that database, we should turn on logging. This is quickly done by adding the following code to the **dynamodb.py** module:

```
import logging

logger = logging.getLogger(__name__)
logger.setLevel(logging.INFO)
```

This will let us add logging to our database functions to see what is going on inside them.

Next, we need to add the code to initialize the DynamoDB persistence adapter, as follows:

```
from ask_sdk_dynamodb.adapter import DynamoDbAdapter

adapter = DynamoDbAdapter('CalendarItem', partition_key_name="PersonId")
```

Now we can create a function to read the user profile from the database:

```
def read_user_profile(handler_input):
    validity = AccessTokenValidity.NONE
    attr = []

    hasAccessToken = has_access_token(handler_input)
    logger.info(f"AccToken: {hasAccessToken}, Response: {attr}")

    if hasAccessToken:
        amgr = handler_input.attributes_manager
        attr = amgr.persistent_attributes
        if attr:
```

```
            logger.info(f"{attr}")
            validity = AccessTokenValidity.VALID
            if type(attr["Birthday"]) == str:
                attr["Birthday"] = datetime.fromisoformat(attr["Birthday"])
        else:
            validity = AccessTokenValidity.NEW
    else:
        validity = AccessTokenValidity.NONE

    return validity, attr
```

Finally, we need to handle persistence errors. This is done by wrapping the preceding code in a try…except block, as shown here:

```
from ask_sdk_core.exceptions import PersistenceException
from datetime import datetime

def read_user_profile(handler_input):
    validity = AccessTokenValidity.NONE
    attr = []
    try:
        hasAccessToken = has_access_token(handler_input)
        logger.info(f"AccToken: {hasAccessToken}")

        if hasAccessToken:
            amgr = handler_input.attributes_manager
            attr = amgr.persistent_attributes
            if attr:
                logger.info(f"{attr}")
                validity = AccessTokenValidity.VALID
                if type(attr["Birthday"]) == str:
                    attr["Birthday"] = datetime.fromisoformat(attr
                    ["Birthday"])
            else:
                validity = AccessTokenValidity.NEW
        else:
            validity = AccessTokenValidity.NONE
```

```
    except PersistenceException as e:
        logger.error(e)
        validity = AccessTokenValidity.ERROR
        #TODO: Handle PersistenceExceptions gracefully

    except Exception as e:
        logger.error(e)
        validity = AccessTokenValidity.ERROR
        raise e
    return validity, attr
```

After adding this code, *Save* both modules and *Deploy* them. Then run the Launch test we created in Chapter 12. You should see your welcome response. If you do not, then fix the bugs before moving on.

Now that we know whether the token exists and is valid, we can use this to determine what to say to the user in the Launch Request handler.

A Trio of Launch Request Handlers

Now that we can read the user profile, we can create the additional Launch Request handler when there is one. Specifically, we need a different Launch Request handler when the account is not linked, when it has just been linked, and when it was already linked with a saved profile.

Switch to the **lambda_function.py** module and add the following line to import the functionality from the **dynamodb.py** module:

```
from dynamodb import adapter, read_user_profile, AccessTokenValidity, has_
access_token
```

Now change the original LaunchRequestHandler(). Rename it to LaunchRequestHandlerUnlinked() and modify the can_handle() method to say

```
def can_handle(self, handler_input):
    return not has_access_token(handler_input) and ask_utils.is_request_
    type("LaunchRequest")(handler_input)
```

In the handle() method, change the speak_output and add a new attribute named "question," like this:

```
def handle(self, handler_input):
    speak_output = """Welcome, if you link your account, you can
    personalize your calendar.
        Would you like to link now?
        If not, just tell me your birthday, and I'll tell you something
        interesting."""
    handler_input.attributes_manager.session_attributes["question"] =
    "LinkAccount"

    handler_input.attributes_manager.session_attributes["last_speech"] =
    speak_output
```

The finished LaunchRequestHandlerUnlinked() will look like this:

```
class LaunchRequestHandlerUnlinked(AbstractRequestHandler):
    """Handler for Skill Launch when the Account is not linked."""

    def can_handle(self, handler_input):
        return not has_access_token(handler_input) and ask_utils.is_
        request_type("LaunchRequest")(handler_input)

    def handle(self, handler_input):
        speak_output = """Welcome. If you link your account, you can
        personalize your calendar.
            Would you like to link now?
            If not, just tell me your birthday, and I'll tell you something
            interesting."""
        handler_input.attributes_manager.session_attributes["question"] =
        "LinkAccount"

        handler_input.attributes_manager.session_attributes["last_speech"]
        = speak_output
```

```
    return (
        handler_input.response_builder
        .speak(speak_output)
        .ask(speak_output)
        .response
    )
```

Next, add a Launch Request handler for when the account has just been linked. We'll call this LaunchRequestHandlerNew():

```
class LaunchRequestHandlerNew(AbstractRequestHandler):
    """Handler for Skill Launch when the account is newly linked."""

    def can_handle(self, handler_input):
        validity, profile = read_user_profile(handler_input)
        return (validity == AccessTokenValidity.NEW) and ask_utils.is_
        request_type("LaunchRequest")(handler_input)

    def handle(self, handler_input):
        speak_output = "Welcome new user! Tell me your birthday, and I'll
        tell you something interesting."
        handler_input.attributes_manager.session_attributes["last_speech"]
        = speak_output

        return (
            handler_input.response_builder
            .speak(speak_output)
            .ask(speak_output)
            .response
        )
```

Now add the third Launch Request handler for when we already have a Valid token and a user profile:

```
class LaunchRequestHandlerValid(AbstractRequestHandler):
    """Handler for Skill Launch when we already know the birthday."""

    def can_handle(self, handler_input):
        validity, profile = read_user_profile(handler_input)
```

```
    return (validity == AccessTokenValidity.VALID) and ask_utils.is_
    request_type("LaunchRequest")(handler_input)

def handle(self, handler_input):
    speak_output = "Welcome back! You can add an event or view your 90-
    year Calendar. What would you like to do?"
    handler_input.attributes_manager.session_attributes["last_speech"]
    = speak_output

    return (
        handler_input.response_builder
        .speak(speak_output)
        .ask(speak_output)
        .response
    )
```

With these three Launch Request handlers defined, we need to modify the SkillBuilder() code at the bottom of the **lambda_function.py** module. Remember, whenever you add or modify a request handler, you must update the SkillBuilder() code. We're going to change this:

```
from ask_sdk_core.skill_builder import SkillBuilder

...

sb = SkillBuilder()
sb.add_request_handler(LaunchRequestHandler())
```

Into this:

```
from ask_sdk_core.skill_builder import CustomSkillBuilder

...

sb = CustomSkillBuilder(persistence_adapter=adapter)
sb.add_request_handler(LaunchRequestHandlerUnlinked())
sb.add_request_handler(LaunchRequestHandlerNew())
sb.add_request_handler(LaunchRequestHandlerValid())
```

Note the changes to the import and the declaration to use CustomSkillBuilder instead of SkillBuilder.

Adding the Yes Intent Handler

In the `LaunchRequestHandlerUnlinked()`, we ask the user, "Would you like to link now?" If they answer "Yes," this will trigger the Yes intent, so we need to add a `YesIntentHandler()`. This will check for the value of the "`Question`" attribute, so it knows the context for the Yes intent.

Start the handler by defining the class and the can_handle and handle methods:

```
class YesIntentHandler(AbstractRequestHandler):
    """Handler for Yes Intent."""

    def can_handle(self, handler_input):
        # type: (HandlerInput) -> bool
        return ask_utils.is_intent_name("AMAZON.YesIntent")(handler_input)

    def handle(self, handler_input):
```

Then get the value of the "`Question`" attribute:

```
question = handler_input.attributes_manager.session_attributes["question"]
```

If the question value is "LinkAccount," we will need to open a Card in the Alexa app.

Using Cards in the Response

There are several different kinds of Cards in the Alexa app. These are usually used to summarize a set of values. For example, a card can show a stock price. A different card can show the upcoming weather for the day. Cards are displayed on the Alexa device (if it has a screen) or in the Alexa app on the user's smartphone.

When you want to instruct the user to set up account linking, you will use a special card notification called the `LinkAccountCard`. This card is then returned in the response so that the Alexa app leads the user to link their account. The code to do this is

```
card_output = ui.link_account_card.LinkAccountCard()
...
return (
    handler_input.response_builder
    .set_card(card_output)
...
```

We need to check if the question variable has the value "LinkAccount," and then use the card as shown previously. Here is the finished code for the handle() method.

```
def handle(self, handler_input):
    question = handler_input.attributes_manager.session_
    attributes["question"]

    # Initialize the response variables
    speak_output = ""
    endSession = False
    card_output = None

    if question == "LinkAccount":
        # Handle the LinkAccount response
        speak_output = "OK, I've sent some information to the Alexa app.
        Open your Alexa app and click on the link to connect your account."
        endSession = True
        card_output = ui.link_account_card.LinkAccountCard()

    else:
        # Handle a Yes response with no question value set
        speak_output = "Sorry, I got confused, please tell me what you want
        to do or say Help."
        endSession = False

    handler_input.attributes_manager.session_attributes["last_speech"] =
    speak_output
    # Clear t
    handler_input.attributes_manager.session_attributes["question"] = ""

    return (
        handler_input.response_builder
        .speak(speak_output)
        .ask(speak_output)
        .set_card(card_output)
        .set_should_end_session(endSession)
        .response
    )
```

And, of course, we need to add the Yes intent request handler to the Skill Builder at the bottom of the module:

```
sb = CustomSkillBuilder(persistence_adapter=adapter)
...
sb.add_request_handler(YesIntentHandler())
```

The next thing we need to do in this chapter saves the user's profile after telling us their birthday, so they don't have to tell us twice.

Saving the User's Profile

To save the user's profile, we need to add a method to the dynamodb.py module. This is done by using the Alexa Persistence Manager, as shown here:

```
def save_user_profile(handler_input, profile):
    if has_access_token(handler_input):
        try:
            attr = {}
            attr["Birthday"] = str(profile["Birthday"])
            attr["Events"] = profile["Events"]
            amgr = handler_input.attributes_manager
            amgr.persistent_attributes = attr
            amgr.save_persistent_attributes()

        except PersistenceException as e:
            logger.error(e)
            # TODO: Handle PersistenceExceptions gracefully

        except Exception as e:
            logger.error(e)
            raise e
```

In this method, we pass in the handler_input, the user's birthday, and an array of events. If there is a valid Access Token, we define an attribute variable (attr) as a dictionary of key:value pairs, one pair for the birthday, and another for the events array. Then we get the attributes manager out of the handler input and assign it to the amgr variable. Next, we assign our attr dictionary to the amgr.persistent_attributes property and then use the amgr to save the persistent attributes. And that's it. The rest of the code is the error handler logic, which you should always use when saving or loading data from a database just in case there's a problem with the database or the connection to the database.

Now that we've defined the save_user_profile method, we need to switch back to the lambda_function.py module and modify the import, the GiveBirthdayIntentHandler(), and add a new View Calendar intent handler.

First, we will modify the dynamodb import to include the new save method. This line

```
from dynamodb import adapter, read_user_profile, AccessTokenValidity, has_
access_token
```

becomes

```
from dynamodb import adapter, read_user_profile, AccessTokenValidity, has_
access_token, save_user_profile
```

In the GiveBirthdayIntentHandler(), we need to make some major changes. Specifically, we need to split the Handle Function so that all the logic for calculating and displaying the calendar is in a separate function. Find the line of code that says

```
today = datetime.today()
```

In front of it, add the declaration:

```
def ShowCalendar(handler_input, bday, events):
```

At the bottom of it, change the return value to just return the response builder, not the response. So change this

```
handler_input.attributes_manager.session_attributes["last_speech"] = speak_
output
return (
    rb
    .speak(speak_output)
    .response
)
```

to

```
handler_input.attributes_manager.session_attributes["last_speech"] =
speak_output
rb.speak(speak_output)
return rb
```

Now change the GiveBirthdayIntentHandler's handle() method to

```
def handle(self, handler_input):
    # type: (HandlerInput) -> Response
    validity, profile = read_user_profile(handler_input)
    logger.info(f"Validity: {validity}")

    bday_str = handler_input.request_envelope.request.intent.
    slots["birthday"].value
    logger.info(f"Birthday: {bday_str}")
    bday, _, _, _ = period_from_amazon_date(bday_str)
    logger.info(f"bday: {bday}")
    profile["Birthday"] = bday
    if validity == AccessTokenValidity.NEW:
        profile["Events"] = []
    save_user_profile(handler_input, profile)

    # Handle the ask and terminate options
    ask = None
    terminate = True
    if validity == AccessTokenValidity.VALID or validity ==
    AccessTokenValidity.NEW:
        ask = "Would you like to add some events to your calendar?"
        handler_input.attributes_manager.session_attributes["question"] =
        "AddEvents"
        terminate = False
    rb = ShowCalendar(handler_input, bday, profile["Events"])
    if ask:
        rb.ask(ask)
```

```
if terminate:
    rb.set_should_end_session(True)
return (rb.response)
```

In the third Launch Request handler, for when the linked account is valid and not new, we offer the user the opportunity to answer this question: "Welcome back! You can add an event or view your 90-year calendar. What would you like to do?" We need to add a View Calendar intent and intent handler to cover this.

Adding the View Calendar Intent

Before we add the View Calendar intent handler, we should pop over to the Alexa Developer Console and add the View Calendar intent. To do this, follow these steps:

1. Launch and log in to the Alexa Developer Console.

2. Edit your 90-year calendar skill.

3. Select *Interaction Model* on the left nav bar.

4. Select *Intents* on the left nav bar.

5. Click + *Add Intent*. (See Figure 13-9.)

6. Enter the name of the intent: **ViewCalendar**

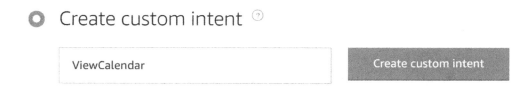

Figure 13-9. *Adding the ViewCalendar intent*

7. Click *Create custom intent*.

8. Add a couple of sample utterances:

    • View calendar

    • View my calendar

9. Click the *Save Model* button at the top.

10. Click the *Build Model* button at the top.

Now add the ViewCalendarIntentHandler class after the GiveBirthdayIntentHandler class in the lambda_function.py module:

```python
class ViewCalendarIntentHandler(AbstractRequestHandler):
    """Handler for ViewCalendar Intent."""

    def can_handle(self, handler_input):
        # type: (HandlerInput) -> bool
        return ask_utils.is_intent_name("ViewCalendar")(handler_input)

    def handle(self, handler_input):
        # type: (HandlerInput) -> Response
        validity, profile = read_user_profile(handler_input)
        logger.info(f"Validity: {validity}")

        ask = "Would you like to add some events to your calendar?"
        handler_input.attributes_manager.session_attributes["question"] =
        "AddEvents"
        rb = ShowCalendar(handler_input, profile)
        rb.ask(ask)
    return (rb.response)
```

And add it to the Skill Builder at the bottom of the lambda_function.py module:

```python
...
sb.add_request_handler(GiveBirthdayIntentHandler())
sb.add_request_handler(ViewCalendarIntentHandler())
sb.add_request_handler(YesIntentHandler())
...
```

And add the "AddEvents" code to the if statement in the Yes intent handler:

```
def handle(self, handler_input):
    question = handler_input.attributes_manager.session_
    attributes["question"]

    speak_output = ""
    ask = None
    endSession = False
    card_output = None

    if question == "LinkAccount":
        speak_output = "OK, I've sent some information to the Alexa app.
        Open your Alexa app and click on the link to connect your account."
        endSession = True
        card_output = ui.link_account_card.LinkAccountCard()

    elif question == "AddEvents":
        speak_output = "To add an event to the Calendar, I need to know
        the event date, type, and description. The date doesn't have to be
        exact if you only know the month or year. When was the event?"
        ask = "When was the event?"

    else:
        speak_output = "Sorry, I got confused, please tell me what you want
        to do or say Help."

    handler_input.attributes_manager.session_attributes["last_speech"] =
    speak_output
    handler_input.attributes_manager.session_attributes["question"] = ""

    if not ask:
        ask = speak_output

    return (
        handler_input.response_builder
        .speak(speak_output)
        .ask(ask)
```

```
        .set_card(card_output)
        .set_should_end_session(endSession)
        .response
    )
```

Save and Deploy your code. Run your Unit Tests. With the code added and unit tested, we should also test the new View Calendar intent.

Testing the View Calendar Intent

Flip back to the Alexa Developer Console. Make sure you are logged in and that your account is currently linked to the 90-year calendar skill in the Alexa app on your phone.

Select the Test tab and launch your skill (90 kilo). Alexa should say, "Welcome back! You can add an event or view your 90-year calendar. What would you like to do?"

You should answer, "view calendar."

She should then say your interesting thing (from the saved profile) and display the calendar.

Figure 13-10 shows this dialog.

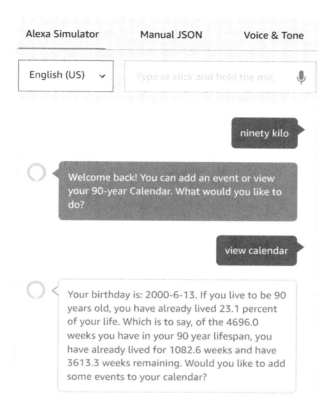

Figure 13-10. *The Valid Launch Request handler and View Calendar intent*

Now you have the Json code you need for the Unit Test in the lambda function. (See Figure 13-11.)

```
86 ▾                    Alexa.Presentation.APL : {
87 ▾                        "runtime": {
88                             "maxVersion": "1.5"
89                         }
90                     }
91                 }
92             },
93             "apiEndpoint": "https://api.amazonalexa.con
94             "apiAccessToken": "eyJ0eXAiOiJKV1QiLCJhbGci
95         }
96     },
97 ▾    "request": {
98         "type": "IntentRequest",
99         "requestId": "amzn1.echo-api.request.01e3e727-2
100        "locale": "en-US",
101        "timestamp": "2021-03-13T09:36:50Z",
102 ▾      "intent": {
103            "name": "ViewCalendar",
104            "confirmationStatus": "NO
105        },
106        "dialogState": "STARTED"
107    }
108 }|
```

Figure 13-11. *ViewCalendar Json for a Unit Test*

Copy the Json and paste it into a new Unit Test in the Lambda Function Editor. (See Figure 13-12.)

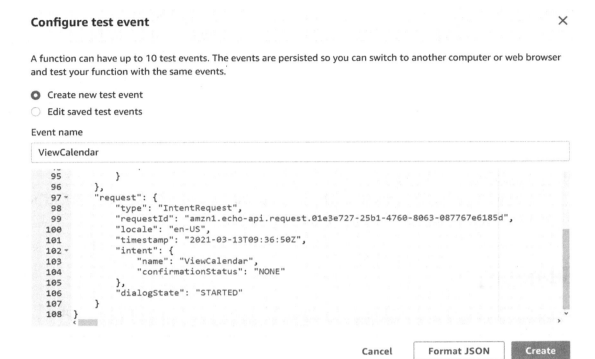

Figure 13-12. *Configuring the new Unit Test*

Run your new Unit Test by clicking the Test button. You should see the Json response for the `ViewCalendarIntentHandler`.

If all is well, we're ready to move on.

What You Can Do Next

At this point, you could go in a variety of directions. You could add the No intent handler. Similar to the Yes intent handler, you need to know to which Question your user is answering No. You could start to add the Add Event intent handlers (Date, Type, Description). Note: The Date handler is a bit of a problem because we already have a Birthdate handler (the GiveBirthdayIntentHandler).

How will Alexa know the difference between a user utterance for the Give Birthday Intent and one for the Give Event Date intent? In short, she won't, so you will need to make sure that only one of the intents allows the user to say just the date. The other requires additional words. For example, Give Birthday has an utterance that is just the {birthday} slot. Give Event Date should not have an utterance that is just the {eventDate} slot. Instead, the GiveBirthday intent handler should disambiguate that the date is coming from a GiveBirthday intent or coming from a GiveEventDate intent. You do this by passing a session attribute, similar to the way we did for the Question attribute, so that the Yes intent handler could figure out which question was asked.

You should also add the GiveEventDescription and GiveEventType intent handlers. Then give the AddAnEvent intent handler a try. As you develop more code, be sure to Save and Deploy often, run your existing Unit Tests, and create more from the Json in the Alexa Developer Console Test tab.

When you have completed testing, change your skill's launch phrase from "90 kilo" to something more useful. For example, "90-Year Calendar."

Summary

Congratulate yourself on your progress so far. You've come a long way. In this chapter, we learned how to get the Access Token to check if an account is linked and what to do when it isn't linked. We learned how to read and write data to a DynamoDB table using the Alexa persistence adapter. We modified the Launch Request handler to work when the user is not linked, is newly linked, and has an established profile. Lastly, we added the View Calendar intent and its handler.

PART III

Using APIs in Advanced Skills

## CHAPTER 14

A Personal Net Worth Skill

In this chapter, we're going to design and implement a Personal Worth skill. In the next chapter, we will wire up the skill to some APIs (Application Programming Interfaces) that will get us the value of our assets. At the end of this section, Alexa will be able to tell you your net worth.

Note You cannot publish this skill to the Skill Store because Amazon will not allow you to create a finance skill if you are not a financial institution. However, you can create the skill for personal use.

Also If you do not want to use real accounts, all the APIs used in the next chapter allow you to create and use Test accounts and Test data, so you can still work the examples without giving Amazon/Alexa access to your personal data.

First, let's discuss the requirements for this skill.

Requirements

Imagine Alexa being able to tell you your net worth. She would need to know the value of your home, the value of your investment portfolio, and the value of your bank accounts, mortgage, and credit card balances. To get the value of your home, she'll need your address. To value your investment portfolio, she'll need a list of your stock symbols and the quantity of each stock you hold. To value your other accounts, she'll need access to their balances.

Starting with security, we'll need to use a linked account. This skill does nothing if it's not linked.

Just like the Calendar skill, we'll need a DynamoDb table to store the user profile.

© Simon A. Kingaby 2022
S. A. Kingaby, *Data-Driven Alexa Skills*, https://doi.org/10.1007/978-1-4842-7449-1_14

Next, we need an intent for getting your address, and we need an intent for adding a stock ticker and the number of shares held. Again, you don't have to use real accounts if you don't want to. We do need an intent for getting our net worth, though.

That's a very brief overview of the requirements for this skill.

Next, we will design the VUI.

VUI Design

In Botmock, there are many ways to diagram this flow. See Figure 14-1 for one example flow.

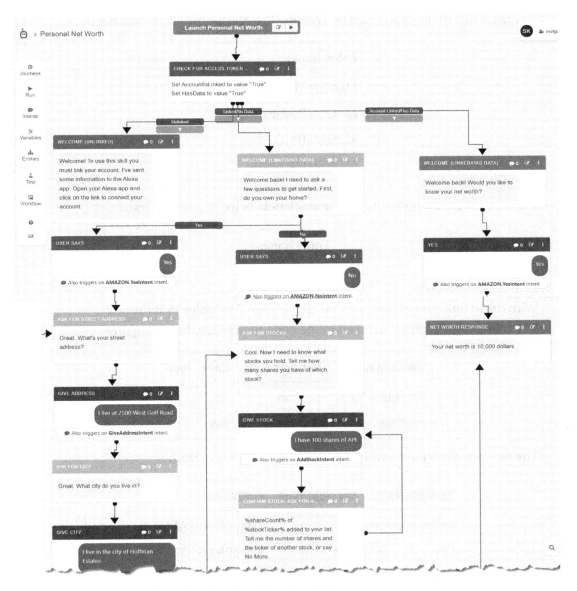

Figure 14-1. *Dialog flow for the Net Worth skill*

To create this dialog flow, start by creating the Alexa Entities we will need.

Entity Name
AMAZON.NUMBER
AMAZON.PostalAddress
AMAZON.US_CITY
AMAZON.US_STATE

Then create a custom entity for the stock tickers we're going to track.

Entity Name
StockTicker

With these Entities defined, we can create some Variables in Botmock. The following variables are used in the code to manage the dialog flow.

Variable Name	Variable Type	Entity Type
AccountIsLinked	Boolean	Any
HasData	Boolean	Any

The next set of variables will become Slots in the Alexa Skill.

Variable Name	Variable Type	Entity Type
street_address	Text	AMAZON.PostalAddress
City	Text	AMAZON.US_CITY
State	Text	AMAZON.US_STATE
zip_code	Text	AMAZON.NUMBER
share_count	Text	AMAZON.NUMBER
stock_ticker	Text	StockTicker

With the slots defined as variables, we are ready to create some intents.

Intent Name	Options
AddStockIntent	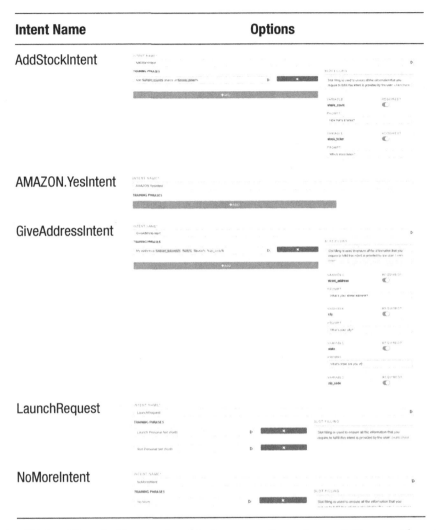
AMAZON.YesIntent	
GiveAddressIntent	
LaunchRequest	
NoMoreIntent	

Start the Dialog Flow in Botmock with the same three Launch Request handlers we saw in the 90-year calendar. (See Figure 14-2.)

1. Unlinked Account

2. Newly Linked Account

3. Linked Account with Data

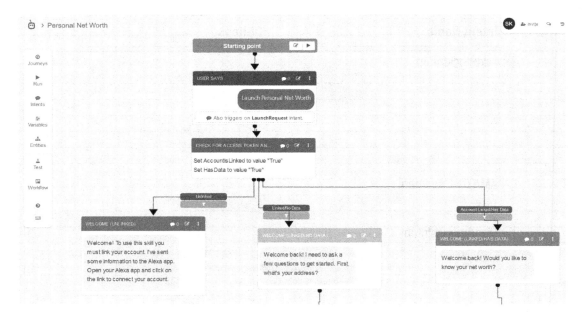

Figure 14-2. *The Launch Request handlers*

Then add the user intents for Give Address, Give Stock, No More, and Yes. See Figure 14-3 for an example.

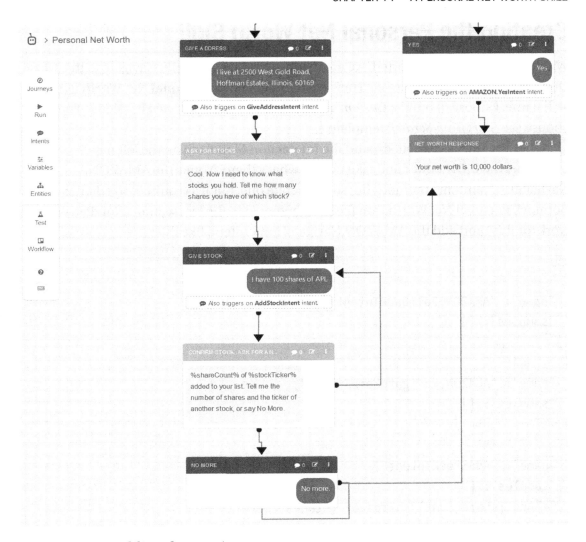

Figure 14-3. *Adding the user intents*

When you are happy with your Botmock diagram, follow the process in Chapter 9 to migrate it to a new skill in the Alexa Developer Console. This mainly involves copying the .env file for API usage from the Botmock Settings menu. Update the Token with the same one we used before. Then run the export-master project from the command line by entering npm start.

Now we can create the bones of the skill.

Creating the Personal Net Worth Skill

With the dialog model exported, we are ready to load it into a skill. Navigate to the Alexa Developer Console. Then create a new custom skill. Enter **Personal Net Worth** as the skill name. Choose to build a *Custom* skill with a *Provision your own* back end. Then choose the *Start from Scratch* template.

Once the skill is created, expand the Interaction Model tab on the left nav bar. Select the JSON Editor and take note of what's there. Notice the AMAZON. NavigateHomeIntent? Botmock doesn't generate one, but it's required, so edit the Botmock Personal Net Worth.json file you generated in the last section (NotePad++ will work for this) and add the AMAZON.NavigateHomeIntent, like this:

```
...
{
  "name": "AMAZON.FallbackIntent",
  "samples": []
},
{
  "name": "AMAZON.NavigateHomeIntent",
  "samples": []
},
{
  "name": "AddStockIntent",
  "samples": [
    "Add {sharecount} shares of {stockticker}"
  ],
...
```

Also, Botmock exported our LaunchRequest, which is not needed in Alexa, so we can safely remove that from the model, as shown here:

```
...
        "My address is {street_address}, {city}, {state}, {zip_code}"
      ]
    }
  ]
},
```

```
{
   "name": "LaunchRequest",
   "samples": [
      "Launch Personal Net Worth",
      "Run Personal Net Worth"
   ],
   "slots": []
},
{
   "name": "NoMoreIntent",
   "samples": [
      "No More"
   ],
   "slots": []
}
...
```

Once these edits are made, copy the entire Json file from NotePad++ to the Alexa Developer Console's JSON Editor window. Then, click the Save Model button at the top and you should see a green message saying, "Skill Saved Successfully." If not, double-check the Json file and try again. In particular, make sure you have the proper punctuation (commas, braces, square brackets, etc.) after adding and removing the parts shown previously.

Next, we need to create the lambda function.

Creating the Lambda Function

Log in to AWS and create a new lambda function. Author it from scratch. Call it **PersonalNetWorthBackend**. Choose the latest version of Python as the runtime. Let it create a new execution role with basic Lambda permissions. Add a trigger. Select the *Alexa Skills Kit* trigger. Paste in the Skill ID from the Alexa Developer Console | Endpoint tab. Then paste the lambda function's ARN into the Alexa Developer Console | Endpoint tab | Default Region field. Don't forget to click the *Save Endpoints* button at the top of the Alexa Developer Console screen.

Now that you've got an empty lambda function and it's connected to your Alexa skill, you can copy in some of the code from the 90-year calendar skill's lambda function to get us started here. Specifically, let's copy in the imports, logging, Launch Request handlers, yes intent handler, built-in intent handlers, SkillBuilder, and persistence code. In fact, we might as well copy both the lambda_function.py and dynamodb.py modules and the requirements.txt file. Then we can modify the Calendar-specific code as we build out the Personal Net Worth specific code. After copying the Calendar files to the Net Worth lambda, I recommend you close the Calendar window so that you don't accidentally modify the files there.

Now, in the dynamodb.py file, after copying it to the **PersonalNetWorthBackend** lambda function, we need to make a couple of changes, as shown here:

```
from ask_sdk_dynamodb.adapter import DynamoDbAdapter
from ask_sdk_core.exceptions import PersistenceException
import logging
from enum import Enum
from datetime import datetime

logger = logging.getLogger(__name__)
logger.setLevel(logging.INFO)

adapter = DynamoDbAdapter('PersonalNetWorth', partition_key_
name="PersonId")

class AccessTokenValidity(Enum):
    NONE = 1
    VALID = 2
    NEW = 3
    ERROR = 4

def has_access_token(handler_input):
    reqEnv = handler_input.request_envelope
    if reqEnv.context.system.user.access_token:
        return True
    else:
        return False
def read_user_profile(handler_input):
```

```python
    validity = AccessTokenValidity.NONE
    attr = []
    try:
        hasAccessToken = has_access_token(handler_input)
        logger.info(f"AccToken: {hasAccessToken}")

        if hasAccessToken:
            amgr = handler_input.attributes_manager
            attr = amgr.persistent_attributes
            if attr:
                logger.info(f"{attr}")
                validity = AccessTokenValidity.VALID
            else:
                validity = AccessTokenValidity.NEW
        else:
            validity = AccessTokenValidity.NONE

    except PersistenceException as e:
        logger.error(e)
        validity = AccessTokenValidity.ERROR
        # TODO: Handle PersistenceExceptions gracefully

    except Exception as e:
        logger.error(e)
        validity = AccessTokenValidity.ERROR
        raise e
    return validity, attr

def save_user_profile(handler_input, profile):
    if has_access_token(handler_input):
        try:
            amgr = handler_input.attributes_manager
            amgr.persistent_attributes = profile
            amgr.save_persistent_attributes()

        except PersistenceException as e:
            logger.error(e)
            # TODO: Handle PersistenceExceptions gracefully
```

```
    except Exception as e:
        logger.error(e)
        raise e
```

Editing the lambda_function.py is a little more complex. We need to remove the following classes and functions:

```
class GiveBirthdayIntentHandler(AbstractRequestHandler)
class ViewCalendarIntentHandler(AbstractRequestHandler)
def ShowCalendar(handler_input, profile)
def load_apl_document(file_path)
def addYears(d, years)
def days_between(d1, d2)
def period_from_amazon_date(iso)
```

Then we need to remove the following lines from the SkillBuilder:

```
sb.add_request_handler(GiveBirthdayIntentHandler())
sb.add_request_handler(ViewCalendarIntentHandler())
```

Next, we need to change all the verbiage in the speak_output lines to reflect our Personal Net Worth skill's intents correctly. In this chapter, we'll focus on your home and the questions, answers, and intents related to your home's value. This will change some code in the following classes:

```
class LaunchRequestHandlerUnlinked(AbstractRequestHandler)
    speak_output = """Welcome, you need to link your account to use the
    Personal Net Worth skill. Would you like to link it now?"""

class LaunchRequestHandlerNew(AbstractRequestHandler)
    speak_output = "Welcome! Thanks for linking your account. Let's get
    started. Do you own your home?"
    handler_input.attributes_manager.session_attributes["question"]  =
    "DoYouOwnYourHome"

class LaunchRequestHandlerValid(AbstractRequestHandler)
    speak_output = "Welcome back! Would you like to know your net worth?"
    handler_input.attributes_manager.session_attributes["question"] =
    "GetNetWorth"
```

```python
        handler_input.attributes_manager.session_attributes["last_speech"] =
        speak_output
class YesIntentHandler(AbstractRequestHandler)
        if question == "LinkAccount":
            speak_output = "OK, I've sent some information to the Alexa app.
            Open your Alexa app and click on the link to connect your account."
            endSession = True
            card_output = ui.link_account_card.LinkAccountCard()

        elif question == "DoYouOwnYourHome":
            speak_output = "Great! What's the street address of your primary
            residence?"
            ask = "What's your street address?"
            handler_input.attributes_manager.session_attributes["question"] =
            "What's your street address?"

        elif question == "GetNetWorth":
            # TODO: CalculateNetWorth
            speak_output = "Your current Net Worth is: "
            endSession = True

        elif question == "ClearAndStartOver":
            # TODO: Clear and Start Over
            speak_output = "I've cleared your personal data. To start with,
            what's the street address of your primary residence?"
            ask = "What's your street address?"
            handler_input.attributes_manager.session_attributes["question"] =
            "What's your street address?"

        else:
            speak_output = "Sorry, I got confused, please tell me what you want
            to do or say Help."

class HelpIntentHandler(AbstractRequestHandler)
        if question == "LinkAccount":
            speak_output = "OK, I've sent some information to the Alexa app on
            your phone. Open your Alexa app and click on the link to connect
            your account."
```

```
    elif question == "What's your street address?":
        speak_output = "Try saying your house number and street name."
class StartOverIntentHandler(AbstractRequestHandler)
    speak_output = "OK. Are you sure you want to clear your personal
    information and start again?"
    handler_input.attributes_manager.session_attributes["question"] =
    "ClearAndStartOver"
    handler_input.attributes_manager.session_attributes["last_speech"] =
    speak_output
class FallbackIntentHandler(AbstractRequestHandler)
    speak_output = """Your Personal Net Worth skill can't help with that,
        but I can help you determine your net worth. Try asking for
        Help."""
class RepeatIntentHandler(AbstractRequestHandler)
    else:
        speak_output = """I can help you calculate your net worth. Try
        asking for Help."""
class CatchAllExceptionHandler(AbstractExceptionHandler)
    speak_output = "Sorry, I had trouble doing what you asked. Please try
    again or try asking for Help."
```

After making these edits, the lamda_function.py module is ready for us to start adding the new intent handlers to capture and save your primary residence address. At this point, the module should look like the listing from the code for this book named lambda_function.py after converting from calendar to net worth.py.

Next, you need to add the resource modules Layer the same way we did in Chapter 12. Select the option to add a custom layer and select the latest version of the CalendarDependencies, since this has all the resources we need for now. (See Figure 14-4.)

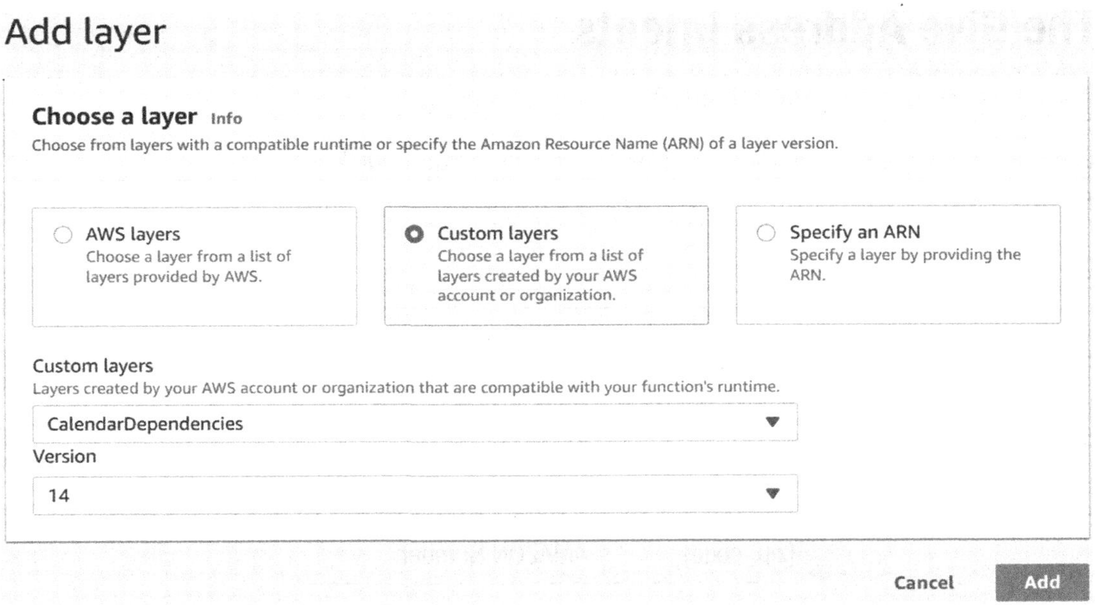

Add layer

Choose a layer Info

Choose from layers with a compatible runtime or specify the Amazon Resource Name (ARN) of a layer version.

○ **AWS layers** Choose a layer from a list of layers provided by AWS.	● **Custom layers** Choose a layer from a list of layers created by your AWS account or organization.	○ **Specify an ARN** Specify a layer by providing the ARN.

Custom layers

Layers created by your AWS account or organization that are compatible with your function's runtime.

CalendarDependencies ▼

Version

14 ▼

Cancel   **Add**

Figure 14-4. *Adding the Custom layer to our lambda function*

Now you should configure a test event based on the *Amazon Alexa Start Session* Event template to test your lambda at this point and make sure you don't have any compile errors and that the unlinked Launch Request handler fires correctly. When you deploy the code and run the test, you should see the "Welcome" response from the LaunchRequestHandlerUnlinked class, as shown in Figure 14-5. If you do not, then fix any bugs before proceeding.

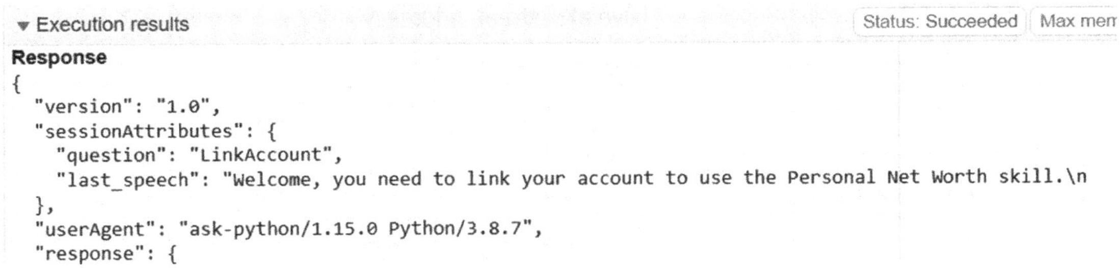

```
▼ Execution results                                        Status: Succeeded   Max mem
Response
{
  "version": "1.0",
  "sessionAttributes": {
    "question": "LinkAccount",
    "last_speech": "Welcome, you need to link your account to use the Personal Net Worth skill.\n
  },
  "userAgent": "ask-python/1.15.0 Python/3.8.7",
  "response": {
```

Figure 14-5. *The "Welcome" response*

With the lambda function well on its way, we are ready to add the handlers and code for the address collection and valuation.

The Give Address Intents

With the GiveAddressIntent defined with two sample utterances:

```
I live at {street_address} {city} {state} {zip_code}
My address is {street_address} {city} {state} {zip_code}
```

and with the slots defined as

Slot Name	Slot Type
{street_address}	AMAZON.PostalAddress
{city}	AMAZON.US_CITY
{state}	AMAZON.US_STATE
{zip_code}	AMAZON.Number

we should test it with the Utterance Profiler (in the Alexa Developer Console, Build Tab, Evaluate Model button). Enter the utterance: 1058 Crossings Circle, Spring Hill, Tennessee 37174. Hmm. That hits the AMAZON.FallbackIntent. Not what we expected. Note: The Utterance Profiler doesn't touch our lambda function. So something else is wrong. We probably need to split this intent into four intents – one for each slot.

Back in Botmock, split the GiveAddressIntent into four pieces:

Intent	GiveAddressIntent
Utterance	My address is %street_address% I live at %street_address%
Slot Prompt	What's your street address?

Intent	GiveCityIntent
Utterance	In %city% I live in the city of %city% In the city of %city%
Slot Prompt	What city do you live in?

Intent	GiveStateIntent
Utterance	In the state of %state%
Slot Prompt	What state do you live in?

Intent	GiveCityIntent
Utterance	My zip code is %zip_code%
	My zip is %zip_code%
Slot Prompt	What's your zip code?

Update the model to use all four slots instead of just one. (See Figure 14-6.)

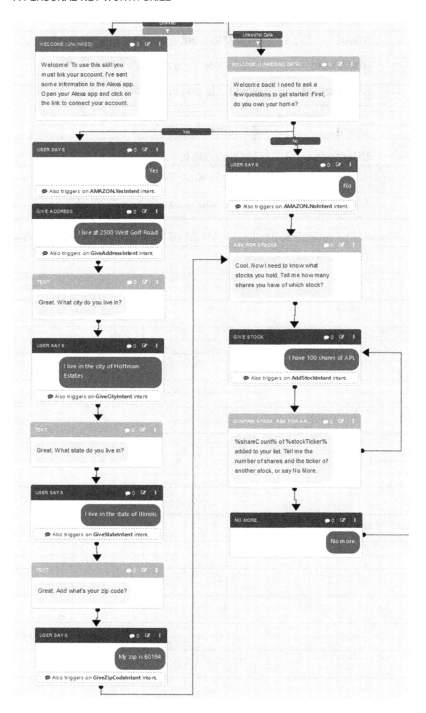

Figure 14-6. *The revised Botmock model*

With the model updated, export it again, edit the Json as previously shown, and copy the Json to the JSON Editor in the Alexa Developer Console. Save the model and build it. Fix any errors. Test the model again in the utterance profiler.

Utterance	Selected Intent
I live at 1058 Crossings Circle.	GiveAddressIntent
In the city of Spring Hill	GiveCityIntent
In the state of Tennessee	GiveStateIntent
My zip is 37174	GiveZipCodeIntent

Now it works as expected. Now we can write the code for the intent handlers. The first three (Address, City, and State) are very similar. They each pull the passed-in slot value out of the `handler_input`, check to make sure the profile has been started, add the slot value to the profile, save the profile, and ask the next question in the progression.

GiveAddressIntentHandler

```python
class GiveAddressIntentHandler(AbstractRequestHandler):
  """Handler for Give Address Intent."""

  def can_handle(self, handler_input):
    validity, _ = read_user_profile(handler_input)
    return (validity == AccessTokenValidity.VALID) and ask_utils.is_
    request_type("GiveAddressIntent")(handler_input)

  def handle(self, handler_input):
    _, profile = read_user_profile(handler_input)
    street_address = handler_input.request_envelope.request.intent.slots[
      "street_address"].value
    if not profile:
      profile = {}
    profile["street_address"] = street_address
    save_user_profile(handler_input, profile)

    speak_output = "Great. What city do you live in?"
    handler_input.attributes_manager.session_attributes["question"] =
    "City"
    handler_input.attributes_manager.session_attributes["last_speech"] =
    speak_output

    return (
      handler_input.response_builder
      .speak(speak_output)
      .ask(speak_output)
      .response
    )
```

GiveCityIntentHandler

```python
class GiveCityIntentHandler(AbstractRequestHandler):
  """Handler for Give City Intent."""

  def can_handle(self, handler_input):
    validity, _ = read_user_profile(handler_input)
    return (validity == AccessTokenValidity.VALID) and ask_utils.is_
    request_type("GiveCityIntent")(handler_input)

  def handle(self, handler_input):
    _, profile = read_user_profile(handler_input)
    city = handler_input.request_envelope.request.intent.slots[
      "city"].value
    if not profile:
      profile = {}
    profile["city"] = city
    save_user_profile(handler_input, profile)

    speak_output = "Cool. What state do you live in?"
    handler_input.attributes_manager.session_attributes["question"] =
    "State"

    handler_input.attributes_manager.session_attributes["last_speech"] =
    speak_output

    return (
      handler_input.response_builder
      .speak(speak_output)
      .ask(speak_output)
      .response
    )
```

GiveStateIntentHandler

```python
class GiveStateIntentHandler(AbstractRequestHandler):
  """Handler for Give State Intent."""

  def can_handle(self, handler_input):
    validity, _ = read_user_profile(handler_input)
    return (validity == AccessTokenValidity.VALID) and ask_utils.is_
    request_type("GiveStateIntent")(handler_input)

  def handle(self, handler_input):
    _, profile = read_user_profile(handler_input)
    state = handler_input.request_envelope.request.intent.slots[
      "state"].value
    if not profile:
      profile = {}
    profile["state"] = state
    save_user_profile(handler_input, profile)

    speak_output = "Awesome. What is your zip code?"
    handler_input.attributes_manager.session_attributes["question"] =
    "ZipCode"

    handler_input.attributes_manager.session_attributes["last_speech"] =
    speak_output

    return (
      handler_input.response_builder
      .speak(speak_output)
      .ask(speak_output)
      .response
    )
```

The zip code intent handler is quite different. First, we need a helper function to deal with zip codes with a leading zero. Specifically, we need to add a right() function that allows us to take the rightmost five characters from the concatenation of "00000" and the numeric value entered for the zip code. For example, if the zip code slot holds 4829, and we prefix it with "00000," we get "000004829," then if we take the rightmost five characters, we get the zip code "04829," which is what the user probably told us in the first place. Here is the right() function:

```
def right(s, amount):
    if s == None:
        return None
    elif amount == None:
        return None  # Or throw a missing argument error
    s = str(s)
    if amount > len(s):
        return s
    elif amount == 0:
        return ""
    else:
        return s[-amount:]
```

The second big difference in the zip code intent handler is that we expect it to come last in the address progression, but the user could fake us out by jumping ahead. In this case, the zip code handler needs to check that we have a complete address and jump back to get the piece(s) of the address we are missing. For example:

```
if not "street_address" in profile:
    speak_output = "I missed your street address. What is it?"
    handler_input.attributes_manager.session_attributes["question"] =
"StreetAddress"
```

The handler would, therefore, be

GiveZipCodeIntentHandler

```
class GiveZipCodeIntentHandler(AbstractRequestHandler):
    """Handler for Give Zip Code Intent."""

    def can_handle(self, handler_input):
        validity, _ = read_user_profile(handler_input)
        return (validity == AccessTokenValidity.VALID) and ask_utils.is_
        request_type("GiveZipCodeIntent")(handler_input)
```

```python
def handle(self, handler_input):
    _, profile = read_user_profile(handler_input)
    zip_code = handler_input.request_envelope.request.intent.slots[
        "zip_code"].value
    if not profile:
        profile = {}
    profile["zip_code"] = right("00000" + str(zip_code), 5)
    save_user_profile(handler_input, profile)

    if not "street_address" in profile:
        speak_output = "I missed your street address. What is it?"
        handler_input.attributes_manager.session_attributes["question"]
        = "StreetAddress"
    elif not "city" in profile:
        speak_output = "I'm missing your city. What is it?"
        handler_input.attributes_manager.session_attributes["question"]
        = "City"
    elif not "state" in profile:
        speak_output = "I'm missing your state. What is it?"
        handler_input.attributes_manager.session_attributes["question"]
        = "State"
    elif not "zip_code" in profile:
        speak_output = "I'm missing your zip code. What is it?"
        handler_input.attributes_manager.session_attributes["question"]
        = "ZipCode"
    else:
        speak_output = f"""Thanks. I have your address as
            {profile["street_address"]},
            {profile["city"]}, {profile["state"]}, {profile["zip_code"]}.
            Is that correct?"""
        handler_input.attributes_manager.session_attributes["question"]
        = "ConfirmAddress"

    handler_input.attributes_manager.session_attributes["last_speech"]
    = speak_output
```

```
return (
    handler_input.response_builder
    .speak(speak_output)
    .ask(speak_output)
    .response
)
```

Next, we'll add your investment portfolio to the Personal Net Worth skill.

The Give Stock Intent

The utterances for the Give Stock intent all have two slots: the stock ticker and the share count. In the Give Stock intent handler, we will need to get both values out of their respective slots, like this:

```
stock_ticker = handler_input.request_envelope.request.intent.slots["stock_
ticker"].value
share_count = handler_input.request_envelope.request.intent.slots["share_
count"].value
```

Then we can add them to a Python dictionary in the profile. We're using a dictionary instead of a list because the key-value pair syntax is ideal for capturing key (stock ticker) and value (share count) for each investment. For example, profile["stocks"]["AMZN"] = 25 would mean you own 25 shares of AMZN. The dictionary allows us to automatically handle updates or additions because if the key is already there, we'll just update the quantity; if not, we'll add the ticker and quantity. For example:

```
profile["stocks"][stock_ticker] = share_count
```

We should probably confirm each addition. In the next chapter, we'll use an API to get the stock name from the ticker so we can confirm with both the ticker and name. For now, we'll just confirm with the ticker. For example:

```
if stock_ticker in profile["stocks"]:
    speak_output = f'The number of shares of {stock_ticker} is updating
    from {profile["stocks"][stock_ticker]} to {share_count}. Is this
    correct?'
```

```
else:
    speak_output = f'Adding {share_count} shares of {stock_ticker} to your
    portfolio. Is this correct?'
```

Suppose the user says "No" when we ask, "Is this correct?" We'll need to undo the assignment of profile["stocks"][stock_ticker] = share_count. Before we change the quantity, let's stash the previous quantity in the session_attributes; if the user says, "No," we can put the previous quantity back. Unless the previous quantity is zero, then we can delete that stock ticker from the dictionary. For example, if we put this code in the Give Stock intent handler:

```
if stock_ticker in profile["stocks"]:
    handler_input.attributes_manager.session_attributes["previous_share_
    count"] = profile["stocks"][stock_ticker]
else:
    handler_input.attributes_manager.session_attributes["previous_share_
    count"] = 0

handler_input.attributes_manager.session_attributes["previous_stock_
ticker"] = stock_ticker
profile["stocks"][stock_ticker] = share_count
save_user_profile(handler_input, profile)
```

then we can put this code in the No intent handler to undo the add/update:

```
elif question == "ConfirmShares":
    if handler_input.attributes_manager.session_attributes["previous_share_
    count"] == 0:
        del profile["stocks"][handler_input.attributes_manager.session_
        attributes["previous_stock_ticker"]]
    else:
        profile["stocks"][handler_input.attributes_manager.session_
        attributes["previous_stock_ticker"]] = handler_input.attributes_
        manager.session_attributes["previous_share_count"]
```

The finished GiveStockIntentHandler would therefore be

```
class GiveStockIntentHandler(AbstractRequestHandler):
    """Handler for Give Stock Intent."""
```

```python
def can_handle(self, handler_input):
    validity, _ = read_user_profile(handler_input)
    return (validity == AccessTokenValidity.VALID) and ask_utils.is_
request_type("GiveStockIntent")(handler_input)

def handle(self, handler_input):
    _, profile = read_user_profile(handler_input)
    stock_ticker = handler_input.request_envelope.request.intent.slots[
        "stock_ticker"].value
    share_count = handler_input.request_envelope.request.intent.slots[
        "share_count"].value
    if not profile:
        profile = {}
        profile["stocks"] = {}
    if stock_ticker in profile["stocks"]:
        handler_input.attributes_manager.session_attributes[
            "previous_share_count"] = profile["stocks"][stock_ticker]
        speak_output = f'The number of shares of {stock_ticker} is
        updating from {profile["stocks"][stock_ticker]} to {share_
        count}. Is this correct?'
    else:
        handler_input.attributes_manager.session_attributes["previous_
        share_count"] = 0
        speak_output = f'Adding {share_count} shares of {stock_ticker}
        to your portfolio. Is this correct?'
    handler_input.attributes_manager.session_attributes["previous_
    stock_ticker"] = stock_ticker
    profile["stocks"][stock_ticker] = share_count
    save_user_profile(handler_input, profile)
    handler_input.attributes_manager.session_attributes["last_speech"]
    = speak_output
    ask = "Is this correct?"
    handler_input.attributes_manager.session_attributes["question"] =
    "ConfirmShares"
```

```
return (
    handler_input.response_builder
    .speak(speak_output)
    .ask(ask)
    .response
)
```

Now we have the Give* intent handlers, and we need to look at the Yes and No intent handlers.

The Yes/No Intents

In the other intents, we ask the user several yes/no questions. Specifically, we ask

```
Would you like to link it [your account] now?
Do you own your home?
Would you like to know your net worth?
Is that correct? [Address confirmation]
Is this correct? [Updating quantity of shares held]
Is this correct? [Adding stock ticker and quantity]
```

In each case, we add the "question" item to the session attributes so that we know to what the user is saying Yes or No. The basic structure of the Yes or No intent handlers is, therefore, a series of if...elif...else statements. For example, here's the first if statement that handles Yes response to the LinkAccount question:

```
if question == "LinkAccount":
    speak_output = "OK, I've sent some information to the Alexa app. Open
    your Alexa app and click on the link to connect your account."
    endSession = True
    card_output = ui.link_account_card.LinkAccountCard()
```

and the corresponding No handler for the LinkAccount question:

```
if question == "LinkAccount":
    speak_output = "OK, you can come back later and link your account to
    get started. Thank you."
    endSession = True
```

One special thing about the Yes/No handlers is if the user's Access Token isn't valid yet and the question is "LinkAccount," we still need to run the handler code. To make this happen, we need to modify the can_handle logic as shown here:

```
def can_handle(self, handler_input):
    validity, _ = read_user_profile(handler_input)
    question = handler_input.attributes_manager.session_
    attributes["question"]
    return (validity == AccessTokenValidity.VALID
        or validity == AccessTokenValidity.NEW
        or question == "LinkAccount") \
        and ask_utils.is_intent_name("AMAZON.YesIntent")(handler_input)
```

This will ensure the code runs, regardless of whether the account is linked yet or not, but only if the question is "LinkAccount."

Putting it all together, we end up with a Yes intent handler that looks like this:

```
class YesIntentHandler(AbstractRequestHandler):
    """Handler for Yes Intent."""

    def can_handle(self, handler_input):
        # type: (HandlerInput) -> bool
        validity, _ = read_user_profile(handler_input)
        question = handler_input.attributes_manager.session_
        attributes["question"]
        return (validity == AccessTokenValidity.VALID
                or validity == AccessTokenValidity.NEW
                or question == "LinkAccount") \
            and ask_utils.is_intent_name("AMAZON.YesIntent")(handler_input)

    def handle(self, handler_input):
        _, profile = read_user_profile(handler_input)
        question = handler_input.attributes_manager.session_
        attributes["question"]

        speak_output = ""
        ask = None
        endSession = False
        card_output = None
```

```
if question == "LinkAccount":
    speak_output = "OK, I've sent some information to the Alexa
    app. Open your Alexa app and click on the link to connect your
    account."
    endSession = True
    card_output = ui.link_account_card.LinkAccountCard()

elif question == "DoYouOwnYourHome":
    speak_output = "Great! What's the street address of your
    primary residence?"
    ask = "What's your street address?"
    handler_input.attributes_manager.session_attributes[
        "question"] = "StreetAddress"
    if not profile:
        profile = {}
    profile["own_home"] = True
    save_user_profile(handler_input, profile)

elif question == "ConfirmAddress":
    speak_output = "Fantastic! Now we can move on to your
    investments. Tell me how many shares you own and the stock
    ticker for each of your investments. Or say No More to stop
    adding shares."
    ask = "Tell me how many shares you own of a certain stock ticker."
    handler_input.attributes_manager.session_attributes[
        "question"] = "AddStock"

elif question == "ConfirmShares":
    speak_output = "That many? Wow! Tell me how many shares you own
    and the stock ticker for another of your investments. Or say No
    More to stop adding shares."
    ask = "Tell me how many shares you own of a certain stock ticker."
    handler_input.attributes_manager.session_attributes[
        "question"] = "AddStock"

elif question == "GetNetWorth":

    # TODO: CalculateNetWorth
```

```
        speak_output = "Your current Net Worth is: "
        endSession = True

    elif question == "ClearAndStartOver":
        profile = {}
        save_user_profile(handler_input, profile)
        speak_output = "I've cleared your personal data. To start with,
        do you own your home?"
        ask = "Do you own your home?"
        handler_input.attributes_manager.session_attributes[
            "question"] = "DoYouOwnYourHome"

    else:
        speak_output = "Sorry, I got confused, please tell me what you
        want to do or say Help."

    handler_input.attributes_manager.session_attributes["last_speech"]
    = speak_output

    if not ask:
        ask = speak_output

    return (
        handler_input.response_builder
        .speak(speak_output)
        .ask(ask)
        .set_card(card_output)
        .set_should_end_session(endSession)
        .response
    )
```

We also need a corresponding No intent handler that looks like this:

```
class NoIntentHandler(AbstractRequestHandler):
    """Handler for No Intent."""

    def can_handle(self, handler_input):
        # type: (HandlerInput) -> bool
        validity, _ = read_user_profile(handler_input)
```

```
    question = handler_input.attributes_manager.session_
    attributes["question"]
    return (validity == AccessTokenValidity.VALID
            or validity == AccessTokenValidity.NEW
            or question == "LinkAccount") \
        and ask_utils.is_intent_name("AMAZON.NoIntent")(handler_input)

def handle(self, handler_input):
    _, profile = read_user_profile(handler_input)
    question = handler_input.attributes_manager.session_
    attributes["question"]

    speak_output = ""
    ask = None
    endSession = False

    if question == "LinkAccount":
        speak_output = "OK, you can come back later and link your
        account to get started. Thank you."
        endSession = True

    elif question == "DoYouOwnYourHome":
        speak_output = "OK. Let's move on to your investments. Tell me
        how many shares you own and the stock ticker for each of your
        investments. Or say No More to stop adding shares."
        ask = "Tell me how many shares you own of a certain stock
        ticker."
        handler_input.attributes_manager.session_attributes[
            "question"] = "AddStock"

    elif question == "ConfirmAddress":
        speak_output = "Ok. Let's try that again. What's the street
        address of your primary residence?"
        ask = "What's your street address?"
        handler_input.attributes_manager.session_attributes["question"]
        = "StreetAddress"
        profile = {}
        profile["own_home"] = True
```

```
        save_user_profile(handler_input, profile)

    elif question == "ConfirmShares":
        speak_output = "Oops. Let's try that again. Tell me how
        many shares you own and the stock ticker for each of your
        investments. Or say No More to stop adding shares."
        ask = "Tell me how many shares you own of a certain stock
        ticker."
        if handler_input.attributes_manager.session_attributes
        ["previous_share_count"] == 0:
            del profile["stocks"][handler_input.attributes_manager.
            session_attributes["previous_stock_ticker"]]
        else:
            profile["stocks"][handler_input.attributes_manager.session_
            attributes["previous_stock_ticker"]
                                 ] = handler_input.attributes_manager.
                                     session_attributes["previous_share_
                                     count"]
        handler_input.attributes_manager.session_attributes[
            "question"] = "AddStock"

    elif question == "GetNetWorth":
        speak_output = "OK. Now's not a good time. I get it. You're
        welcome to come back later and find out your net worth. It only
        takes a minute."
        endSession = True

    elif question == "ClearAndStartOver":
        # Rejected. Don't Clear and Start Over
        speak_output = "Phew. I thought you were going to delete
        everything. But you're not. Great. Would you like to know your
        net worth?"
        ask = "Would you like to know your net worth?"
        handler_input.attributes_manager.session_attributes[
            "question"] = "GetNetWorth"
```

```
    else:
        speak_output = "Sorry, I got confused, please tell me what you
        want to do or say Help."

    handler_input.attributes_manager.session_attributes["last_speech"]
    = speak_output

    if not ask:
        ask = speak_output
    return (
        handler_input.response_builder
        .speak(speak_output)
        .ask(ask)
        .set_should_end_session(endSession)
        .response
    )
```

The last thing we'll cover in this chapter is the No More intent handler.

The No More Intent

When the user wants to stop adding stocks to their portfolio, they need to say "No more."
When they do, we need to stop asking for stocks and offer to get their Net Worth instead.
The No More intent handler will therefore be

```
class NoMoreIntentHandler(AbstractRequestHandler):
    """Handler for No More Intent."""

    def can_handle(self, handler_input):
        validity, _ = read_user_profile(handler_input)
        return (validity == AccessTokenValidity.VALID) and ask_utils.is_
        request_type("NoMoreIntent")(handler_input)

    def handle(self, handler_input):
        speak_output = "Ok. Would you like to know your net worth?"
        handler_input.attributes_manager.session_attributes["question"] =
        "GetNetWorth"
```

```
    handler_input.attributes_manager.session_attributes["last_speech"]
    = speak_output

    return (
        handler_input.response_builder
        .speak(speak_output)
        .ask(speak_output)
        .response
    )
```

Now we need to add the new intents to the Skill Builder. At the bottom of the module, update the Skill Builder section as shown here:

```
sb = CustomSkillBuilder(persistence_adapter=adapter)
sb.add_request_handler(LaunchRequestHandlerUnlinked())
sb.add_request_handler(LaunchRequestHandlerNew())
sb.add_request_handler(LaunchRequestHandlerValid())
sb.add_request_handler(GiveAddressIntentHandler())
sb.add_request_handler(GiveCityIntentHandler())
sb.add_request_handler(GiveStateIntentHandler())
sb.add_request_handler(GiveZipCodeIntentHandler())
sb.add_request_handler(GiveStockIntentHandler())
sb.add_request_handler(NoMoreIntentHandler())
sb.add_request_handler(YesIntentHandler())
sb.add_request_handler(NoIntentHandler())
sb.add_request_handler(HelpIntentHandler())
sb.add_request_handler(NavigateHomeIntentValidHandler())
sb.add_request_handler(NavigateHomeIntentInvalidHandler())
sb.add_request_handler(StartOverIntentHandler())
sb.add_request_handler(CancelOrStopIntentHandler())
sb.add_request_handler(SessionEndedRequestHandler())
sb.add_request_handler(RepeatIntentHandler())
sb.add_request_handler(FallbackIntentHandler())
# make sure the IntentReflectorHandler and CatchAllExceptionHandler
```

```
# are last so they don't override your custom intent handlers
sb.add_request_handler(IntentReflectorHandler())
sb.add_exception_handler(CatchAllExceptionHandler())
```

Your homework is to update the HelpIntentHandler, NavigateHomeIntent*Handlers, and all the other built-in intents' handlers so that they work appropriately for this skill. You should also create unit tests in the lambda environment to test your functions. Remember that this involves using the Alexa Developer Console to get the Json for an intent and then copying that into the Test in the lambda function.

And with that, we've created the front end (the VUI) and the back end (the lambda_ function and dynamodb modules) for our Personal Net Worth skill. There is one glaring omission, though. We have a To-Do item left in the Yes intent handler:

```
# TODO: CalculateNetWorth
```

That's what we'll do in the next chapter.

Summary

In this chapter, we created the beginnings of a Personal Net Worth skill. First, we identified the requirements. This enabled us to design the VUI in Botmock. We then exported that design as Json and brought it into the Alexa Developer Console. Then we created the back-end lambda function, where we coded the Launch Intent handlers. We added a dynamodb module that could read and save the user profile. We added the give address intent handlers and the give stock intent handlers. Then we looked at the Yes and No intent handlers. Finally, we added the No More intent handler and updated the Skill Builder section of the lambda function. In the next chapter, we will use financial APIs to get the value of the assets we collected in this chapter.

## CHAPTER 15

The Real Estate API

In this chapter, we're going to take the Personal Finance skill that we built in the previous chapter and add the first of the asset value calculations that will tell us the value of our home and investments. Again, this skill could have its hands on a lot of our personal data, but all of that data will be safely ensconced in a secured database and encrypted for your protection. **In all cases, you will have the option of using a test account and fake data for development purposes, so no REAL data need to be involved at all.**

We will be using two APIs: a real estate API and a stock market API. This chapter will introduce APIs – how to authenticate to them and how to use them. Then we'll add a module to our lambda function that calls a real estate API to calculate the value of our home so that Alexa can tell us what it's worth.

First up, an introduction to APIs.

Application Programming Interfaces

An Application Programming Interface, most commonly referred to as an API, is a way for a developer to publish functionality, in this case, on the web, in such a way that other developers can access that functionality and use it in their programs. Many APIs are said to be RESTful.[1] This means many things, but for our purposes, it means that they are accessible through a specially crafted URL[2] instead of through a more complex mechanism.

---

[1] RESTful API. REST stands for Representational State Transfer. But no one uses the long form. Almost all the documentation about REST and RESTful APIs uses the acronym.

[2] URL. Another acronym that has lost its meaning to history. URL stands for Uniform Resource Locator, but you know URLs better as simply web addresses.

© Simon A. Kingaby 2022
S. A. Kingaby, *Data-Driven Alexa Skills*, https://doi.org/10.1007/978-1-4842-7449-1_15

For example, the Numbers API is a free service that provides a trivia fact for a given number. This is a RESTful API, so you can access it through a standard Internet browser. Simply navigate to `http://numbersapi.com/100`. You can substitute any number for 100. For example, `http://numberspi.com/8` might respond, "8 is the number of bits in a byte." Some numbers are unremarkable. Many will provide one of several simple trivia facts about the number. You can see the home page and additional functionality of the Numbers API at `http://numbersapi.com/`.

You can also call the Numbers API, or any RESTful API, from Python's `requests` module. For example:

```
import requests
```

```
response = requests.request("GET", "http://numbersapi.com/17")
print(response.text)
```

```
Output:
17 is the number of flames emanating from the grenade cap-badge of the Grenadier
Guards.
```

With an understanding of how we can call APIs with the Python requests module, we can now look for an API that will value our property.

The Real Estate Valuation API

A Google search turns up all sorts of APIs for property valuation. At first, this may seem overwhelming. However, there is a website that makes finding and using API interactions much simpler: `https://rapidapi.com`. Rapid API is a hub for API developers to expose their API in a somewhat standard way. It makes it easy to subscribe to the freemium sites, and it provides example code for calling the API in a variety of programming languages. After registering as a developer, a quick search in Rapid API for a property valuation API turns up a few likely candidates. (See Figure 15-1.)

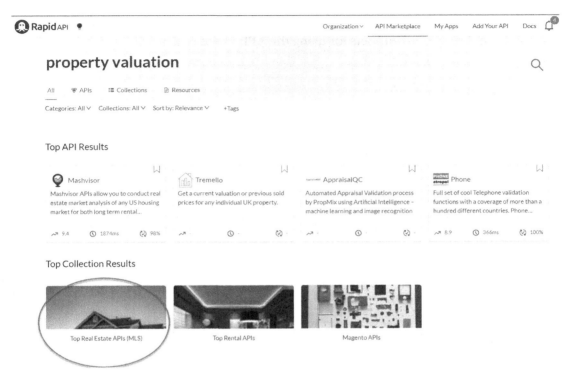

Figure 15-1. *A search for Property Valuation in Rapid API*

Clicking on the Top Real Estate APIs (MLS) collection result, we find several APIs that might fit the bill. One, in particular, is intriguing. Hovering over the Realty Mole (See Figure 15-2), we see a GET Sale Price Estimate method in the API. That's precisely what we're looking for.

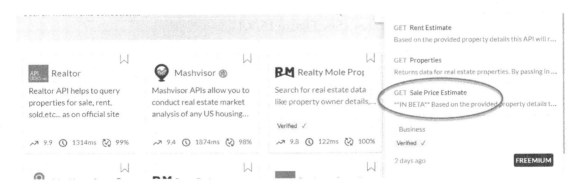

Figure 15-2. *Finding the Sale Price Estimate method*

Clicking through to the Realty Mole API, we find the Documentation, tests for the Endpoints, and the Code Snippets for using the API. There is also a Subscribe to Test button. (See Figure 15-3.)

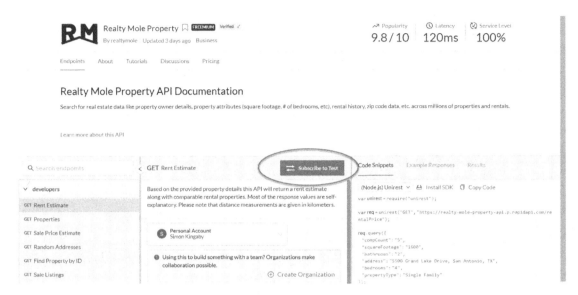

Figure 15-3. *The Realty Mole Property API*

Go ahead and click Subscribe to Test. Then select the Basic (Free) plan. That gives us 50 API calls per month quota which should be plenty for us to test with. After subscribing to the Free plan (yes, you still need to give them a credit card in case you go over your 50 free API calls), you will be redirected back to the API Documentation page, where you now have a Test Endpoint button. Click it. The API should return a Status 200 message on the right with some rental rates. (See Figure 15-4.)

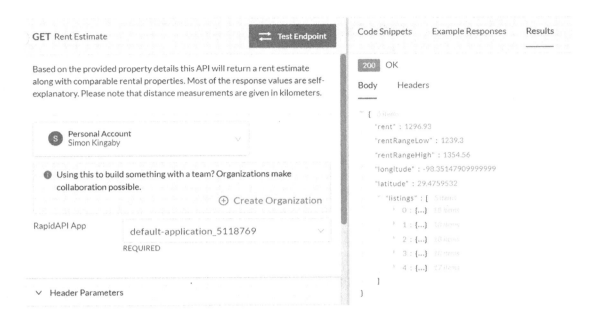

Figure 15-4. *Testing the Endpoint, we get a message with rental rates*

Switch to the Sale Price Estimate method on the left. Scroll down and put in the particulars for your home, specifically square footage, bathrooms, address (excluding the zip code), bedrooms, and property type. Select the Code Snippet for Python | Requests. (See Figure 15-5.)

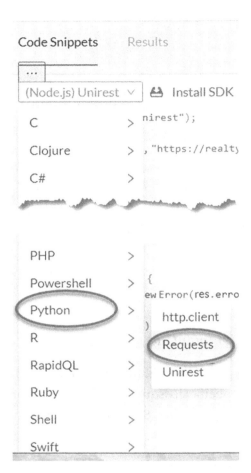

Figure 15-5. *Select Python Requests*

Click Test Endpoint again. This time, see that the Json result has a price in it, not rental rates. (See Figure 15-6.)

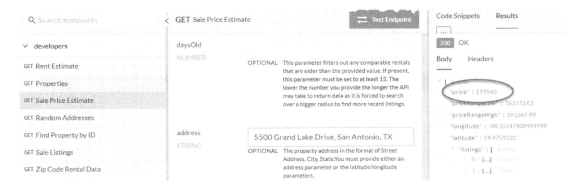

Figure 15-6. *The Sale Price Estimate method returns a price*

This looks exactly like what we need. Now we need to update our VUI to gather the facts.

Adding the Give Home Stats Intent

We need to ask the user to give us square footage, bathrooms, bedrooms, and property type. Since property type has a shortlist of finite values, you will need to add an Entity in Botmock or a Slot Type in the Alexa Developer Console.

Botmock	Alexa Developer Console

EN **EDIT ENTITY**

ENTITY NAME*

PropertyType

POSSIBLE VALUES FOR THIS ENTITY

VALUE*

Duplex-Triplex

VALUE*

Condo

VALUE*

Townhouse

VALUE*

Single Family

VALUE*

Apartment

Slot Types / PropertyType

Custom slot types with values define a representative list of possible values, IDs and synonyms.

Slot Values (5)

VALUE	ID (OPTIONAL)
Duplex-Triplex	
Condo	
Townhouse	
Single Family	
Apartment	

Then add an Intent for Giving the Home Stats.

Botmock

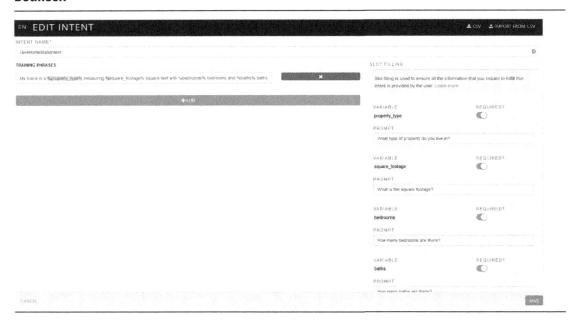

Alexa Developer Console

Botmock

Intents / GiveHomeStatsIntent

Sample Utterances (1)

> What might a user say to invoke this intent?

My home is a {property_type} measuring {square_footage} square feet with {bedrooms} bedrooms and {baths} baths.

Dialog Delegation Strategy

fallback to skill setting

Intent Slots (4)

ORDER	NAME	SLOT TYPE
1	property_type	PropertyType
2	square_footage	AMAZON.NUMBER
3	bedrooms	AMAZON.NUMBER
4	baths	AMAZON.NUMBER

In Botmock, the diagram can be updated as shown in Figure 15-7.

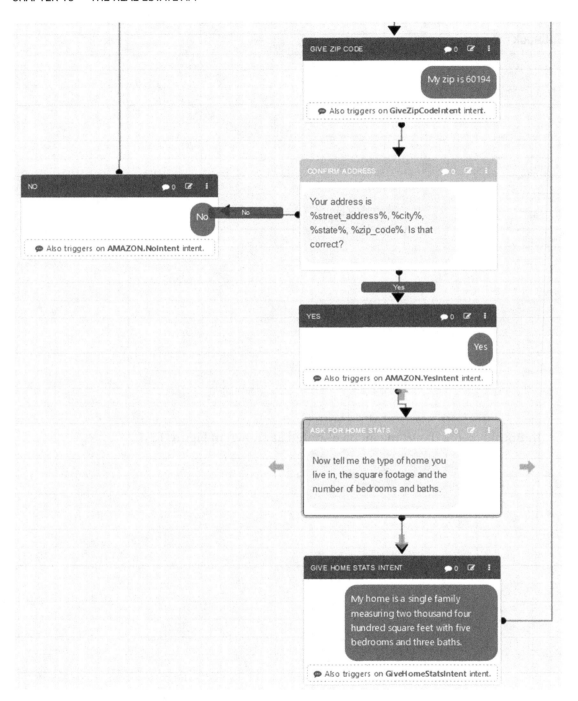

Figure 15-7. *The Botmock diagram updated with the Give Home Stats Intent*

Now we can add the code for the new intent. Since we're collecting all the stats in one utterance, we can process them in a single intent handler.

```python
class GiveHomeStatsIntentHandler(AbstractRequestHandler):
    """Handler for Give Home Stats Intent."""

    def can_handle(self, handler_input):
        validity, _ = read_user_profile(handler_input)
        return (validity == AccessTokenValidity.VALID) and ask_utils.is_
        request_type("GiveHomeStatsIntent")(handler_input)

    def handle(self, handler_input):
        _, profile = read_user_profile(handler_input)
        property_type = handler_input.request_envelope.request.intent.
        slots["property_type"].value
        square_footage = handler_input.request_envelope.request.intent.
        slots["square_footage"].value
        bedrooms = handler_input.request_envelope.request.intent.
        slots["bedrooms"].value
        baths = handler_input.request_envelope.request.intent.
        slots["baths"].value
        if not profile:
            profile = {}
        profile["homestats"] = {
            "property_type": property_type,
            "square_footage": square_footage,
            "bedrooms": bedrooms,
            "baths": baths
        }
        save_user_profile(handler_input, profile)

    speak_output = f"Your home is a {property_type} measuring {square_footage} square
feet with {bedrooms} bedrooms and {baths} baths. Is that correct?"
    handler_input.attributes_manager.session_attributes["last_speech"] =
    speak_output
        ask = "Is that correct?"
    handler_input.attributes_manager.session_attributes["question"] =
    "ConfirmStats"
```

```
    return (
        handler_input.response_builder
        .speak(speak_output)
        .ask(ask)
        .response
    )
```

We'll also need to add a clause to the Yes and No intent handlers.

Yes Intent Handler

```
elif question == "ConfirmAddress":
  speak_output = "Super. Tell me a little about your home. What type
  of home is it, how many square feet, how many bedrooms, and how many
  baths?"
  ask = "What type of home is it, how many square feet, how many bedrooms,
  and how many baths?"
  handler_input.attributes_manager.session_attributes["question"] =
  "HomeStats"

elif question == "ConfirmStats":
  speak_output = "Fantastic! Now we can move on to your investments.
  Please tell me how many shares you own and the stock ticker for each of
  your investments. Or say No More to stop adding shares."
  ask = "Tell me how many shares you own of a certain stock ticker."
  handler_input.attributes_manager.session_attributes["question"] =
"AddStock"
```

No Intent Handler

```
elif question == "ConfirmStats":
  speak_output = "Doh. Let's try that again. What type of home is it, how
  many square feet, how many bedrooms, and how many baths?"
  ask = "What type of home is it, how many square feet, how many bedrooms,
  and how many baths?"
  handler_input.attributes_manager.session_attributes[
    "question"] = "HomeStats"
```

And don't forget to add some help to the Help intent handler and add the new GiveHomeStatsIntentHandler to the Skill Builder.

```
sb.add_request_handler(GiveHomeStatsIntentHandler())
```

Now that we're able to gather the home stats, we can get back to calculating the value of your home.

Back to the Real Estate API

We have the address and the home stats. Now we need to pass that info to the API and get the home valuation. We need two things: (1) the code to call the API and (2) a way to test it. As for the code, we have most of what we need in the API Code Snippet for Python Requests:

```python
import requests

url = "https://realty-mole-property-api.p.rapidapi.com/salePrice"

querystring = {"compCount":"5","squareFootage":"1600","bathrooms":"2",
"address":"5500 Grand Lake Drive, San Antonio, TX","bedrooms":"4",
"propertyType":"Single Family"}

headers = {
    'x-rapidapi-key': "b912ba32xxxxxxxxxxxxxxxxxxxxxxxxxxxxxxxxxxxx899e140d",
    'x-rapidapi-host': "realty-mole-property-api.p.rapidapi.com"
    }

response = requests.request("GET", url, headers=headers, params=querystring)

print(response.text)
```

To test it, we can plug something into our Launch Request handler to ensure the plumbing works. Then we can create the necessary Json in the Alexa Developer Console's Test tab to test it with our data. Then we can hook it up to the missing CalculateNetWorth function, which we'll add. Sounds like a plan.

First, let's put this code in a new module so that we don't bury the API calls in among the intent handlers. In the lambda function, in the PersonalNetWorthBackend folder, next to lambda_function.py and dynamodb.py, add another file: api_calls.py. Then paste in the code from the API Code Snippet (shown previously). Then we have to make one crucial change.

This code includes our API key:

```
headers = {
    'x-rapidapi-key': "b912ba32xxxxxxxxxxxxxxxxxxxxxxxxxxxxxxxxxxxxx899e140d",
```

The API keys are "your keys to the kingdom." Anyone can use your keys to call the API on your behalf, which is fine for your skill but not so fine for you if a hacker gets your keys and puts them on the dark web. You should NEVER leave keys in your code. This is very similar to leaving the keys in your car in a parking lot and hoping your car is still there when you come back. Good luck.

If we can't leave the keys in the code, where can we put them? The best place to put them is in an Environment variable. This gets the keys out of the code itself but puts them where they are still available for use. In AWS Lambda, we can configure the Environment variables quite easily:

1. Select the *Configuration* tab above the code window (see Figure 15-8).

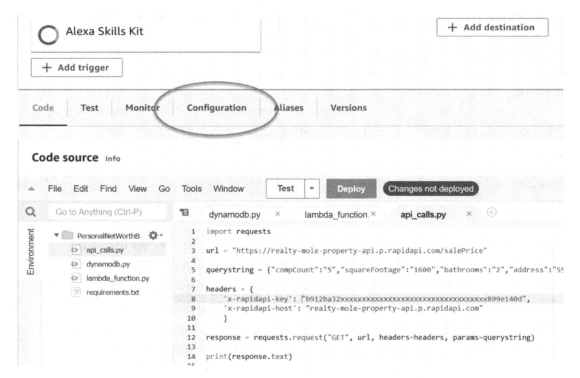

Figure 15-8. *Select the Configuration Tab*

2. Select the *Environment variables* option from the left nav menu (see Figure 15-9).

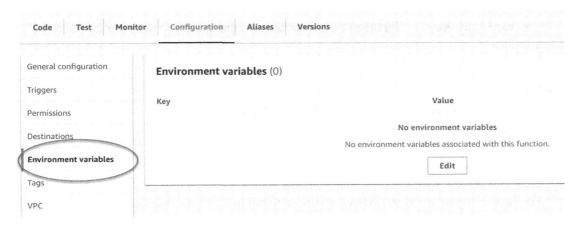

Figure 15-9. *Select the Environment variables menu option on the left*

3. Click the *Edit* button in the center of the screen.

4. Click the *Add environment variable* button.

5. Environment variables are Key-Value pairs. In our case, the Key is the name we will assign to the API key, and the Value is the key itself.

6. In the *Key* slot, enter **RAPID_API_KEY**. (Environment variables are, by convention, all uppercase characters.)

7. In the *Value* slot, paste in the API key from the Code Snippet: **b912ba32xxxxxxxxxxxxxxxxxxxxxxxxxxxxxxxxxxx899e140d**

8. Click the *Save* button in the bottom right.

The environment variable is encrypted at rest with the default Lambda service key. This is sufficient for our purposes. However, if you want to encrypt the key in flight, there is an option to use the AWS Key Management Service (KMS) to encrypt the environment variable. If you want to enable this option, you would then have to supplement the code presented here with the code provided in the KMS examples.

Now that we have stored the API key in an environment variable, we can change the code to use it from there instead of hard-coding the key value. Change this:

```
headers = {
    'x-rapidapi-key': "b912ba32xxxxxxxxxxxxxxxxxxxxxxxxxxxxxxxxxx899e140d",
```

Replace the key value with a call to the environment:

```
headers = {
    'x-rapidapi-key': os.environ['RAPID_API_KEY'],
```

This will require an additional import statement at the top of the module:

```
import os
```

The last thing we need to do is wrap the API call in a function definition that will take a user profile (to be passed in from the intent handler that is calculating the net worth) and return the home value (from the API call). After making these changes, the api_calls. py module should look like this:

```
import requests
import os
import logging
import json

logger = logging.getLogger(__name__)
logger.setLevel(logging.INFO)

url = "https://realty-mole-property-api.p.rapidapi.com/salePrice"

def GetHomeValue(profile):

    querystring = {
        "compCount": "10",
        "squareFootage": profile["homestats"]["square_footage"],
        "bathrooms": profile["homestats"]["baths"],
        "address": f'{profile["street_address"]}, {profile["city"]},
        {profile["state"]}',
        "bedrooms": profile["homestats"]["bedrooms"],
        "propertyType": profile["homestats"]["property_type"]
```

```
}
headers = {
    'x-rapidapi-key': os.environ['RAPID_API_KEY'],
    'x-rapidapi-host': "realty-mole-property-api.p.rapidapi.com"
}
response = requests.request(
    "GET", url, headers=headers, params=querystring)

if response.text:
    logger.info(f"{response.text}")
    result = json.loads(response.text)
    if result["price"]:
        return result["price"]
return None
```

With the environment variable defined and the code in place, we can test the API call.

Testing the API Call

How can we test the API call efficiently? I'd rather not have to have the entire conversation with Alexa just yet, though we will need to a little later. Instead, we can plug the API call into the Launch Request handler and just use the test for that. First, we need to have a test for the Launch Request handler. If you don't have one yet, then you get a slap on the wrist for not testing anything to this point. If you do, give yourself a self-high-five. Thank you for being in the 1% of coders who actually test their code[3] before launching it into production. If you haven't had a chance to create the test for the Launch Request yet, there's still hope. You can create one now:

1. Click the *Test* button's drop-down and select *Configure test event*.

2. Select the radio button to *Create new test event*.

3. Select the **alexa-skills-kit-start-session** Event template.

4. Name your test: **LaunchRequestNoLink**.

---

[3] Not an actual fact. This is a made-up number to make a point. Far too many coders do not test their code sufficiently before deploying it. Don't be that coder. Make sure your code actually works before submitting it for Alexa certification.

5. Click *Save* at the bottom.

6. Click the *Test* button to run the test.

You should see the Welcome message in the Json results:

Response
```
{
  "version": "1.0",
  "sessionAttributes": {
    "question": "LinkAccount",
 "last_speech": "Welcome, you need to link your account to use the Personal Net Worth
skill.\n            Would you like to link it now?"
  },
```

If, instead, you see an error message, then debug your code until you do see the welcome message before proceeding.

Now that we all have a unit test for the Launch Request handler, we can plug in the API call. First, import the GetHomeValue() function at the top of the lamda_function.py module.

Next, we will plug in our API test in the middle of the handle() function in the LaunchRequestHandlerUnlinked class.

```
    def handle(self, handler_input):
    speak_output = """Welcome, you need to link your account to use the Personal Net
Worth skill.
            Would you like to link it now?"""
  handler_input.attributes_manager.session_attributes["question"] =
  "LinkAccount"

        ====> API Call goes here

handler_input.attributes_manager.session_attributes["last_speech"] =
speak_output

        return (
            handler_input.response_builder
```

```
        .speak(speak_output)
        .ask(speak_output)
        .response
    )
```

The call to the API needs to populate the Profile, which we're going to hard-code for this test. It will return the home value, which we will have Alexa speak in the speak_ output of the response.

Loading the profile will look like this:

```
profile = {}
profile["street_address"] = "1234 Main Street"
profile["city"] = "Nashville"
profile["state"] = "TN"
profile["zip_code"] = 37206
profile["homestats"] = {
    "property_type": "Single Family",
    "square_footage": 2250,
    "bedrooms": 4,
    "baths": 3
}
```

And the call to the API function is just one line:

```
homeValue = GetHomeValue(profile)
```

Lastly, we need to output the home value so we can hear/see it in the Alexa response:

```
speak_output = f"The home value is {homeValue}"
```

The finished Launch Request handler will be

```
class LaunchRequestHandlerUnlinked(AbstractRequestHandler):
    """Handler for Skill Launch when the Account is not linked."""

    def can_handle(self, handler_input):
        return not has_access_token(handler_input) and ask_utils.is_
        request_type("LaunchRequest")(handler_input)

    def handle(self, handler_input):
```

```
        speak_output = """Welcome, you need to link your account to use the
        Personal Net Worth skill.
            Would you like to link it now?"""
    handler_input.attributes_manager.session_attributes["question"] =
    "LinkAccount"

        # ====>

        profile = {}
        profile["street_address"] = "1234 Main Street"
        profile["city"] = "Nashville"
        profile["state"] = "TN"
        profile["zip_code"] = 37206
        profile["homestats"] = {
            "property_type": "Single Family",
            "square_footage": 2250,
            "bedrooms": 4,
            "baths": 3
        }
        homeValue = GetHomeValue(profile)
        speak_output = f"The home value is {homeValue}"

        # ====>

        handler_input.attributes_manager.session_attributes["last_speech"]
        = speak_output

        return (
            handler_input.response_builder
            .speak(speak_output)
            .ask(speak_output)
            .response
        )
```

We can rerun the Launch test. We should see an estimate of the home value in the response, as shown in Figure 15-10.

```
Response
{
  "version": "1.0",
  "sessionAttributes": {
    "last_speech": "The home value is 646941.6"
  },
```

Figure 15-10. *The Launch Request handler is running the API test code*

Now that we have the test running, we can put the code in the right place. First, comment out the code we added to the Launch Request handler. Then, in the Yes intent handler, find the elif for "GetNetWorth" and modify it to call the GetHomeValue() function.

With the code commented out in the Launch Request handler and modified in the Yes intent handler, we are ready to test in the Alexa Developer Console Test tab. Give it a try. Fix any bugs you encounter. You should be able to give the entire skill a try. Remember, you will need the full address, the type of home, square footage, number of bedrooms, and number of bathrooms. Debug any problems you encounter. When you've finished testing your skill, we can move on to the next chapter to add the stock portfolio's value to your net worth.

Summary

In this chapter, we looked at APIs. We looked at the Numbers API. We introduced a real estate valuation API from Realty Mole, where we could call the Sale Price Estimate endpoint of the Realty Mole Property API and get an approximate price for a home. We added the necessary intent to the VUI and handler to the lambda function to gather the stats. Then we learned how to test the API call directly by putting it in the Launch Request handler. Then, once it was working, we moved it to the correct location in the Yes intent handler and tested the skill in the Alexa Developer Console. With that working, we are ready to move on to the next chapter to call the stock valuation API.

CHAPTER 16

The Stock Market API

In this chapter, we're going to take the Personal Finance skill that we built in the previous chapters and add the second of the asset value calculations to tell us the value of our investments. Again, this skill could have its hands on a lot of our personal data, but all of that data will be safely ensconced in a secured database and encrypted for your protection. **In all cases, you will have the option of using a test account and fake data for development purposes, so no REAL data need to be involved at all.**

To calculate your stock portfolio's current value, we need to know each stock ticker, share quantity, and current closing price. The first two we are collecting in our skill. For the third, we will need to find an API.

A search for stock market APIs turns up hundreds of them. A popular one is the Yahoo Finance API.

The Yahoo Finance API

In Rapid API, you can find the Yahoo Finance API here: `https://rapidapi.com/apidojo/api/Yahoo-Finance1`.

Browsing through the API calls available under the heading for stock on the left, the first one, `stock/v2/get-summary`, seems promising. Subscribe to the API and test the `get-summary` call. In the results, we see a lot of data. Under the "`price`" section, there's a "`regularMarketPrice`" section, with the price in `raw` (numeric) and `fmt` (formatted string) formats. That's what we need. There are several other calls in the stock category that return the `regularMarketPrice`. However, the Yahoo Finance API is very "noisy" – it returns a lot more data than we need.

© Simon A. Kingaby 2022
S. A. Kingaby, *Data-Driven Alexa Skills*, https://doi.org/10.1007/978-1-4842-7449-1_16

It's also worth looking at the pricing. (See Figure 16-1.) Yahoo Finance has a Freemium model. The Free (Basic) tier has a 500/month quota with a Hard Limit. This means that we can only make a total of 500 API calls per month, or an average of 25 calls per business day. At 500, we're cut off. Also, note the rate limit of five requests per second, which means that if you invest in 20 stocks, it will take 4 seconds to make the price requests. Lastly, the Pro tier (the lowest paid tier) costs $10/month.

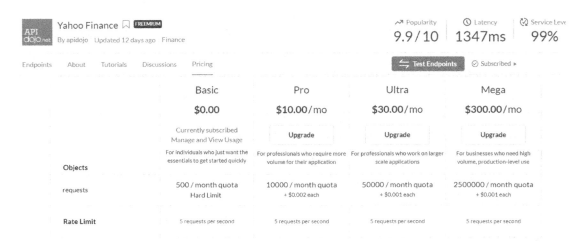

Figure 16-1. *Yahoo Finance's pricing model*

Let's look for another API that has better free options and returns a more straightforward response.

The Alpha Vantage API

In Rapid API, you can find the Alpha Vantage API here: `https://rapidapi.com/alphavantage/api/alpha-vantage/`.

This API has a default endpoint that provides pricing for stocks, forex, crypto, and more. The result that comes back is very clean and easy to read:

```
{
    "Global Quote": {
        "01. symbol": "TSLA",
        "02. open": "688.3700",
```

```
    "03. high": "692.4203",
    "04. low": "659.4200",
    "05. price": "661.7500",
    "06. volume": "35298378",
    "07. latest trading day": "2021-04-01",
    "08. previous close": "667.9300",
    "09. change": "-6.1800",
    "10. change percent": "-0.9252%"
  }
}
```

A glance at the pricing looks promising. (See Figure 16-2.) The 500 calls per day quota is 30 times more than the limit allowed by Yahoo. However, we are only allowed five free requests per minute. That means 20 stocks will take 4 minutes. And the first Pro level is almost $50/month.

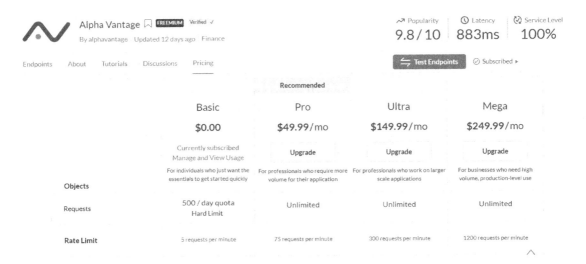

Figure 16-2. *Alpha Vantage's pricing model*

In this chapter, we'll see the code for both APIs. The Yahoo API provides much more information and has a faster poll rate. The Alpha Vantage API returns more concise results but has a slower poll rate. Both will let us calculate the stock price as of the last market close. In the next section, we'll create the Stock API module.

The Stock API Module

To keep the Stock API code organized and separate from the main skill code in the lambda_function.py, we will append it to the api_calls.py module that we added in the last chapter.

We'll start by creating a module-level constant for which STOCK_API we want to use:

```
STOCK_API = 'YAHOO' # OR
# STOCK_API = 'ALPHA'
```

Then, we will need to move the URL for Realty Mole inside the GetHomeValue function. (In the previous chapter, it was the only URL we cared about, and we put it at the module level.) So the code should now read:

```
def GetHomeValue(profile):

    url = "https://realty-mole-property-api.p.rapidapi.com/salePrice"

    querystring = {
        "compCount": "10",
```

Now we can add a function that loops through the profile["stocks"] dictionary. If there aren't any stocks, then we return 0. If there are, we need to look up the most recent closing price, multiply it by the number of shares held, and add that to a running total.

Remember, when we stored the stock in the profile, we used the stock ticker as the key and the share count as the value, like so:

```
profile["stocks"][stock_ticker] = share_count
```

Now, in the api_calls.py, we need to define a function that will calculate the total share value from the profile:

```
def GetStockValue(profile):
```

Next, we'll define a set of variables to hold the request info:

```
stockUrl = ''
querystring = {}
headers = {}
```

Pulling the request samples directly from the Rapid API Python definitions for each API and substituting our environment variable for the key, we get the following:

```python
if STOCK_API == 'YAHOO':
    stockurl = "https://apidojo-yahoo-finance-v1.p.rapidapi.com/stock/v2/
    get-summary"
    querystring = {"symbol":"TSLA","region":"US"}
    headers = {
        'x-rapidapi-key': os.environ['RAPID_API_KEY'],
        'x-rapidapi-host': "apidojo-yahoo-finance-v1.p.rapidapi.com"
        }

else:
    stockurl = "https://alpha-vantage.p.rapidapi.com/query"
    querystring = {"function":"GLOBAL_QUOTE","symbol":"TSLA"}
    headers = {
        'x-rapidapi-key': os.environ['RAPID_API_KEY'],
        'x-rapidapi-host': "alpha-vantage.p.rapidapi.com"
        }
```

With the API request configured, we can start checking for the presence of stocks:

```python
if not "stocks" in profile:
    return 0

if len(profile["stocks"]) == 0:
    return 0
```

Then we can loop through the stocks in the profile:

```python
for ticker, quantity in profile["stocks"].items():
```

and call the `requests.request` method for each ticker symbol:

```python
querystring["symbol"] = ticker
response = requests.request("GET", stockurl, headers=headers,
params=querystring)
```

Depending on which API we're using, we have to pull a different property out of the returned Json. For Yahoo, it's price.regularMarketPrice.raw; for Alpha Vantage, it's "Global Quote"."05. price". The resulting code might look like this:

```
totalValue = float(0)
for ticker, quantity in profile["stocks"].items():
    if quantity != 0:
        querystring["symbol"] = ticker
        response = requests.request("GET", stockurl, headers=headers,
        params=querystring)
        if response:
            if response.text:
                result = json.loads(response.text)
                price = float(0)
                if STOCK_API == 'YAHOO':
                    try:
                        price = float(
                            result["price"]["regularMarketPrice"]["raw"])
                    except:
                        price = 0
                else:
                    try:
                        price = float(result["Global Quote"]["05. price"])
                    except:
                        price = 0
```

Next, we can do the math to keep track of the running sum for the total value:

```
totalValue += price * float(quantity)
```

After the for loop completes, we can return the total value:

```
return round(totalValue, 2)
```

And that completes the function. Or does it? What about that constraint on how many API requests we can make over time?

Adding a Delay to the For Loop

To add a delay so that we don't make too many calls over time, we will need to import the `time.sleep()` function. Start by importing the time module:

```
import time
```

Next, we need to figure out how long the delay should be in seconds. For Yahoo, the rate is five requests per second. Therefore, the rate is 1 second divided by five requests or 0.2 seconds per one request. For Alpha Vantage, it's five requests per minute. This rate is computed as 60 seconds divided by five requests, or 12 seconds per one request. The code to add would look like this:

```
if STOCK_API == 'YAHOO':
    rate = 1.0 / 5.0
else:
    rate = 60.0 / 5.0
```

Having calculated the rate per request, we can add the delay to the for loop with this line of code:

```
time.sleep(rate)
```

Now, we have completed the function, as shown in the next section.

The Completed GetStockValue Function

Putting it all together, we get the following function:

```
def GetStockValue(profile):

    stockurl = ''
    querystring = {}
    headers = {}
    rate = 0

    if STOCK_API == 'YAHOO':
        stockurl = "https://apidojo-yahoo-finance-v1.p.rapidapi.com/stock/
        v2/get-summary"
```

```
        querystring = {"symbol": "TSLA", "region": "US"}
        headers = {
            'x-rapidapi-key': os.environ['RAPID_API_KEY'],
            'x-rapidapi-host': "apidojo-yahoo-finance-v1.p.rapidapi.com"
        }
        rate = 1.0 / 5.0

    else:
        stockurl = "https://alpha-vantage.p.rapidapi.com/query"
        querystring = {"function": "GLOBAL_QUOTE", "symbol": "TSLA"}
        headers = {
            'x-rapidapi-key': os.environ['RAPID_API_KEY'],
            'x-rapidapi-host': "alpha-vantage.p.rapidapi.com"
        }
        rate = 60.0 / 5.0

    if not "stocks" in profile:
        return 0

    if len(profile["stocks"]) == 0:
        return 0

    totalValue = float(0)
    for ticker, quantity in profile["stocks"].items():
        if quantity != 0:
            querystring["symbol"] = ticker
            response = requests.request(
                "GET", stockurl, headers=headers, params=querystring)
            if response:
                if response.text:
                    result = json.loads(response.text)
                    price = float(0)
                    if STOCK_API == 'YAHOO':
                        try:
                            price = float(
                                result["price"]["regularMarketPrice"]["raw"])
                        except:
                            price = 0
```

```
            else:
                try:
                    price = float(result["Global Quote"]["05. price"])
                except:
                    price = 0
                totalValue += price * float(quantity)
        time.sleep(rate)
    return round(totalValue, 2)
```

Now we need to test this function in several different ways.

Unit Testing the GetStockValue Function

We need to test the GetStockValue function with the following conditions:

1. A missing profile["stocks"] dictionary

2. An empty profile["stocks"] dictionary

3. A profile with one stock with a valid (nonzero) quantity (to test the API request)

4. A profile with an invalid stock ticker and a valid quantity (to test the error handling)

5. A profile with one stock with a zero quantity (to test the skip logic)

6. A profile with three stocks, each with a valid quantity (to test the loop)

7. A profile with three stocks, one of which has a zero quantity (to test the skip logic in the loop)

8. A profile with 20 stocks (to test the delay properly)

Whew! That's a lot of tests. It will clutter our Launch Request handler if we insert the tests there like we did for the home value. What can we do instead?

One common way to create unit tests is to put them in a parallel module, i.e., right next to the api_calls.py module, we can add an api_calls_tests.py module. (See Figure 16-3.)

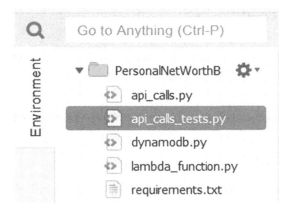

Figure 16-3. *Adding the api_calls_tests.py module*

In the new tests module, add the logging and api_calls imports (including the new GetStockValue function):

```
import logging
from api_calls import GetHomeValue, GetStockValue

logger = logging.getLogger(__name__)
logger.setLevel(logging.INFO)
```

Then add a function called UnitTests():

```
def UnitTests():
```

Now move all the code for the GetHomeValue test from where we inserted it into the Launch Request handler into a test function in this new module. Afterward, the module should look like this:

```
import logging
from api_calls import GetHomeValue, GetStockValue

logger = logging.getLogger(__name__)
logger.setLevel(logging.INFO)

def UnitTests():
    TestGetHomeValue()

def TestGetHomeValue():
```

```
profile = {}
profile["street_address"] = "1234 Main Street"
profile["city"] = "Nashville"
profile["state"] = "TN"
profile["zip_code"] = 37206
profile["homestats"] = {
    "property_type": "Single Family",
    "square_footage": 2250,
    "bedrooms": 4,
    "baths": 3
}
logger.info(f"Calling GetHomeValue with profile: {profile}")
homeValue = GetHomeValue(profile)
logger.info(
    f"Back from calling GetHomeValue, asserting homeValue is non-zero.
    HomeValue is {homeValue}")
assert homeValue != 0, "Home Value is 0, expected a non-zero result."
```

Note the use of logging to make the unit test progress explicit. Also, note the use of the assert statement in the last line. This is how Python will ensure we get a value when we call the GetHomeValue function with our sample address.

To run the test, edit the lambda_function.py. Modify the same Launch Request handler as before. Now it will call the UnitTests function instead of doing the testing itself. First, edit the imports section:

```
from api_calls import GetHomeValue, GetStockValue
from api_calls_tests import UnitTests
```

Add a flag to the module to turn unit tests on or off:

```
RUN_UNIT_TESTS = True
```

And modify the Launch Request handler as shown here:

```
class LaunchRequestHandlerUnlinked(AbstractRequestHandler):
    """Handler for Skill Launch when the Account is not linked."""
```

```
def can_handle(self, handler_input):
    return not has_access_token(handler_input) and ask_utils.is_
    request_type("LaunchRequest")(handler_input)

def handle(self, handler_input):
    speak_output = """Welcome, you need to link your account to use the
    Personal Net Worth skill.
        Would you like to link it now?"""
    handler_input.attributes_manager.session_attributes["question"] =
    "LinkAccount"

    # ====>

    if RUN_UNIT_TESTS:
        UnitTests()
        speak_output = "The Unit Tests have Passed."

    # ====>

    handler_input.attributes_manager.session_attributes["last_speech"]
    = speak_output

    return (
        handler_input.response_builder
        .speak(speak_output)
        .ask(speak_output)
        .response
    )
```

You should get a message that says, "The Unit Tests have Passed." If you do not, debug before proceeding. With the TestGetHomeValue function moved out of lambda_function.py into the api_calls_tests.py, we can start building out the test cases for the GetStockValue function.

Start by adding a TestGetStockValue function that will call the other GetStockValue tests. Then add that function call to the main UnitTests() function. Add each specific unit test for GetStockValue to the TestGetStockValue() function. For example:

```
def UnitTests():
    TestGetHomeValue()
    TestGetStockValue()
```

```
def TestGetStockValue():
    delay = 0.2  # 0.2 seconds for Yahoo API, 12 seconds for Alpha Vantage
    TestGetStockValueMissingProfile()
    TestGetStockValueEmptyStocks()
    TestGetStockValueOneValidStock()
    time.sleep(delay)
```

A missing profile["stocks"] dictionary

```
def TestGetStockValueMissingProfile():
    # A missing profile["stocks"] dictionary.
    profile = {}
    logger.info(
        f"TestGetStockValueMissingProfile: Calling GetStockValue with
        profile: {profile}")
    stockValue = GetStockValue(profile)
    logger.info(
        f"-   Back from Calling GetStockValue. StockValue is {stockValue}")
    assert stockValue == 0, f"Stock Value should be 0, got {stockValue}
    instead."
```

An empty profile["stocks"] dictionary

```
def TestGetStockValueEmptyStocks():
    # An empty profile["stocks"] dictionary.
    profile = {}
    profile["stocks"] = {}
    logger.info(
        f"TestGetStockValueEmptyStocks: Calling GetStockValue with profile:
        {profile}")
    stockValue = GetStockValue(profile)
    logger.info(
        f"-   Back from Calling GetStockValue. StockValue is {stockValue}")
    assert stockValue == 0, f"Stock Value should be 0, got {stockValue}
    instead."
```

A profile with one stock with a valid (non-zero) quantity (to test the API request)

```
def TestGetStockValueOneValidStock():
    # A profile with one stock with a valid (non-zero) quantity (to test
      the API request).
    profile = {}
    profile["stocks"] = {"TSLA": 10.0}
    logger.info(
        f"TestGetStockValueOneValidStock: Calling GetStockValue with
        profile: {profile}")
    stockValue = GetStockValue(profile)
    logger.info(
        f"-    Back from Calling GetStockValue. StockValue is {stockValue}")
    assert stockValue != 0, f"Stock Value should be non-zero, got 0 instead."
```

Note   You should Deploy and Test your Unit Tests often. Even after each function has been added. Also, don't forget to add the delay between calls to the API so you don't go over the speed limit.

A profile with an invalid stock ticker and a valid quantity (to test the error handling)

```
def TestGetStockValueOneInvalidStock():
    # A profile with an invalid stock ticker and a valid quantity (to test
      the error handling).
    profile = {}
    profile["stocks"] = {"Bustopher Jones": 10.0}  # Invalid Ticker
    logger.info(
        f"TestGetStockValueOneInvalidStock: Calling GetStockValue with
        profile: {profile}")
    stockValue = GetStockValue(profile)
    logger.info(
```

```
    f"-    Back from Calling GetStockValue. StockValue is {stockValue}")
assert stockValue == 0, f"Stock Value should be 0, got {stockValue}
instead."
```

Note   This test takes a little longer and is likely to time out before it completes. To fix this, edit the Function I Configuration I General Configuration I Timeout (see Figure 16-4). Bump it up to 5 minutes (up to a maximum of 15 minutes).

Figure 16-4. *Setting the Timeout for the function*

A profile with one stock with a zero quantity (to test the skip logic)

```
def TestGetStockValueValidStockWithZeroQuantity():
    # A profile with one stock with a zero quantity (to test the skip logic).
    profile = {}
    profile["stocks"] = {"TSLA": 0.0}  # Zero Quantity
    logger.info(
        f"TestGetStockValueValidStockWithZeroQuantity: Calling
        GetStockValue with profile: {profile}")
    stockValue = GetStockValue(profile)
    logger.info(
        f"-    Back from Calling GetStockValue. StockValue is {stockValue}")
    assert stockValue == 0, f"Stock Value should be 0, got {stockValue}
    instead."
```

A profile with three stocks, each with a valid quantity (to test the loop)

```
def TestGetStockValueThreeValidStocks():
    # A profile with three stocks, each with a valid quantity (to test the
      loop).
    profile = {}
    profile["stocks"] = {"TSLA": 10.0, "MSFT": 20, "AAPL": 15.5}
    logger.info(
        f"TestGetStockValueThreeValidStocks: Calling GetStockValue with
        profile: {profile}")
    stockValue = GetStockValue(profile)
    logger.info(
        f"-    Back from Calling GetStockValue. StockValue is {stockValue}")
    assert stockValue != 0, f"Stock Value should be non-zero, got 0 instead."
```

A profile with three stocks, one of which has a zero quantity (to test the skip logic in the loop)

```
def TestGetStockValueThreeValidStocksOneWithZeroQuantity():
    # A profile with three stocks, one of which has a zero quantity (to
      test the skip logic in the loop).
    profile = {}
    profile["stocks"] = {"TSLA": 10.0, "MSFT": 0, "AAPL": 15.5}
    logger.info(
        f"TestGetStockValueThreeValidStocksOneWithZeroQuantity: Calling
        GetStockValue with profile: {profile}")
    stockValue = GetStockValue(profile)
    logger.info(
        f"-    Back from Calling GetStockValue. StockValue is {stockValue}")
    assert stockValue != 0, f"Stock Value should be non-zero, got 0 instead."
```

A profile with twenty stocks (to test the delay properly)

```
def TestGetStockValueTwentyStocks():
    # A profile with twenty stocks (to test the delay properly).
    profile = {}
```

```
profile["stocks"] = {"TSLA": 10.0, "MSFT": 20, "AAPL": 15.5, "GE": 4,
"NKE": 5,
                      "MCD": 6, "AMZN": 7, "GOOG": 8, "GMWKF": 9,
                      "SONY": 10,
                      "RRGB": 11, "TACO": 12, "DPZ": 13, "DIS": 14,
                      "WMT": 15,
                      "WFC": 16, "BAC": 17, "TD": 18, "C": 19, "JNJ": 20}
logger.info(
    f"TestGetStockValueTwentyStocks: Calling GetStockValue with
    profile: {profile}")
stockValue = GetStockValue(profile)
logger.info(
    f"-   Back from Calling GetStockValue. StockValue is {stockValue}")
assert stockValue != 0, f"Stock Value should be non-zero, got 0 instead."
```

After adding all the subordinate test functions to the main test function for the stock value, we get the following:

```
def TestGetStockValue():
    delay = 0.2  # 0.2 seconds for Yahoo API, 12 seconds for Alpha Vantage
    TestGetStockValueMissingProfile()
    TestGetStockValueEmptyStocks()
    TestGetStockValueOneValidStock()
    time.sleep(delay)
    TestGetStockValueOneInvalidStock()
    time.sleep(delay)
    TestGetStockValueValidStockWithZeroQuantity()
    time.sleep(delay)
    TestGetStockValueThreeValidStocks()
    time.sleep(delay)
    TestGetStockValueThreeValidStocksOneWithZeroQuantity()
    time.sleep(delay)
    TestGetStockValueTwentyStocks()
```

Run your tests as you did in the previous chapter, debugging any errors you encounter. I found that when I ran all the tests for the Yahoo API, it took about 42 seconds. When I ran them for the Alpha Vantage API, which has a much lower speed limit, it took approximately 6.5 minutes. If all your unit tests pass, you have completed the code for this chapter. Select an API and contemplate what you'll do next.

What Can I Do Next?

There are several things we can do next to improve our skill.

First, we can return all the prices for all the stocks as part of the profile. This will allow us to save the price in the database, which, in turn, affords us the opportunity to (a) make sure that each stock ticker is returning the correct price and (b) calculate yesterday's value vs. today's and tell the user whether their portfolio is up or down.

Second, we can expand our stocks feature to include mutual funds, cryptocurrencies, and more. The Yahoo API exposes all of these.

Third, we can add a stock inquiry feature to the dialog model so that when the user gives us a ticker, we try to pull a price for it from the Yahoo API. We can then confirm that we have the correct ticker by echoing the stock name and price back to the user.

Fourth, we can add more tests. Especially adding a test to audit the GetStockValue method's results to make sure they are 100% correct all the time. We can also make sure that all parts of the process handle decimal values properly.

Fifth, the world is your oyster. Think of ways to use these APIs to provide more information to the user. What is the necessary dialog (intents and utterances) to support that?

Summary

In this chapter, we looked at two different financial APIs that can be used to get stock prices. We wired them up to get the total stock portfolio value from the ticker symbols and share quantities that we gathered in Chapter 15. We also spent some time expanding our understanding of program structure where unit testing was concerned. We created a parallel module that is used to contain unit tests. Then we set up a variety of unit tests to exercise our new GetStockValue function.

CHAPTER 17

What's Next?

Conclusion

In Part I, we started out learning about the world of Voice User Interfaces. We then looked at Alexa Routines and Blueprints. We then created and published a Body Mass Index Alexa skill. This also introduced Alexa Conversations.

Then, in Part II, we went beyond Hello World with the 90-year calendar skill. We designed a VUI with Botmock, created a visual interface with Alexa Presentation Language, and programmed a back-end lambda function. We then saw several ways to unit test our lambda function and our Alexa skill.

Finally, in Part III, we pulled data from real estate and stock market APIs to build a Personal Net Worth skill.

What's Next?

Within this book, you have worked with various data sources, including databases like DynamoDb, and APIs like the Realty Mole Property API. In addition, you have created and tested lambda functions that are back-end applications in the cloud. These Lambda back-ends can pull data from anywhere and expose it through an Alexa skill interface.

What's next? You could, for example, pull in FBI Crime data from the Crime Data Explorer (`https://crime-data-explorer.app.cloud.gov/`), creating an Alexa Crime Explorer. Then, perhaps add geospatial data to that from the Google Maps Platform (`https://developers.google.com/maps/gmp-get-started`) and build a "What's the crime rate in this city?" skill.

© Simon A. Kingaby 2022
S. A. Kingaby, *Data-Driven Alexa Skills*, https://doi.org/10.1007/978-1-4842-7449-1_17

You could also work with your favorite enterprise cloud application's API and create an Alexa skill that works with that application's data. For example, develop a skill that queries and updates Salesforce through their Lightning Platform REST API (`https://developer.salesforce.com/docs/atlas.en-us.api_rest.meta/api_rest/intro_what_is_rest_api.htm`).

Perhaps build an Alexa Conversations interface to log ServiceNow tickets through their Now Platform Rest API (`https://docs.servicenow.com/bundle/rome-application-development/page/integrate/inbound-rest/concept/c_RESTAPI.html`).

You could extend the Personal Net Worth skill by adding stock market details from the Quandl API (`www.quandl.com/tools/api`). You can have Alexa make trades for you through the Alpaca API (`https://alpaca.markets/docs/api-documentation/api-v2/`). Add in some machine learning with AWS Sagemaker (`https://sagemaker.readthedocs.io/en/stable/`), and you could have Alexa become your algorithmic-trading partner and smart broker. Imagine having this conversation:

You: Alexa, what are my stock recommendations for today?

Alexa: Hi Dave, I would recommend OTRK. Ontrak Inc. is an AI and tele-health-enabled, virtualized outpatient healthcare treatment company. Their market cap is nearly 500 million dollars, and they have 18.6 million shares out. In March 2021, their stock dropped from 93.46 to 24.39. Based on their current price of 32, you should short them at 30 because their stock is still on a downward trend.

You: Great. Short 1000 OTRK at 30, with a stop loss of 31 and a target of 28.

Alexa: Short sell 1000 shares of OTRK, Ontrak Inc., at a price of 30 dollars, with a stop loss of 31 dollars and a target price of 28 dollars. I need your PIN to confirm this trade.

You: 1234.

Alexa: PIN confirmed. I have placed the order.

This book is just the beginning of your data-driven Alexa skill journey. I can't wait to hear what you build.

Index

A

Y, Z

Printed in the United States
by Baker & Taylor Publisher Services